Becoming an Evidence-based Practitioner

Too oft ... hers and
provide ... ctitioner
shows h ... earchers
and uni ... e studies
of class ... l science
and dra ... tnership
with the ... primary
curricul

Posit ... umental
in conce ... research.
Full of i ... thods, it
also cap ... ce-based
Practiti ... ndertake
research

Olwen ... opolitan
Univers

Becoming an Evidence-based Practitioner

A framework for teacher-researchers

Edited by
Olwen McNamara

London and New York

First published 2002 by RoutledgeFalmer
11 New Fetter Lane, London EC4P 4EE

Simultaneously published in the USA and Canada
by RoutledgeFalmer
29 West 35th Street, New York, NY 10001

RoutledgeFalmer is an imprint of the Taylor & Francis Group

© 2002 Edited by Olwen McNamara

Typeset in Sabon and Gill Sans by
Prepress Projects Ltd, Perth, Scotland
Printed and bound in Great Britain by
TJ International Ltd, Padstow, Cornwall

British Library Cataloguing in Publication Data
A catalogue record for this book is available from the British Library

Library of Congress Cataloging in Publication Data

A catalog record for this book has been requested

ISBN 0–415–25243–1 (hbk)
ISBN 0–415–25244–X (pbk)

Contents

Tables and boxes

Boxes

Tables

Contributors

Mike Berry received a Diploma in Art from St Martins School of Art in London in 1970. In 1973, he returned to Manchester, where he qualified as a teacher at Mather College and in 1994 completed an MA in Art Education. He has taught mostly in schools with large multiethnic populations and was Deputy Head at Cheetham Community School, Cheetham Hill, Manchester, at the time of writing. He is now Headteacher at Sparrow Hill Community School, Manchester. His main interests include research into Islamic Art and its use in the primary art curriculum.

Sarah Brealey graduated from University College of North Wales in 1997. She then moved to Manchester, where she was employed to teach Year 2 children at St Malachy's RC Primary School, Collyhurst, Manchester, a challenging city centre school. Currently, she is using research – her own and that of others – to develop her practice.

Brian Corbin, after teaching for ten years in primary schools, went into the secondary and then the tertiary sectors. He was awarded a PhD for research at Manchester Metropolitan University, and is now involved in research projects at the Institute of Education, Manchester Metropolitan University, particularly those concerned with the impact of recent national innovations on primary teachers' practice, professionalism and identity.

Anne Campbell is Head of Quality Assurance and Academic Standards at the Institute of Education, Manchester Metropolitan University. Her research interests centre on the professional development of teachers, mentoring and teachers as researchers. She is involved in the evaluation of Early Excellence Centres and the management of the DfES Best Practice Research Scholarship programme. Publications include *School-Based Teacher Education: Telling Tales from a Fictional Primary School* (London: David Fulton, 1998) and *Researching Professional Development* (London: Sage/Paul Chapman, forthcoming).

Peter Foster (deceased) was a Senior Lecturer at the Crewe School of Education at Manchester Metropolitan University. His research interests lay in the areas of ethnography and research methods and methodology. He was well known for rigorous academic critique of research findings and he held a deep commitment to all matters pertaining to social justice and equal opportunities. The clear principles he brought to all his professional work are sorely missed.

Gary Gornell began teaching in 1987 and has worked for three LEAs in both mainstream schools and schools for children with emotional and behavioural difficulties. He has been a co-ordinator for eight subject areas and is now Deputy Headteacher at Temple Primary School, Manchester, with responsibility for curriculum development and behaviour management.

Rob Halsall is currently Head of Research Development for the Institute of Education, Manchester Metropolitan University. His main research interests are in the areas of social inclusion, school improvement and teacher research. He is currently leading the external evaluation of two Education Action Zones and of the Healthy Schools initiative across five LEAs. He had edited and contributed to *Education and Training 14–19: Chaos or Coherence?* (London: David Fulton, 1996) and *Teacher Research and School Improvement: Opening Doors from the Inside* (Buckingham: Open University Press, 1998).

Gudrun Heatley started teaching in 1988, having completed a BEd at Manchester Metropolitan University, which included a final teaching practice at Cravenwood Primary School. In 1990 she returned to Cravenwood as a teacher, only to leave again in 1998 to take up her first Headship at St Augustine's CE Primary School. She has now returned to Cravenwood for the third time, this time as Headteacher.

Dave Heywood, after commencing teaching in secondary science, moved into the primary sector, where he worked as an advisory teacher and in senior management. He now teaches across a wide range of courses at the Institute of Education, Manchester Metropolitan University, including post-graduate and higher degrees. He is a core researcher and completed his PhD thesis in 2000. He has published widely in international science journals in the area of language in science learning and the development of teacher subject and pedagogic knowledge.

Sandy Holt started teaching in 1991 after training at Derby College of Education. She subsequently moved to Manchester and took up her first teaching position at St Augustine's where she remained for 9 years. During this time she was curriculum coordinator for many subjects and, additionally, for the last 4 years was Acting Deputy Head. At the end of 2000 she moved to Spain to continue her teaching career in the British School of Barcelona.

Dave Hustler is Professor of Education and Head of Research at the Institute of Education, Manchester Metropolitan University. He has taught in primary, secondary and further education. His research interests are in formative evaluation and professionally focused research (in 1986 he edited *Action Research in Classrooms and Schools*). Currently he is involved in a project for the DfES researching teachers' perceptions of continuing professional development. He is co-editor of the *British Educational Research Journal* and *Research in Education*.

Susan Jennings initially trained as a Russian teacher and subsequently retrained in special needs and has since worked as a specialist teacher of literacy at primary level. In 1999 she became a member of the DfEE's Teacher Research Panel.

Liz Jones is Senior Lecturer at the Manchester Metropolitan University, where she teaches in the areas of educational studies and early years education. Her teaching career spans over 20 years and she has worked in mainstream and special education and as an advisory teacher. More recently, she taught in an inner-city nursery while studying for her PhD. Liz has published widely for both academic and practitioner audiences.

Olwen McNamara taught mathematics in secondary schools for over 20 years, latterly combining her teaching career with work in HEI while studying for a doctorate. Post-doctorally she managed a school improvement partnership of local LEAs and universities. She is currently employed as a Senior Research Fellow at the Institute of Education, Manchester Metropolitan University, where her main interests are professionally focused in the areas of practitioner research and mathematics education.

Anne-Marie Roberts trained at Christ's and Notre Dame College, Liverpool, where she taught for 9 years before moving to Manchester to take up her present post as Deputy Headteacher at St Chad's RC Primary School. She was science co-ordinator at the time of writing and her present role encompasses responsibility for special educational needs and Key Stage 1. She has nearly completed an MA in Leadership in Education.

Bill Rogers is Head of Manchester School Improvement Service, where his primary role is in managing a service dedicated to support, challenge and intervention. He has a strong commitment to the development of teacher-practitioner networks and schools as collaborative learning communities. His publications include *An Introduction to Careers Education and Guidance* (CRAC), *Careers Education* (COIC), *Success Against The Odds: Effective Schools in Disadvantaged Areas* (London: Routledge, 1996) and *Success Against the Odds Revisited* (edited by M. Madden: London, Routledge 2001).

Ian Stronach is a Research Professor at the Institute of Education, Manchester Metropolitan University. His main research interests are in the areas of qualitative research and evaluation. He is an editor of the *British Educational Research Journal*, and has co-published (with M. MacLure) *Educational Research Undone: the Postmodern Embrace* (Buckingham: Open University Press, 1997).

Claire Van-es graduated from Newman College, Birmingham, and in 1996 moved to Manchester, where she is currently employed at St Malachy's RC Primary School, teaching a Year 3 class. Now in her fifth year of teaching, she has found that engagement in research has helped her to develop her own style of teaching. In March 2000 whe was presented with the Lloyds/TSB Teaching Award for the North West Primary Teacher of the Year.

Mandy Walsh qualified at Notre Dame College in 1979 and moved back to Manchester, where she has worked ever since, being currently employed at St Anne's RC Primary School. She has worked in all areas of the primary sector but has particular experience in the lower years of Key Stage 2 and has responsibility for literacy across the curriculum. She became interested in children's language development early in her career and her research work has given her insight into this vital area and into reviewing her own practice.

Helen White (deceased) qualified as a teacher in 1972 and continued the study of education by completing a Post Graduate Diploma in Education in 1996. In a teaching career that spanned nearly 30 years she taught in both secondary and primary phases. She was appointed to Cheetham Community School in 1984 and rose to be Senior Teacher. Her great interest was music and she held responsibility for teaching of the music curriculum throughout the school.

Acknowledgements

We, the authors, gratefully acknowledge the support of the staff and pupils of our partner primary schools in Manchester and Salford, without whose commitment and encouragement this project could not have succeeded. We also appreciate the support of colleagues, too numerous to mention, at Manchester and Salford LEAs, the Victoria University of Manchester and the Institute of Education at Manchester Metropolitan University. Special thanks go to Trish Gladdis, ever cheerful and patient, for her assistance in compiling this book. Our final thanks go to the TTA, our sponsors, and in particular Philippa Cordingley and her colleagues at Curee for their comments on earlier drafts of this book. Our final thoughts must be to remember Helen White and Peter Foster, who both died before this book was published.

Introduction

Inviting research

Olwen McNamara and Bill Rogers

It was a foggy February morning when a large cream envelope dropped though the door to brighten our day. 'We' were a group of university researchers and LEA (local education authority) School Improvement Officers who had been waiting for just such an opportunity. It had been 4 years since we had formed a partnership with the primary intention of developing a critical mass of teacher practitioner researchers in local schools as a vehicle for school improvement. Despite having engaged a sizeable cohort of primary and secondary schools in a variety of small research-based projects, we had not yet attracted funding to enable us to pilot rigorously what we had already learnt.

What had we learnt? Well there had been some real successes. We had seen the enthusiasm of one or two teachers in a primary school transform assessment practice across the whole school and raise the profile of action research with their colleagues. We had seen a small-scale research project by two high school special educational needs staff tackle the low level of boys' literacy skills on entry, and develop it into a major strategy for improving literacy across Key Stage 3. We had seen many cases of individual teachers (re)discovering the benefits of supported reflection on their own practice. Although this had left us with the firm belief that improvement should be underpinned by engagement in research-based practice, there were also a number of salutary lessons that had been learnt. The most important, perhaps, was that it was not easy to engage teachers, let alone whole schools, in action research at a time when the pressures of league tables and impending OfSTED inspections competed for their attention. The prospects in this respect certainly did not appear likely to improve in the foreseeable future! In addition, there was not a bedrock of experience in the area on which to build, and new teachers were still not coming out of training with their research skills honed!

Nationally the 'teacher-as-researcher' movement had become well established over the previous two decades. Teachers had been involved as researchers in a number of curriculum initiatives, such as the FordT and the Schools' Council Curriculum Project depicted by John Elliott in his seminal book *Action Research for Educational Change* (1991). In general, however, the teachers' involvement with research was mainly in relation to award-bearing courses, and it was one thing to respond to the needs of individual teachers seeking higher degrees and quite another to encourage classroom teachers, and indeed whole schools, to engage with research in relation to their everyday work. Our experience showed that it was not enough simply to provide guidelines and encouragement. Active support was needed from colleagues who understood the nature of the complex demands on teachers and had ways in which to access existing research findings and the methodologies necessary to carry out research. Such support required funding, and that was hard to come by. Nobody, it seemed, was willing to support the necessary infrastructure. Yet here, in the large cream envelope, was an invitation to bid for a 3-year project funded by the Teacher Training Agency (TTA) (Box 1). The first major grant to be offered to support a research partnership of schools, LEAs and HEIs (Higher Education Institution) such as ourselves. Who could resist?

Box 1 A very brief sketch of the history behind the invitation to bid

---

The School-based Research Consortia was one of a number of projects supported by the TTA in order to promote teaching as a 'research based profession' – an initiative which it had launched in 1996 with the announcement of a pilot scheme of individual Teacher Research Grants. The message promoted by the TTA was clear – if teachers engaged in research and with knowledge from the wider evidence base they would improve the quality of their teaching and thereby the standard of pupil outcomes. The TTA aimed, through a number of strategies, to improve the existing stock of knowledge, extend the quality and relevance of research on schools and help teachers play a more active role in conceiving, implementing, evaluating and disseminating that research.

The deal was £105K over a 3-year period to fund consortia of schools, HEIs and LEAs. The goals were (1) to encourage teachers to engage both *in* research and *with* research and evidence about pupils' achievements; (2) to increase the capacity for high-quality, teacher-focused classroom research by supporting teacher involvement in the development of research proposals for external funding; and (3)to develop long-term, medium-scale data sets to provide evidence about what teachers and pupils do and how that affects pupil achievement. The expectation was that the consortia would match the TTA funding both 'in-kind' and 'in-cash'. The latter was to be acquired by drawing down funding from external sources in order to sustain further engagement of teachers *with* and *in* research.

Developing a vision

The funding offered by the TTA was, in relative terms, not very much and the time scale for submission of the outline bid, impossible. Our first task was to find a group of schools willing and ready to embark on this journey with us – the Cheetham and Broughton Regeneration Area, which crossed Manchester and Salford LEAs, seemed ideal in a number of ways. You will be hearing more of the history and context of the individual schools, but a brief portrait of the area is given below (Box 2).

These broad statistics hide a diversity of opportunities and challenges afforded in the eight primary schools that expressed an interest in joining the project. A major challenge was their almost total lack of previous involvement in research activity. Our outline bid, we learnt later, was one of sixty-three submitted in April 1997. A few weeks later, another large cream envelope fell through the door. The good news was that we had been short-listed, the bad news was that the bid-writing had to begin again. Our deadline to flesh out themes – relating to the improvement of pedagogy and practice – and contexts – relating to TTA priorities – was to be mid-July.

Box 2 The local context

> The majority of children in the Manchester schools were drawn from the Cheetham ward, which in 1991 had the third highest level of deprivation in Manchester. Broughton, the corresponding ward in Salford, has a similar profile. On the Jarman index, which acts as an indicator of relative deprivation assessment, Cheetham scores +56, in a range from a low of −60 and to a high of +60. For example, the average entitlement to free school meals across the schools is up to three times the national average. Attendance figures range from 95 per cent to 85 per cent. The percentage of pupils gaining Level 4+ in the Key Stage 2 English tests in 1996 ranged from 13 per cent to 73 per cent. The percentage of ethnic minority children in individual schools is up to 95 per cent. The level of pupil mobility into and out of many of the schools is exceptionally high, and several receive a significant proportion of children from traveller families (fairs, circuses, seasonal occupations.) Over the course of the 3-year project, ten schools have been involved in some way, including seven voluntary-aided church schools. Although there are many similarities, there are also a number of notable differences. While some of the schools have a very small proportion of pupils from a non-white cultural heritage, two served almost exclusively Muslim communities. Many of the schools are housed in late-Victorian and early-Edwardian buildings, but some are in 1960s and 1970s open-plan buildings.

It seemed essential to us that the schools should address individual needs focused on their priority areas identified in their School Development Plan, and although the group had a number of common objectives their particular curriculum/teaching/learning priorities did not make for a single cohesive focus. As a consequence, in the event, we were forced to submit a bid that was more diverse than we had anticipated, and this lack of coherence across the projects perhaps inhibited cross-fertilisation in the early stages. It was also evident from the onset that it could create difficulties with common data sets, baselines and benchmarks. We knew that the route we had chosen was a compromise and to a certain extent it would increase the complexities of the project.

The vision

We, like the TTA, firmly believed that engagement in the processes of research and with the wider evidence base would promote the professional development of staff, raise the quality of teaching and, most importantly, improve pupil attainment. We even had specific goals for the creation of 'research rich environments':

- A significant proportion of consortium teachers would become actively *engaged in* doing research in their own classrooms.
- All consortium teachers would become aware of the potential of *engaging with* the research and evidence base relevant to primary school classroom practice.
- The school, HEI and LEA partnership would be promoted as a way forward in developing high-quality classroom research and would thus contribute to a culture in which research was done *by* or *with* schools rather than done *to* them.

- We would attempt to influence those involved in education and education research by employing our expertise in research initiatives in order to generate funding to support more classroom based research projects.

Behind these specific objectives we set out a clear rationale in the bid. We wanted to generate a culture of teacher research in partner schools, because we saw research, and in particular action research, as one basis for improving practice by informing the process of change and developing the nature of professionalism. Recent OfSTED reports had consistently commented on the absence of systematic monitoring and evaluation procedures in many schools. Indeed the pace of curriculum and management change in recent years had compelled schools to take action without the safeguard of building such procedures into their development plans. Our consortium was to be committed to the idea of teachers becoming actively involved in research as a means of providing a powerful method for determining useful and effective action and a systematic and thoughtful framework for monitoring and evaluating the improvement process. Practitioner research was a real opportunity to develop an evidence-based approach to our craft. This was improvement through 'doing': *engaging in research*. We also believed that partnerships, such as ours, should seek improvement through 'using': *engaging with research*. Our intention was that we should help teachers to become more 'research aware'. We hoped to encourage schools to use research relevant to classroom practice in order to test the beliefs, norms and understandings that presently underpinned the knowledge base about teaching upon which pedagogy was traditionally based. More will be said of problems with regard to the knowledge base in the next chapter. Over and above that, however, many accounts of the problems of disseminating research to practitioners assume that the findings are unproblematic and consider the key issue to be access and communication. We felt the problem was deeper and that solutions would, by necessity, lead to the development of different 'cultures' and 'roles'.

Research evidence regarding the management of change was beginning to accumulate to support the view that models of effectiveness could not be imposed upon schools and that along the road to improvement 'school culture' was of crucial significance. An important factor, for example, in achieving both the shift from tradition-based understandings to evidence-based knowledge, and the embedding of change strategies, was the way teachers think and talk about teaching in schools. Such 'talk' both creates and reflects the professional climate. We thought it important that 'teacher talk' should focus more on pedagogy and the curriculum and be more 'subject-centred' and 'pupil outcome' orientated. Rob Halsall, one of the HEI members of the consortium, makes two important points in his book *Teacher Research and School Improvement: opening doors from the inside*. First, in order to make an impact, evidence needs to be related to things other than the measurement of performance in a narrow, mechanistic way. Second, we need to recognise that change is 'messy', and thus flexibility and openness to uncertainty are needed to cope with the unstable internal and external conditions and environments in which many schools, particularly urban schools, operate. We proposed that the dominant research culture, in so far as it related to supporting school improvement, needed to change and such change was best negotiated practically in an HEI/LEA/school partnership. It would offer a combination of tightly focused school-based and -owned projects, with the rigor, expertise and access to the evidence base and methodologies which LEAs and HEIs could provide. Each partner institution, whatever its other agendas, was committed to school improvement and understanding more deeply the contexts within which the other institutions worked and the repertoire of skills they had to offer. Three partners with well defined, appropriate and mutually supportive roles? Only time would tell!

Finally, and not surprisingly, the project had a political dimension. The TTA wanted to influence the education and research communities by promoting the school/LEA/HEI partnership as a model for educational research of the future. We believed that given a change in the culture between schools, HEIs and LEAs, and a change in the perception that government and funding bodies held of that culture, partnerships such as our own would be able to raise funds from external sources for further classroom-based research projects. We were very clear then about our research aims and processes; we had a research plan that included existing data sets; and we had a strong experiential base for the dissemination of outcomes. Now all that remained was for us to have an opportunity to deliver the goods!

Sure enough, late in the summer of 1997 a third cream envelope fell through the letterbox – we had been successful! The Manchester and Salford Schools Consortium was one of the three [shortly to become four as an additional consortium was to be funded by CfBT (Centre for British Teachers)] school-based research consortia to be funded nationally by the TTA. Of the other consortia one, similar to ourselves in the primary phase but with a focus on 'mathematics', was based at Leeds University. A second, focused upon 'disaffection' in the secondary phase, was based at the University of East Anglia and the third, based in the Northeast at Newcastle University, was also secondary and focused upon 'thinking skills'.

Making the vision a reality

The level of compromise built into the design of our bid was apparent very quickly: tensions between our contractual obligations to the TTA and the demands of school ownership could not easily be reconciled. Supportive as the TTA proved to be about our focus on school improvement, our requirement that individual school research foci should be in an improvement priority area was to prove a 'hostage to fortune'. Small primary schools, particularly those in challenging urban areas, are characteristically very unstable. School priorities change, sometimes very quickly, in response, for example, to a post-OfSTED Action Plan; and we were to find that by the start of the project two schools had already announced their intention to change their substantive curriculum focus. Our already eclectic set of projects was in danger of becoming even more so, and, in retrospect, we did not fully appreciate just how important those common themes and objectives would be in the establishment and nurturing of a robust partnership of schools. In addition, it soon became apparent that the TTA's conception of 'pedagogically' focused research was somewhat narrower than our own. So, for example, the project at Cheetham School (Chapter 11) that focused on the effects of streaming/setting for maths and English hovered uncomfortably on the contested 'pedagogic' boundary for many months. Such conflicts with the TTA were resolved only as a result of a good deal of listening and learning on both sides.

Research partner, rather than sponsor, is perhaps how the TTA, and in particular its Chief Professional Research Advisor, Philippa Cordingley, would actually prefer to characterise the relationship, for, almost uniquely among such funders, the TTA was deliberately proactive in its steering capacity. We have already alluded to the fact that they were openly critical of some aspects of educational research and they were not on their own: two official reports commissioned by the DfEE (Hillage *et al.*, 1998) and OfSTED (Tooley and Darby, 1998) were also disapproving to a degree. The high profile vested in this project was partly as a result of such tensions and partly related to the vulnerability of the TTA, about to undergo its quinquennial review. The combination of these circumstances made the venture an interesting foray into the national political arena (more of which will be said in Chapter 12) and the tensions were particularly apparent at meetings of the National Steering Group, which included representatives from HMI, OfSTED, QCA (Qualifications and Curriculum Authority), schools, universities, etc.

The Consortium 'launch' in September 1997 took the form of a large and rather formal Consortium Management Group (CMG) meeting at St Malachy's, an imposing Victorian primary school, with spare capacity and a large car park. Consortium meetings were always held in one of the schools in order to cut down on travelling times, at least for teacher colleagues, and make twilight meetings a realistic possibility. Despite the geographical compactness of the consortium schools, communication was nevertheless a problem. None had access to the Internet, and for some months one did not even have a fax machine. The euphoria surrounding its acquisition was short-lived as, sadly, it was just as soon to disappear!

The membership of the CMG included everyone involved in the project: eight teacher research coordinators; eight link tutors from HEI/LEA; a TTA link officer; and an administration support person. Headteachers were, of course, always welcome, and on a number of occasions a specific invitation went out to all staff. The presence of a TTA 'link officer' was an additional strain in the early days, but rapidly we got to know John Ferguson (a retired Chief Education Officer), and later Vanessa Wright (a retired Headteacher), and appreciate their role as broker/trouble shooter between us and the TTA. The CMG had as its remit accountability; resource deployment; systems and procedures such as quality assurance and control; financial management; reporting; monitoring and evaluation of research, dissemination activity, etc. The meetings were programmed to take place monthly in the first year and were initially heavily bureaucratic, and somewhat laboured; so we acted quickly to refocus them onto the critical friendship side of their role: discussing concerns and offering mutual advice/challenge/support. In addition, the opportunity was used for dissemination of insights from the wider evidence base. At one meeting, Sue Jennings and Mandy Walsh gave a report on a seminar they had attended about a transatlantic research project on teacher types. At another, Anne-Marie Roberts presented a report about a British Educational Research Association day conference of science education researchers. Gary Gornell and four colleagues from Temple Primary School attended the Association of Teachers of Mathematics conference in the Easter holiday, 1999, reported back and persuaded the consortium schools to enrol as a cluster member.

Occasionally we invited outside speakers to the CMG meetings. We heard, for example, about the National Oracy Project from a researcher who had been centrally involved. On another occasion an LEA literacy advisor on questioning skills held a workshop. We also had a session with a teacher and a researcher working on a 'sister' project studying the implementation of the National Numeracy Strategy in another group of six schools in Manchester and Salford. This project was funded by one of the two research grants that we, as a consortium, were awarded by the Economic and Social Research Council.

The second main structural feature of the consortium was the linking of an HEI/ LEA tutor with each teacher research coordinator in order to provide individual support with the research process including the initial design of the project and collecting, analysing and interpreting data, report writing and conference presenting. This structural device embedded into the consortium design established and cemented many individual relationships between LEA/HEI colleagues, teachers and, in some cases, whole schools. The linked pairs operated discretely to a great degree, which was, we felt, a strength, but also a weakness, of the structure. It potentially isolated individual school research-coordinators, making points of contact more difficult to engineer successfully given the diversity of the research foci.

The third support feature in the consortium design was a monthly meeting of school coordinators with key consortium officials. The sessions were very important in the early days of the consortium as they provided an opportunity to share anxieties, give support and develop friendships in a 'cosier', less intimidating setting than the CMG. In the first year of operation they took the form of research training sessions, and school coordinators met together monthly with Olwen McNamara, the consortium coordinator, for a workshop led by Ian Stronach, HEI link to Cravenwood Primary. The research training programme complemented the support offered to school coordinators by their HEI/LEA link and was designed to be practical and focused on 'learning by doing'. Research tasks were planned to be as uncontaminated as possible by the technical concepts; thus, the teachers' initial induction was into action research practice as opposed to the jargon (triangulation, validity, etc.) and complex stages/ cycles. We hoped that such practice, devoid of the academic mystique that so often disempowers teachers working with HEI colleagues in research projects, would connect more readily with the ways in which teachers reflected upon, talked about and acted in their professional lives. In addition, we hoped it would be viewed not as a 'paternalistic' simplification but as empowering. The sessions included discussion of research foci and baseline data collection; questionnaire construction; semi-structured interview techniques; research diaries; survey, interview and classroom transcript data analysis, etc. Initially, for example, we conducted a baseline 'attitude to research' survey across all project schools that functioned as a training exercise in developing research tools and analysing data, and also acted as an awareness-raising strategy in the schools as a whole. Where possible, sessions were based around self-generated project data from schools, and this ensured not only relevance but also that the research effort was advanced. Inevitably there were times when things did not go according to plan: data were not always available and research processes were, on occasions, introduced before the need arose.

Moving on, changing visions

As needs changed support mechanisms responded, and at the end of the first year of the project the monthly meeting changed in focus and timing. The shift in focus arose from a need for us all to become more skilled at observing teacher behaviours in the classroom and developing a common language with which to think and talk about the pedagogic processes. The change of timing, from afternoon to twilight spot, was brought about by the increasing strain of releasing teachers from classes: although money for supply cover was readily available the same could not be said of supply staff of a calibre sufficient to teach in such challenging schools. In addition, Year 2 and Year 6 teachers were particularly reluctant to leave their classes, because of the Key Stage 1 and 2 National Tests; and Headteachers were generally anxious about having too many staff out of the classroom, overburdened as they were with the need to release teachers for literacy training. In order to address the supply cover problem creatively, we devised a plan to employ classroom assistants for the schools under the Government's 'New Deal' initiative. Our bid was accepted by the Local Training and Enterprise Council, but it eventually fell prey to local political agendas.

Pressure from the TTA to achieve more coherence across the research projects had abated, after the initial period of intense negotiation, but at the first annual review in the spring of 1999 the National Steering Group suggested adopting a common theme of 'speaking and listening' as an overall focus. It would have felt more of an imposition had it not been for the fact that we, as a consortium, were already moving in this direction. A number of schools, like St Malachy's and St Chad's, were beginning to question whether the understanding of scientific concepts was the key obstacle for their pupils. Or, whether a more fundamental problem was their inadequate listening and comprehension skills, their impoverished vocabulary and their inability to articulate even in non-specialist language. Thus 'speaking and listening' was embraced, it would appear quite happily, as a unifying focus. It seemed that the TTA was keen that the new focus should replace individual projects, but this was firmly resisted in most schools. An early reflection, perhaps, of the sense of ownership already developed by the school coordinators and, to a lesser degree, the successful embedding of some of the projects in the schools more generally. Developing a critical mass of teachers within each school actively engaged in doing or using the research was always our greatest challenge.

We had also, encouraged by the TTA, increasingly begun to see video recording as a way to collect and share evidence that was particularly relevant to our research foci and especially so in view of our central focus on 'speaking and listening'. Two of our individual school projects had used videotaped evidence during their first year of operation and video data sets were being used in an extensive and systematic way by the Northeast Schools Consortium in its 'thinking skills' project. Only one of our schools had use of a video camera, however, and we simply did not have the capacity to collect such systematic data with the resources available at the time. It was at this stage, nearly half-way through the project, that we were fortunate enough to recruit Liz Jones, an HEI colleague, to work with the consortium one day per week and she took charge of supporting the collection of video evidence in the schools. Although we did not see the relevance, in our particular situation, of systematically coding our data in the way that the Northeast Consortium was intending to do, we did see it as a way of collecting evidence in individual classrooms and successively homing in on improvement strategies. A useful idea we did adopt and adapt from the Northeast Consortium was the use of pupil logs to record the children's perceptions of the classroom activity. The rest of this story is related in Chapter 3 by Liz herself.

Overview of this book

Indeed, much of the remainder of the story is related, bit by bit, in the ensuing chapters. The book itself is a case study that offers a reflexive critique of the use of collaborative teacher research partnerships as a vehicle for school improvement. It gives an account of evidence-based practice through five major strands. First, it describes the teachers' experience of engaging *in* and *with* research. Second, it explores what for them counts as evidence and the kind of evidence that they find compelling. Third, it gives an account of some of the pedagogic strategies used and relates them to effectiveness in terms of pupil outcomes. Fourth, it considers notions of professionalism, how teachers can intervene as professionals, and the ways in which structural and cultural factors within the school relate to the development of effective communities of professional practice. Finally, it critiques the notion of partnership and analyses the themes that have emerged as a result of our attempts to engage together as HEIs, schools and LEAs in this project. Importantly, all of the accounts offered are grounded within particular contexts, so that they provide not recipe knowledge but insights into ways of knowing and thinking that can be added to the repertoire of skills that all teachers need to have at their fingertips.

Thus although not intended to be a 'how to' manual, with regard to either research or pedagogy, the book explores frankly, and we hope honestly, the consortium's attempts to develop the skills required to 'do' and 'use' research; 'develop' effective pedagogy; and create a shared language of pedagogy. Our fundamental purpose has been to observe, describe, analyse and, ultimately, intervene in areas of the primary curriculum spanning mathematics, English and science. Concrete and practical, but not necessarily generalisable, the book can be dipped into for insights into research methods as well as generic professional issues about teaching and learning. The first section of the book sets the context of the initiative. Chapter 1 explores notions of evidence-based practice drawing on data collected in the consortium schools, which highlight, in particular, the problematic and contested nature of evidence, and includes results of the baseline and mid-project attitudinal surveys towards research. Chapter 2 explores notions of professionalism and the shifting nature of professional development. It draws together project data that illustrate the extent to which, at both individual and collective levels, engagement in research has affected teachers' notions of self, relations with colleagues, careers and schools cultures. Chapter 3 describes the collection and analysis of evidence relating to the common 'speaking and listening' theme: outlining the development of first a language, then a common understanding and finally frameworks for analysing and assessing listening and speaking across the consortium schools. In Chapters 4–11 we present a series of individual school case studies with substantive foci in a variety of contexts, including narrative writing, reading, comprehension, mental maths, forces, listening and speaking, etc. Each gives an account of some aspects of the research undertaken, a reflection or discussion that focuses on particular pedagogic and/or methodological issues and, where appropriate, substantive findings. We intend that this account will record both successes and the areas in which we have not done as well as we would have liked. Areas in which structural, cultural and contextual features of the school and the life histories of its teachers have conspired to inhibit progress and then sometimes accelerate it in unexpected ways. Attempts to collect survey data in one school, for example, were resisted by staff but succeeded in promoting valuable professional discussion, and beginning a very significant process of shifting the talk-culture in the school. In identifying and analysing experiences such as these, we have learnt to question the very nature of what counts as success.

Finally, Chapter 12 explores the dynamics of partnership and in particular the model depicted by the Manchester and Salford Schools Consortium. It begins by critiquing representations of partnership to be found in the literature using a variety of analytical tools, and then looks at the historical context of the project exploring the perils and pitfalls of HEI/LEA/school/TTA colleagues 'working together'.

The dynamics of the partnership can be usefully illustrated by exploring the unproblematic narrative genre adopted in this introduction, which has involved the suppression of endless crises of identity. As the story evolved and the envelopes fell though the letterbox the characters were put in place one by one. The 'we' who planned the consortium and agreed terms and conditions were the authors of this chapter together with the Headteachers of the schools and some of the teacher research coordinators. The 'we' who actually wrote the bid were largely the authors. The 'we' who signed the contract was Bill Rogers, Head of Manchester School Improvement Service, on behalf of Manchester City Council. The resulting consortium involved a cast too numerous to mention across, initially, two universities and two LEAs. The attempt to reconcile these manifold identities at times involved the consortium in open and productive dissonance. Difference and ambiguity in the 'meshing subplots', not only between partners but also within institutions, became part of the lived experience. Where conflict occurred in the writing of the narrative accounts in this book, for example, the resolution involved not agreeing an 'authentic' reality, but agreeing what could not be said. Luckily, or unluckily, as the case may be, virtually all meetings even from the early bidding phase were either minuted or taped, providing ample data for the authentication of 'accounts' and the interpretation of events.

What, of course, the tape recorders do not capture, nor chapters narrate, other than obliquely, are the human interest stories that inevitably become part of the life history of any relatively long-term project such as ours. Things that are of intense meaning to the participants but of no more than vague interest to the reader. The tragic deaths early in 1999 of Helen White and Peter Foster, research coordinator and HEI link at Cheetham Community School, were heartfelt blows to colleagues. Then there were the joyous events: the birth of Josh, long-awaited first child for Anne-Marie Roberts; promotion to Headteacher and Deputy Headteacher, respectively, for Gudrun Heatley and Gary Gornell; and, a new life in Spain at an international school for Sandy Holt.

Allegiance to the consortium survived much upheaval in a number of schools, perhaps a testament to the value vested in it. However, understandably Cheetham County School withdrew in 1999 and a number of cases of long-term illness among staff caused another of the original schools to withdraw after the first year. The latter school was replaced, but a change of Headteacher, combined with the promotion of the research coordinator, caused the replacement school to withdraw from the project. Finally, another of the original schools left the consortium when the research coordinator was promoted to the headship of a neighbouring school, taking the project with her. Most consequential of all, perhaps, was a degree of 'innovation fatigue' never before experienced in the education sector. In the first year of the project, five of the schools were to experience OfSTED inspections; the second year saw the introduction of the National Literacy Strategy, and the third the National Numeracy Strategy. All this was accompanied by a plethora of Standards Fund initiatives! Both LEAs also experienced their first major inspection during the project, and the HEIs were, as ever, always being inspected by someone or other! All part of life's rich pageant!

References

Elliott, J. (1991) *Action Research for Educational Change*. Buckingham: Open University Press.

Halsall, R. (ed.) (1998) *Teacher Research and School Improvement: Opening Doors from the Inside*. Buckingham: Open University Press.

Hillage, J., Pearson, R., Anderson, A. and Tamkin, P. (1998) *Excellence in Research on Schools*. Research Report RR74. London: DfEE.

Tooley, J. and Darby, D. (1998) *Educational Research: a Critique*. London: OfSTED.

Part I

Emerging issues in teacher research

Chapter 1

Evidence-based practice through practice-based evidence

Olwen McNamara

Introduction

The last few years have seen a sea change in the opportunities available for teachers to engage both *in doing* teacher research projects and *in using* existing findings from the wider research and evidence base. A number of recent initiatives have signposted the Government's intention to support a form of evidence-based practice (EBP) which incorporates both of these elements. Performance Threshold Assessments, for example, require the evidencing of systematic engagement in professional development which could include research and evidence-based activities with a principal focus on teaching in the classroom (DfEE, 2000). In addition, the DfEE announced a new Professional Development Programme for 2000/01, now extended for a further three years, to improve classroom practice by funding Best Practice Research Scholarships which will support teachers in undertaking research and development work and becoming more informed by existing research (DfEE, 2001). The TTA itself, of course, has a relatively long history of supporting teachers' engagement in and with research. The TTA's Teacher Research Grants scheme has, since 1996, supported about thirty teachers a year, and in 1997 our own School-based Research Consortia initiative was launched. Finally, the DfEE has established the Evidence for Policy and Practice Information and Coordinating Centre (EPPI Centre) to commission and maintain systematic reviews of, in the first instance, school-based education research, in order to build resource databases and help practitioners and policy makers to locate and access relevant research.

Against this broad backdrop of recent initiatives the relative absence of a research-informed culture in schools is marked. A range of approaches has been advocated since the 'teachers-as-researchers' movement began in the 1970s (e.g. Stenhouse, 1975; Carr and Kemmis, 1986; Elliott, 1991); however, a number of weaknesses have been evident. First, the issue of teachers engaging *with using* research and evidence, as opposed to engaging *in doing* research, has been widely neglected. Only in recent years has the former been facilitated by the publication of a number of accessible and brief research summaries in hard and electronic copy from the TTA, DfEE, SCRE (Scottish Council for Research in Education), NFER (National Foundation for Educational Research), etc. Second, research-based practice over the last three decades has been a temporary and voluntary activity for the majority of its practitioners. Initial opportunities for teachers to engage in research were through funded projects in the 1970s and 1980s but involved limited numbers of, often specially selected, individuals. Continued support for practitioner research in the late 1980s was mainly resourced from HEI lecturers' own research time, often in collaboration with LEAs (Elliott and Sarland, 1995). The effects of changes in funding bases for LEA and HEI have made such collaboration less likely in the last decade and teachers' experience of research has mainly involved award-bearing Continuing Professional Development courses, and, to a more limited degree because of pressures of time, Initial Teacher Training. A potential failing of this HEI accreditation model of 'teacher research' is that research methodology and theory can easily become decontextualised from practice.

Attitudes to research

When we first embarked upon this project we were interested in exploring teachers' attitudes to research. So, as mentioned briefly in the Introduction, we conducted a baseline questionnaire survey in the consortium schools. The same questionnaire was subsequently repeated, on a smaller scale, towards the end of the project. One of our first corporate activities then was to devise the questionnaire. We were interested to ascertain teachers' perceptions and experiences of, and beliefs and attitudes towards, *doing* and *using* research. The reason for this was fourfold. First, it was an exercise in constructing a questionnaire, even worse an exercise in constructing a questionnaire collaboratively! (You can see the end result in Toolkit 1). It was our intention to collect both descriptive and explanatory data so we devised a mixture of open and closed questions. [Munn and Driver (1995) is a useful sourcebook, which gives a practical guide to using questionnaires in small-scale research]. There are a number of other reasons why it can be useful to conduct a questionnaire, apart from the obvious one of wanting to collect information and elicit views. A second, and for us important, reason was that we hoped that the arrival of the questionnaire would raise the profile of the project within the schools and, on a more general level, get staff to begin thinking and talking about the value of doing and using research. Third, we wanted to collect data that could be used in the research training sessions in order that data analysis would be relevant and illuminating and not simply an academic exercise. Finally, there was always the option to repeat the questionnaire, at a later date, to detect whether any shifts in attitudes had occurred within the schools as a result of the project. We had 100 questionnaire returns (about 80 per cent), which was a very high response rate; characteristically 30 per cent is not uncommon in the teaching profession.

Images of research

Perhaps the question that overall gave us the richest data was 'What image does educational research hold for you?' These images, we discovered, varied enormously, and responses to this very open question included insights on the nature of the data, the findings, the research processes and indeed quite a lot upon researchers themselves.

Two prominent, and largely negative, themes that emerged were that research was seen as 'academic work' and that data were often imagined to be 'statistical' in nature. Academic work involving 'Professors undertaking tests and surveys and making reports' was berated because 'people in universities' were 'out of touch with real classrooms'. 'Academia' was depicted as a 'utopia irrelevant to actual classroom situations'. Research was characterised as 'dry facts' that 'failed to influence practice'. Statistics were mistrusted because 'statistics can prove anything' and can be manipulated. One respondent in particular displayed a very negative image of educational research: 'statistics/research carried out in isolation resulted in misinterpretation/sometimes manipulation of findings. Depending on who is using the statistics/research useful findings can be ignored for political reasons or because they are not in fashion'. Statistical data were seen as a stick with which to beat teachers, 'telling us how bad we are with no ideas of how to improve', and were thus 'very demoralising'. 'Raising confidence' and 'self-esteem' were currently felt to be the highest priority in teaching!

The processes involved in research were often depicted as technical:

- 'controlling variables'
- 'questionnaires'
- 'graphs, surveys and videos'
- 'making observations, asking questions, testing hypothesis'
- 'jargon'.

Such technical processes were not always viewed negatively; they were sometimes seen as 'exciting', 'positive' or 'interesting' when they involved 'analysing data and processing to workable suggestions'.

Research was perhaps viewed most positively when it was linked directly to practice: 'Action research is most useful, teacher-based and school-based.' It could be a source of new ideas, an instrument of change mostly as a means to better performance, and was thought to involve:

- 'assessment of current practice'
- 'justification for good practice'
- 'looking in detail at teaching'
- 'finding out about how children learn a subject'.

Occasionally, however, implementation of research findings was thought to bring about 'change in curricula content and teaching methods which [was] not always in the best interest of children' or was 'impractical on a day-to-day basis'. Linked to this was a concern about the practical use to which the findings were generally put. The perception was that involvement with others in research involved 'hard work and very little feedback'; and concern was expressed that sometimes 'not much was done with the findings'. Again this was linked to 'the wrong people coming up with the wrong suggestions, poorly researched and then left to teachers on the ground to implement'.

Doing research

Surprisingly, 35 per cent of teachers responding to the questionnaire claimed some experience of carrying out research. This was almost entirely related to either Initial Teacher Training, just under half, or Continuing Professional Developments/Masters level work, just over half. Overall, 40 per cent of teachers found the thought of being involved in educational research was 'very valuable' and 30 per cent found the thought of being involved 'very interesting'. On the whole, although such activity was viewed positively in principle, on a practical level pressures of time and workload meant that only 4 per cent of teachers who responded felt that being involved in educational research would be 'very manageable'. The pressure of time necessary to engage in the research process was an ever-present theme in most responses: 'lots of books' and 'paperwork' but 'teachers don't have time to read'. Even a number of the individual positive responses involved a 'yes but', and the 'but' was usually the time that research was seen to involve, 'important, necessary – but yet another addition to workload'.

Information about teaching

Teachers felt that currently their most valuable sources of information about teaching were:

1   'colleagues', a substantial 85 per cent;
2   'books' were cited by 80 per cent ;
3   'LEAs', 'professional journals', 'press and media' and 'DfEE' between 60 and 70 per cent;
4   'conferences' and 'OFSTED' were perceived to be slightly less informative;
5   'TTA' and 'universities' were at the bottom of the heap with only 30 per cent, partly perhaps reflecting disenchantment with academia and teachers' perceived current use of research findings and literature.

Using research

Despite teachers' apparent current lack of use of research, it appeared that they perceived the potential impact of educational research on teaching as quite substantial and also beneficial. Some 50 per cent of teachers claimed that research increased 'teacher effectiveness' and 'teacher knowledge'. On the down side, 60 per cent of those who responded felt that research did not increase the public's esteem of teachers 'at all'. The vast majority of respondents felt that teaching would improve considerably if teachers knew more about *using* research. There was the perception that 'Single class teaching can result in the teacher's approach becoming insular – the more we know of education in other areas, the better'; 'Sometimes I think you can get stuck into a routine of doing things a certain way, finding out about research findings will help teachers, give them fresh ideas and different view points'. Research was not viewed so much as a 'stick with which to beat teachers' but as an aid: it would show teachers where they were 'barking up the wrong trees', reduce 'unproductive work', and stop them 'reinventing the wheel'. Research, it was felt, could improve:

- 'quality of teaching';
- 'pupil learning';
- 'teacher confidence';
- 'ownership' of developments in educatio;n
- understanding of the 'rationale of change';
- underpinning of 'decision-making, planning and organising'.

Only one respondent rejected outright the advantages of research in terms of professional development: 'If you have been teaching for a long time I think you have a pretty good idea what works'. Another teacher thought such dated knowledge unsafe as 'teaching is not static; it needs to use all support available to meet the needs of an ever-changing society'.

There were some clear messages for researchers about current practice and the importance of 'relevance', 'accessibility', 'transferability', 'validity' and 'applicability'. Research, it was felt:

- must offer 'practical advice/ways forward';
- should 'summarise [findings or] they will not, in reality, be accessible';
- should not produce just 'long reports' full of 'educational jargon' and 'unexplained statistics [that] just turn people off';
- should ensure 'outsiders' 'listen to/take note of what teachers have to say';
- should bridge the gap between theory and practice - 'useful research' was 'disregarded in practice' because 'putting into practice research findings in the classroom can be very difficult'.

How attitudes changed

Towards the end of the project we chose to canvass opinion regarding attitudes to research again. We repeated certain of the questions used in the baseline questionnaire survey and added additional ones (see Toolkit 2) designed to provide some evaluative information (although the project was, of course, subject to a major external evaluation and other internal assessments). The survey was conducted on a smaller scale than previously, with only five rather than eight schools taking part (two schools had dropped out over the course, and by dint of circumstances another school was unable to complete the questionnaire at the time). In addition, the response rate fell to about 50 per cent; our strategic timing of the survey during the last 2 weeks of the summer term was necessary but far from ideal!

Images of research

Taking into account that the responses may well have come from the most positive and supportive teachers there was still a noticeable shift in attitude in response to the question 'What image does educational research conjure up now?'. 'Statistics' was only cited once and 'professors in ivory towers' did not feature at all. About 60 per cent of the responses were positive; the themes that could be seen to be emerging were practical relevance and partnership:

- 'far more positive with practical implications in the classroom';
- 'can practically impact on teaching practice/perceptions';
- 'a way forward for educational progress, which is central to teachers' own interests';
- 'progress and development';
- 'working in liaison with other educational bodies to coordinate research based on informed opinion';

- 'working as a team to further the development of education with particular reference to the children's progress and practitioner's practice'.

More equivocal responses included a number of 'not positive' and 'neutral' statements:

- 'some useful stuff. Not as daunting – can be useful when small-scale. Generalisations can be very dangerous';
- 'statistics';
- 'people with tape recorders';
- 'very open-ended tasks'.

The more negative responses were:

- 'hard work on the researcher involved – a great amount of time involved';
- 'a boring waste of time – involving loads of paperwork';
- 'people being paid to invent new names for tried and tested practices and then presenting them as innovations'.

'Doing' and 'using' our schools' own research

Nearly 60 per cent of teachers claimed that they had been 'directly involved in data gathering and interpretation', and the same amount claimed that they had used the findings. When asked about the benefits of the project they were, in rank order:

1   'professional development of staff';
2   'pupil gains';
3   'increased self confidence of staff';
4   'support for development work';
5   'better collaboration with HE';
6   'better collaboration within school';
7   'improved management of school / subject area'.

Areas where little movement was perceived were 'better collaboration with LEA', 'raised esteem from OfSTED' and 'raised esteem from parents and the local community'. Regarding the perceived costs of the project, 40 per cent claimed none (as far as they knew); time out of class featured in 15 per cent of responses; and pressure on project coordinator 30 per cent.

Was it all worthwhile?

Respondents concluded overwhelmingly (93 per cent) that involvement in the project had been worthwhile for themselves and/or their school. However, there was an acknowledgement that recent changes in education had brought with them increased pressures that made involvement in research activity more challenging at present. One of the new questions included in the repeat questionnaire was 'What, if any, recent changes in education have made you feel differently about *doing* research?' Responses recorded in respect of 'more inclined to be involved' were 'financial incentive'; 'because of SATs results and raising standards'; 'cooperation between educational agencies'. There were slightly more responses in respect of being 'less inclined to be involved' and they were all associated with increased workload and pressures from new initiatives: 'pressure and stress of work'; 'Literacy Strategy/ Numeracy Strategy/Curriculum 2000'; 'number of new initiatives being introduced'.

Evidence-based practice

In the Introduction we referred briefly to the initiative launched by the TTA in 1996 and promoted by Hargreaves (1996) in his annual TTA lecture. This sought to make teaching a research-based profession in order to improve the quality of teaching and thereby the standard of pupil outcomes through engaging teachers *in doing* research and *with using* knowledge from the wider evidence base. The notion was based largely upon ideas imported from other professional areas, like medicine and to a lesser degree nursing, where evidence-based practice was more robustly established. For example, the British Government recently established a statutory body known as the 'National Institute of Clinical Excellence' to identify and prescribe 'best practice' methods and procedures to be implemented by doctors. The EPPI Centre, referred to earlier, was modelled upon the well-established international Cochrane Collaboration, which prepares, maintains and disseminates systematic reviews of effective health care interventions.

Even in medicine, however, such approaches remain controversial and are still not universally accepted and acclaimed. A small UK pilot questionnaire survey, of sixty-eight teachers, GPs and surgeons, devised to test whether doctors make more use of research than teachers, revealed that surgeons (83 per cent response rate) were considerably more involved, both as consumers of research and as active researchers, although they too 'bemoan lack of time' and have doubts about 'its applicability and purpose'. The 37 per cent of teachers and 50 per cent of GPs who responded showed 'no evidence of a difference ... in terms of their taking part actively in the research process'. The researchers suggested that the incentive GPs and teachers have to engage in research and/or publication activity is slight, whereas surgeons reap rewards from such investments in terms of career development (Hannan *et al.*, 1998, p. 17).

In education EBP is still in an embryonic phase and this is signalled, in part, by the fluidity of the language used to describe it. Terminology with respect to policy and practice has, in the last few years, shifted from 'research-based' (TTA 1996) to 'research and evidence-based' (TTA, 1999) and even to 'evidence-informed' (Sebba, 1999). Davies (1999, p. 108–9), for example, defines 'Evidence Based Education' as 'a set of principles and practices for enhancing educational policy and practice ... [that] operates on two levels. The first is to utilise existing evidence from worldwide research and literature ... The second is to establish sound evidence'.

Two crucial issues, however, underpin the current debate. First, 'How will EBP inform teaching and what effect will it have upon the teaching profession?' Educational stakeholders have many different views on this. At one extreme, some present it as an 'empowerment' strategy, a formal and specialised knowledge base, which would enhance professional autonomy and status and develop in the teacher a 'repertoire' of skills. At the other extreme, some expose it as an 'entrapment', a technology of teaching that would deny craft knowledge and reduce the capacity for professional action by providing 'recipe' knowledge (McNamara and Stronach, 1999a). Second, an issue to which I will return later and again one where no agreement would be found between, or within, groups of educational stakeholders: 'What counts as evidence?' To this I might add three supplementary questions:

- For whom is the evidence intended, e.g. policy makers, practitioners, parents, educational researchers, etc.?
- In what context is the evidence to be employed, e.g. schools, individual teachers, etc.?
- For what purpose is the evidence to be used, e.g. to inform policy, to develop theory, to open new pedagogic possibilities, etc.?

Evidence-based practitioners?

We wondered whether teachers in the consortium schools viewed themselves as evidence-based practitioners and in order to find out we conducted a further small questionnaire survey to augment other data we had from a series of focus group seminars held in consortium schools. First, it appeared that virtually all consortium teachers had some notion of what EBP might be. Their notions ranged from, at one extreme, the 'scientific and experimental', generated by 'experimental pre- and post-testing of initiatives before wide-scale implementation' and grounded in knowledge of 'teaching methods that are proved by results' using 'agreed standardised measures/targets against which children's performance could be measured'. At the other extreme teachers saw EBP as based upon a sort of 'reflective practitioner' model in which, for example, ongoing monitoring and assessment was seen as an essential element of the teacher's role. There was a considerable amount of agreement that teaching should, largely at least, be based on evidence, and a few teachers claimed that all their judgements were currently based on evidence. A significant number of teachers, however, identified 'experience-based intuition' as an essential part of their skill base. Teachers felt that if this element of their repertoire of skills became marginalised to a significant degree then the profession risked the consequence that 'only elements that could be tested by tick lists etc. would be valued and measured'.

From these responses it seemed that, first, teachers in general understood EBP to encompass insights derived from both research findings and the wider evidence base that encompassed information such as audit data. Thus they used the term to include judgements and understandings based upon both 'research evidence' and 'other evidence'. Second, that 'experience-based intuition', intuitive practitioner understandings and skills, were still deemed an essential part of the teachers' repertoire. This seemed to indicate that, in their view, 'evidence-informed' practice (Sebba, 1999) would be a more appropriate model for the teaching profession than 'evidence-based'.

Teachers were particularly sensitive to the implications that EBP had with regard to their status as 'professionals'. The expectation they held of teaching as a profession was characterised first by the way it acted: it should be 'a profession that reflects upon its own practice' and takes 'action upon evidence', continually questioning, adapting and updating good practice to increase standards. Second, it should be treated as a profession in its relations with associated external bodies: evidence should be taken from teachers as professionals; they should be 'listened to', 'respected' and 'consulted'. Politicians, DfEE, TTA and LEA officials were all seen as guilty, at times, of ignoring teachers' professional judgements. Ironically, it was felt that support and encouragement from just such powerful policy making bodies was essential to make EBP a more realistic possibility.

Aspirations to make teaching an evidence-based profession were clearly not to be realised without difficulty. Obstacles were seen to centre primarily around four issues:

- time constraints – time to 'absorb', 'evaluate' and 'utilise' research findings – which was thought to be a particular problem in the primary phase;
- financial constraints and resource implications;
- the 'accessibility', 'reliability', 'credibility', 'transferability' and 'applicability' of research findings;
- the political nature of research findings – not only what the findings were 'about' but also what they were 'for'. 'Why was the research done?', 'Who is going to benefit and how?', 'How are the findings going to be used?'. In this respect teachers were very clear about whom they did trust – 'only other teachers', 'my union' – and whom they didn't… . Findings were political statements that could be, and were it was felt, 'manipulated'. Yet it was not always overt manipulation that teachers feared, some felt the findings could be 'slanted' as a result of researchers' attitudes, beliefs and preconceptions.

What counts as evidence?

Thus it was that teachers challenged the nature of what was to count as evidence. Much is recorded in the chapters that follow about the kinds of evidence that teachers in individual school projects found compelling when it came to persuading them, and their colleagues, to change their classroom practice and, further, what convinced them that the change strategies they had implemented were effective. For some it was staff room discussion, for others it was videos or interview data from the children, for others still it was National Test results. Many teachers responding to the survey made a clear distinction between 'evidence' and the whole range of factors that 'influenced' them in making judgements about classroom practice: class profile (academic/behaviour/ability/personality, etc.), resources, curricula, policies, pedagogy, colleagues, etc.

'Evidence' comprised a mix of 'external' standardised measures and 'internal' professional judgements. The external measures were clearly quantitative in nature and concerned auditable commodities such as skills, National Test results, targets, OfSTED ratings, local and National League Tables and (self)-audit processes. Most schools appeared to conduct a highly sophisticated level of analysis of their position in the 'League Tables' based upon these 'hard' data. Quantitative data such as National Test results, PANDA, Autumn Package and LEA context-specific benchmarking data were analysed at school, key stage, class and individual pupil levels. Teachers also made 'internal' professional judgements based on practitioner-orientated 'soft' data that were often, but not always, qualitative in nature. These analyses were based on personal judgement, understandings of local context, educational values/beliefs and intuitive experience. They included professional assessment of standards, knowledge, skills, understanding, progress and motivation of both individual children and whole cohorts.

Schools, and individual teachers with them, appeared to 'juggle' with a combination of these two ways of 'warranting' their professional judgements (McNamara and Corbin, 2001). For example, one school attempted to characterise a 'Level 4 pupil' in terms of not only 'hard' data (reading, spelling, non-verbal reasoning, etc.) but also 'soft' data (motivation, learning style, personality, etc.). In another school auditable commodities such as 'targets', although acknowledged as problematic in terms of audit processes because of the highly transient school population, were felt to be strategically important in terms of raising corporate awareness of achievement and attainment. The distinction between quantitative auditable commodities and qualitative practice-based understandings was, in part, also evident in the way that teachers reflected upon the potential of research evidence to inform practice.

Teachers identified a number of dilemmas relating to the problematic nature of the 'evidence' upon which they made judgements; and upon which they in turn were held accountable. A significant divergence was identified in what the various educational stakeholders (Headteachers, policy makers, parents, pupils, etc.) were perceived to count as valid evidence. Teachers weighed evidence that they, as practitioners, found compelling alongside evidence that they believed policymakers found persuasive. They felt that 'auditable' commodities like National Test results were privileged by 'the powers that be'. In contrast, teachers felt that evidence which they personally found compelling, such as that grounded in professional judgements like teacher assessment of pupil performance, was marginalised or no longer 'trusted'.

Practice-based evidence

Reflecting on the teacher research movement 'ten years on' in the USA, Cochran-Smith and Lytle (1999, p. 22) conclude that as pedagogic and assessment prescriptions have proliferated so too has an underlying assumption that has often seemed to:

> de-emphasise differences in local cultures, de-emphasise the construction of local knowledge in and by school communities, and de-emphasise the role of the teacher as decision maker and change agent.

Yet it was just such local cultures and contexts to which Cochran-Smith and Lytle (1999) refer that emerged as a very significant theme in consortium discussions and data-gathering exercises. The issue was particularly vexed because researchers and governments alike were perceived by teachers to pay scant attention to the importance of contextual variables such as cultural and socioeconomic norms etc. For example, optimum class size, often the focus of research enquiries, was felt to be dependent on teaching style, age group, school population, etc. Yet the problem of accessing this detailed information, if indeed it was included, from long, inaccessible research reports was seen as a considerable problem for busy teachers. On the other hand, the dangers of 'soundbite' reporting were also noted, for example: failure to define terms, such as 'progress' and 'effective'; or supply contextual information, such as class size; or disclose methodology, such as sample size. The dilemma faced here was explicitly articulated by one teacher who observed: 'headlines in the press… blown out of proportion… always something controversial. Yet we haven't honestly got time to sit down and read research documents'. Additionally, when teachers did read research documents they were often disappointed in that they were rarely explicit in offering implications for practice, a 'way forward'. For example, research had identified 'a dip [drop in pupil learning gains] in certain years, yet no idea of how, why or what to do about it, and all the other extraneous effects that might result in the dip'.

Discussion with teachers about engaging with insights from the wider evidence base in their own classroom practice often revisited the problem of contextualisation. They felt that findings from research reports, newspapers, conferences and journal articles could not be passively and unquestioningly accepted and transferred from one socio-cultural context to another. There were concerns, as noted earlier, about the political motives, and the lack of methodological transparency, behind some research studies, but just as important was the process of 'owning' research: the need to contextualise findings. In order to engage effectively *with* research, the findings needed to be actively interpreted, adapted, implemented, monitored and evaluated in relation to the school context and the teacher's classroom practices. Likewise, if teachers were to engage effectively *in doing* research it was felt that they should also engage *with* existing literature and relevant research evidence in order to gain insights, and build research questions cumulatively upon existing knowledge. So the distinction drawn between engagement *in doing* research and *with using* the wider research and evidence base appeared, on close inspection, a little fuzzier than was sometimes presented.

'Top-down' formulations for engaging *in* research and, more particularly, *with* the wider evidence base do not then, at present, connect with the experience of the vast majority of practitioners in education. The same is thought to be true in some areas of the health care professions. The Department of Health, for example, appears to present a notion of evidence-based practice that privileges external evidence and theory over practitioner-based knowledge: 'Many members of the nursing profession undertake small scale projects on issues which interest them… However, it must not be seen as a substitute for the generalisable and cumulative research which we would place at the heart of a strategy for advancing research in nursing' (Department of Health, 1993, p. 6). Rolfe (1998) suggests that the 'top-down' research-based practice advocated by the Department of Health is an unhelpful model and advocates instead clinical practitioner–based research and personal and experiential judgement in applying knowledge locally to individual patients. Many teachers in consortium schools also, as noted previously, identified a disjunction between theory and practice; and resolutions offered were similar to those suggested by Rolfe. They felt that teaching would only be improved if research was 'carried out' or 'contextualised' by actual teachers and using 'first-hand experience, supported by school-generated data' which could 'relate closely to context and needs'. In this way, the prototypes such as those offered by the TTA-funded Research-based Schools Consortia and the more recent DfEE Best Practice Research Scholarships, patterned on the TTA Teacher Research Grants Scheme, were seen as promising models of evidence-based practice grounded securely in practice-based evidence.

Acknowledgements

Sections of this chapter are based upon McNamara and Corbin (2001) and an earlier paper McNamara *et al.* (2000) presented at BERA, Cardiff. The findings of the baseline questionnaire were first reported in a paper presented by McNamara and Stronach (1999b) at BERA, Sussex.

References

Carr, W. and Kemmis, S. (1986) *Becoming Critical: Knowing Through Action Research*. London: Falmer Press.

Cochran-Smith, M. and Lytle, S. (1999) The teacher research movement: a decade later. *Educational Researcher*, 28(7): 15–25.

Elliott, J. and Sarland, C. (1995) A study of teachers as researchers, in the context of award-bearing courses and research degrees. *British Educational Research Journal*, 21(3): 371–386.

Davies, P. (1999) What is evidence-based education? *British Journal of Educational Studies*, 47(2): 108–121.

Department for Education and Employment (2000) *Threshold Assessment: Guidance on Completing the Application Form*. London: DfEE.

Department for Education and Employment (2001) *Learning and Teaching: a Strategy for Professional Development*. London: DfEE.

Department of Health (1993) *Report of the Task Force on Strategy for research in Nursing, Midwifery and Health Visiting*. London: DoH.

Elliott, J. (1991) *Action Research for Educational Change*. Milton Keynes: Open University Press.

Hannan, A., Enwright, H. and Ballard, P. (1998) Using research: the results of a pilot study comparing teachers, general practitioners and surgeons, in 'EducatiON-LINE' at http://www.leeds.ac.uk/educal.

Hargreaves, D. (1996a) Teaching as a research-based profession: possibilities and prospects. Teacher Training Agency Annual Lecture London 1996. London: TTA.

McNamara, O. and Stronach, I. (1999a) Working together: short straw and long spoons. Paper presented at the BERA Research-based school university partnership for continuing teacher education conference, Kingston.

McNamara, O. and Stronach, I. (1999b) Teachers: thinking, using and doing research. Paper presented at the BERA annual conference, Sussex.

McNamara, O., Jones, L. and Van-Es, C. (2000) Evidence-based practice through practice-based evidence: the global and the local. Paper Presented at BERA, Cardiff.

McNamara, O. and Corbin, B. (2001) Warranting practices: teachers embedding the National Numeracy Strategy. *British Journal of Educational Studies*, 49(3): 260–284.

Munn, P. and Drever, E. (1995) *Using Questionnaires in Small Scale Research: a Teacher's Guide*. Edinburgh: SCRE.

Rolfe, G. (1998) The theory–practice gap in nursing: from research-based practice to practitioner-based research. *Journal of Advanced Nursing*, 28(3): 672–679.

Sebba, J. (1999) Developing evidence-informed policy and practice in education. Paper presented at BERA, Brighton.

Stenhouse, L. (1975) *An Introduction to Curriculum Research and Development*. London: Heinemann.

Teacher Training Agency (1996) *Teaching as a Research-based Profession*. London: TTA.

Teacher Training Agency (1999) *Improving Standards: Research and Evidence Based Practice*. London: TTA.

Chapter 2

Research and the professional self

Anne Campbell

> Development is an elusive phenomenon. Who can say that any behaviour or thought signifies development if we have no indication of its predecessors? Having spoken with conviction of Vicki's growth through the research at many levels and in many ways, one has to be tentative in the argument, for it is impossible to say whether these qualities that gave rise to the research and to the subsequent actions were ready formed, if latent, in Vicki, waiting to emerge in their fullness, or whether they were just glimmers, laying dormant like seeds of actualisation, waiting for the right conditions to grow and develop into more substantial expression.
>
> Dadds (1995, p. 152)

Introduction

This chapter is based on group and individual interviews and discussions, undertaken by the author, with teachers, HEI tutors and LEA advisors participating in the Manchester and Salford Schools Consortium. The author acted as a 'critical friend' and participant observer, collecting and collating the data during the life of the project, attending meetings, residential writing weekends, listening to the teachers' stories and visiting schools when appropriate. It may be of interest to note that the author, through her previous research and development work in teacher education in the Greater Manchester area, had existing relationships with some of the schools and teachers, which facilitated her role as 'critical friend'. Informal group and individual interview sessions took place midway through the project and at the final residential session. These interviews were taped, transcribed and then used as the basis for this chapter. Following consultation with the teachers in the project, it was decided not to use either actual or fictional names but to simply report verbatim, through quotes, the teachers' views of their professional development.

At the outset of the project the participants had little idea of how researching their chosen topics would affect their lives and careers. Like Vicki, the action researcher in Marian Dadds's (1995) story of one teacher's journey and 'passionate enquiry', it is difficult to prove that participation in the project caused 'amazing' developments to occur. In the views of the teachers themselves towards the end of the project, it was apparent that they thought the experience of 'doing research' and investigating the evidence base of their practice had had a significant effect on their professional lives.

For some it has meant a long hard slog to see the light at the end of the tunnel; for others, while not quite equating to a 'Damascus' type of experience, it has certainly resulted in enlightenment. For a few others it has seemed to be the start of many changes in their professional and personal lives – a change of school, promotion or in one case a change of country of domicile. These are not uncommon occurrences in groups of teachers who are researching their work and evaluating their professional development. The shifting, changing nature of professional development groups is familiar to those engaged in supporting teachers' professional development.

It would be tempting just to accept the surface evidence, to not probe beyond the first layer and to take the easy path of reporting the obvious, observable benefits of teacher participation in research. But often it is the hidden and covert layers which are more interesting and indicative of development. Clandinin and Connolly (1996) talk of 'secret, sacred, cover stories' where teachers talk among themselves in their communities, perhaps obscuring the professional issues. Teachers in the project felt the need to tell anecdotes and stories about their research and its impact on their own and colleagues' professional development. 'Doing research' legitimised talking about teaching and professional issues and gave teachers the reason to engage in precise, concrete professional dialogues: '... We have also developed a language of professional discussion which we didn't use before. We had it, but we didn't use it. I think we've always had it. We neglect it; it is a criticism of us'; 'Now ... we talk about what we are doing, sharing ideas, but really looking at it closely and planning. We never talked like this before.'

Behind these statements we can detect a previous reluctance to engage in 'professional' dialogue. Yet the quality of teachers' interactions with each other, according to Little (1982, 1990), is one of the major factors in successful schools and environments where change and innovation thrive. Paradoxically, although the 'new managerialism' can put pressure on individuals and cause isolation, it can also, as David Hargreaves (1994) discusses, demand that teachers' planning is more collaborative, their teaching more outcomes orientated and their relationships with pupils and parents more contractual.

Timing is a crucial factor. At the time of writing, the teachers in the project are only beginning to realise the impact of the project: some to start on another journey on a 'formal' course at the university; others to enthuse their colleagues to embrace the methods developed during the project; others to reflect and gather their thoughts for the future.

This chapter will attempt to examine from the data collected what the teachers actually identified as the impact on their professional development and thinking. It will also speculate, in the light of literature in the field, and with a bit of 'crystal ball gazing', what might happen in the future, as time elapses and the experience of doing research 'embeds' itself into teachers' practice. In doing so, first this chapter will undertake an exploration of the power of the 'personal' in professional development and will hope to raise important issues concerning the need for teacher ownership, engagement and identity in research projects. Second, a consideration of the relevance of contexts, cultures and collaborations, which characterise the experiences of the teachers, will be discussed. Third, an investigation of autonomy, agency and accountability in relation to participants' experiences of research will help to locate the project in the current educational arena.

The power of the 'personal' in professional development

> Teachers' work is deeply embedded in teachers' lives, in their pasts, in their biographies, in the cultures or traditions of teaching to which they have become committed. Developing the teacher, therefore involves developing the person, developing the life.
>
> Hargreaves (1992, p. 233)

In the current turbulent educational climate, sometimes openly hostile to teachers and where there is more public accountability than ever before, it is heartening to listen to the individual, personal, voices of teachers who are, against the many odds, engaging in projects to improve and develop their professional practice. Much has been written of the value of teachers' narratives, stories and life histories in documenting and understanding teacher development (Ball and Goodson, 1985; Day, 1993; Thomas, 1995; Clandinin and Connolly, 1996; Campbell and Kane, 1998). Dadds (1995, p. 145), in the study of the teacher action researcher, claims her study helped to 'illuminate the contextualised nature of professional development within the shifting ecology of the school culture and within the motivation and power of personal, historical and autobiographical agenda' and demonstrated the inter-relatedness of the personal and the professional when evaluating development. These studies make assertions which underline the importance of teachers' personal beliefs, attitudes and experiences to their professional development, and it is just such personal stories and histories that this chapter turns to in order to investigate participants professional development.

Understanding of professional development is related to current definitions and policies and subject to the political and social influences prevalent in society. Whitty (1999), in his recent paper 'Teacher Professionalism for New Times', argues that, following a period of heavy regulation of teachers, it is time to seek alternative forms of professionalism and professionality (after Hoyle, 1974) by espousing 'democratic decision-making in education' to counter fragmentation and the commercialisation of the profession as manifested in performance management initiatives and in the 'new managerialism'. Bolam (1999, p. 1) identified the main features of this 'new public management' as including the centralisation of decision making; reduced collegial involvement; increased line management; less teacher autonomy; the delegation of routine tasks to 'para-professionals'; more distinct managerial and bureaucratic layers; and an emphasis on target setting and 'rational' accountability. Campbell and Kane (2000, p. 294) agreed with Bolam's summary by likening it to a well-known London 'folly', 'Life has become very Domelike: increasingly robotic, with constant breakdowns making it more hyperactive than interactive'.

The teachers in the project similarly felt strongly about the changes with regard to the demands of a 'new' professionalism:

> ... introducing competition into the system, like Performance Related Pay, or publishing league tables, is changing professionality at all levels. You have got Ofsted coming into schools ... I've got a top set, year 6 in maths, and the teacher in the next class has a bottom set – it's easy for me to teach and I might get a 'good' because of the attainment of the children and the other teacher might get a 'satisfactory' or less because of the low ability of children. There is supposed to

be a marrying of what is happening with the teaching and learning, with the attainment and progress, but it doesn't work like that. League tables call professionality into question and raise issues about 'cheating' or 'teaching to the tests too much'

Participants in the project had well-developed ideas about how the current climate had affected their professionality and agreed that one of the major gaps in recent official documents and pronouncements was the lack of real 'insider' perspectives. There were many external views of what being a professional meant but not enough reflection of the reality of what teachers thought. Much of this 'insider' perspective related to teachers' experiences in implementing National Literacy and Numeracy Strategies and their personal feelings of being 'swamped' and having to 'survive' the juggernaut of recent innovations is evident: 'I have just sort of felt swamped by the Literacy Hour, if you know what I mean'; 'in some ways the pressure you experience brings you together in order to survive …. But it's more than survival – all of us together are better than an individual'.

But there was light at the end of the tunnel! The experience of doing research had provided 'an oasis' for the project teachers, giving them increased 'self confidence' to talk about their practice in informed ways. They had felt 'the luxury of sitting down and discussing their own professional development' and felt they had been able to 'develop a language of professional discussion'. Many agreed that regular reflection and evaluation of their practice had contributed to the raising of standards of teaching and learning in their schools and classrooms. Some had experienced a 'wake up call': 'I have found that reading the research of other teachers, about the nitty-gritty of classroom practice has really, as you say, woken me up again to looking at what I do in a much more detailed way'.

And some refreshment: 'I am in my fourth year of teaching and this is the first time since I have actually left college that I have looked at my own teaching skills'; 'I don't think at my school we would have seriously implemented and looked at outcomes had it not been for the research. For myself there has been a lot of professional development'.

A sort of therapy? Or refreshing of skills once known but since forgotten?

All learning involves risks, which at times can feel uncomfortable for the individual. Not all teachers found talking about their professional development through research easy, they found it difficult to develop an awareness of what they did in the classroom and to identify 'growth points'. The use of video evidence was a valuable aid for teachers who found it helped to observe their classroom practice and discuss their teaching with a colleague from school or university: 'She was very demoralised by an inspection report, and actually going back and looking at herself on video and noting the many tactics and strategies which she used as a teacher in order to teach her class, reaffirmed her notion of herself as a teacher'.

Therapy was having the time to 'think about and develop, to reflect upon, to regroup the children and try again … it doesn't always mean that you can walk in and implement a strategy and it works'. And having the confidence to admit, 'I've looked at the evidence, it has increased my knowledge and understanding, it has affected my practice but I've hit a wall – I don't know what to do next'. And living with uncertainty: 'it feels so messy. You don't think you are going anywhere or doing anything'.

In many of the teachers' stories there was a sense of the loneliness of the 'long distance teacher' and of isolation in their classrooms as they tried to tackle their problems at the beginning of the project. It was suggested by members of the project team that there should be web site entries about investigating teaching along the lines of 'It works for me!' and another 'It doesn't work for me but it may work for you!' in order to share experiences and reduce the 'loneliness' factor. A 'small steps' approach, which recognised the need for time, commitment and perseverance was, it was argued, required for success in researching classrooms. Day (1999) recognised that professional identity and self-esteem are essential features of teachers' lives and of the process of professional development and he emphasised the contribution of sustained critical reflection and evaluation to teacher growth and development. It would appear that small steps and a degree of success and achievement are key to keeping 'on task' with projects.

Individual support and positive, constructive feedback on their own personal project were much sought after by teachers. This support fuelled the development of collaborative strategies later in the project, which helped reduce the isolation. These are addressed in the next part of the chapter. It is important not to view the emphasis on personal critical appraisal of practice as self-indulgent, though at times this could be construed as a weakness, leaving teachers vulnerable to being criticised as individuals lacking skills and knowledge. It is widely recognised that teaching requires a big investment of personal skills, qualities and knowledge. Taking the risk of openly appraising and evaluating one's practice in order to improve it is arguably risky and those doing so need to be confident of support and understanding. This involves the 'head and the heart'.

Hargreaves (1992, p. 236) reminds us of the importance of the personal and individual to the success of developments:

> Attempts at teacher development and educational change will meet with little success unless they engage with the purposes of the teacher, unless they acknowledge the person that the teacher is and unless they adjust to the slow pace of human growth that takes place in the individual and collective lives of teachers. Short of relocating in-service training somewhere on the road to Damascus, there are few better starting points for proponents of teacher development than this.

Teachers researching their own classrooms have the potential to locate development where it arguably should be, in the hearts and minds of the teachers, in their everyday lives and work. But let us not forget there is more to research than planning and implementing developments. There is a need for wider perspectives beyond the school, and for critical reflection and evaluation, engagement with thinking, literature and other studies, and systematic, sustained inquiry within a critical peer group, the keystones of teacher research.

Contexts, cultures and collaborations

The contexts of the school, the LEA and the national climate are of great importance to the ways in which teachers' research and professional development are received, nurtured and sustained. There can be little doubt that the context of the late twentieth and early twenty-first century is one of constant change and innovation, of multiple government proposals aimed at raising standards in education. These greatly affect the education of pupils and teachers. Dadds (1995, p. 160) is optimistic about how the current climate, which despite the pressures of responding to many initiatives, supports joint planning, thinking, agreeing and action and can help the emergence of collaborative action research. Certainly it is no longer possible, or desirable, 'to close one's door and get on with it' as often in the past.

In these 'real worlds', which individual teachers inhabit, the prevailing culture of the school is of paramount importance and can make or break the success of a project. Teachers in the project experienced varying degrees of support and encouragement from within their schools. They felt they were viewed differently especially when they 'brought the project to the school'. This sometimes resulted in a whole school involvement in development, particularly in schools where there was a culture of sharing and discussing new ideas. Perhaps a sort of Group Therapy?

There were incidences of teacher-researchers contributing to whole school practice:

> When we took the ideas and discussions back to school after research meetings, when we were doing a lot of 'hands on' stuff in the early days, because it was so alien to us, we needed to discuss it – how we had gone about it, collecting the data, breaking down the data, trying to analyse it – that was certainly taken back to school. I know my colleagues are now able to analyse NFER test data and share the analysis with others. That would not have gone on before.

And stimulating lively discussion:

> Just on the level of using articles or even quotes like this on professionalism [from Whitty, 1999]. I will go back and put the cat amongst the pigeons by having this out, in forthcoming discussions about Performance Related Pay.

Although the project was successful in some aspects of whole school development, as will be evident in Part 2 of this book, it is appropriate to acknowledge the difficulties of time and conflicting priorities which plagued many of the attempts to 'embed' the research in whole school practice.

Finding the time to do the research, even in a funded project was an issue for all participants. The busy life of primary schools, assessment requirements, parents' evenings, planning, marking, staff meetings, all make calls on primary school teachers' time. Responding to initiatives such as the Literacy and Numeracy Strategies took up a lot of teacher time and energy, but participants had been under pressure to prioritise their work in order to engage in researching their classrooms. In cases where schools had dropped out of the project, the context of the school – long-term illness and other stress factors – had been the major reasons for leaving. Any research or development project in schools is subject to changing priorities, staff changes and external factors out of the teachers' control which often make for volatile and tenuous environments in school. There are often so many initiatives in a primary school at any time that living with the conflicting priorities can cause the 'professional identity crises', which Campbell and Kane (2000) discuss. They suggest a way forward as 'investment in schools, leaders and teachers in order to enable partnerships and networks between schools, universities and other players in the professional development field, to develop ways which will help teachers transform themselves and their institutions into learning communities.'

In the partnerships or 'learning communities' which formed the consortium, the role of HEI and LEA staff was interesting to chart. Two LEA and some eight HEI staff were involved in collaboration with teachers while they researched in schools and attended the group sessions. There were many heated discussions and soul-searching sessions as the collaborations between HEI, LEA and teachers began to take shape. The teachers felt that their LEA and HEI partners 'mediated' between themselves and the TTA, helped them to make sense of the project and supported them in their tentative moves to begin the research in their schools. There was an acknowledgement from LEA and HEI staff that the 'process of identifying a focus which teachers felt was relevant to their situation, their children and their schools' had taken a long time. There had been a necessary period of 'working things through and understanding the reflective process and collaborative work'.

Teachers felt that LEA and HEI colleagues brought valuable, wider, critical perspectives, experience of research and inquiry methods and 'the big picture' to the collaborations. It is important to engage in critical appraisal and dialogue with a variety of educationalists in order to avoid what Smyth (1991, p. 133) refers to as working in unthinking and unquestioning ways. This happens, he asserts, 'because of the way in which teaching is construed as being a technical process that only requires fine-tuning in order to achieve predetermined educational objectives'. One of the benefits of the collaborative work was the opportunity for LEA and HEI staff to review their own practice in the light of their experience of facilitating and supporting the school-based projects.

However, it was not 'all roses in the garden'. Collaboration is not always easy. There is often a delicate balance between how things used to be and how they might be in the future and all participants were mindful that often schools were sometimes 'conservative' places where 'fitting in' is often more expected than challenging the status quo. Colleagues suffering from 'innovation fatigue' could not always be positive about 'yet another project'. One participant speculated about his colleagues, 'If all of our staff would have been involved in discussions like this, would it have changed their attitudes to research or frightened them and made them even more critical?'

Holly (1991) wrote about how action researchers became part of a 'deviant subculture' unsupported by their colleagues in school, underlining the importance of whole school approaches to school improvement and development. This aspect also serves to remind us of the tensions between individual, personal professional development needs and the collective, school development needs. It can be seen that both are important and both need nurturing, supporting and funding. Teachers in the project experienced these tensions in their lives. What they felt was required was a complex and diverse variety of professional development activities which ranged from informal self- and peer-review, to individuals or groups of interested staff engaging in action research, to taught courses at a variety of levels and venues. It is important to recognise the diverse nature of teachers' professional development needs and accept the need for a rich diet of experiences, individual and personal, collective and collegial, which meet short-term and longer-term requirements. There does not appear to be a simple recipe for this! That much was apparent from observing and listening to teachers in the project. The experience of doing research had 'changed' these teachers. They felt that the research process had involved them in worthwhile professional development which had affected their teaching and their thinking.

Autonomy, agency and accountability

> One of the big advantages of doing research for me and my school has been, at this time of unprecedented accountability and people feeling that monitoring is threatening and is attempting to catch people out rather than helping them move forward, is that as a result of all the discussions and sharing of practice in the research project, there is a kind of sub culture growing in the school where there are regular class slots for people going to watch each other teach. People have listed what they feel are the areas which they think they would like to improve in, who they might want to watch teach to improve their practice, and that is happening all the time.

The above comment from one of the teacher-researchers documents an emerging culture of collegiality as a result of a research project with a focus on numeracy, which is about an organic accountability rather than an imposed one. Teachers are arguably in need of improving their self-image and building up their self-esteem through recognition of the value of their own ability to plan, teach and assess learning in their classrooms. It seems timely to redress the balance, and for teachers to construct collegial accountability cultures in their schools and to engage in the practices of self-accountability in the pursuit of professional development. The researchers in this project were, through their own agency, changing and developing their own and colleagues' notions of research and development. Self-determination, the right to identify one's own development needs and to organise one's own teaching within the collective accountability structure of a school and a profession is arguably an important aspect in the development of professional agency:

> Teachers are the best judge of their own professional development, although they are not the only judges. Schools, authorities and training providers need systematic data on how teachers view their professional development but this has to be much more than feedback on in-service events. It must essentially be about the school as a place, which encourages and sustains professional growth.
>
> MacBeath (1999, p. 6)

A key part of teachers' agency is their professional autonomy. Doing and using research allowed participants a degree of autonomy to make informed decisions about their teaching and 'have the freedom to try things out' and find out 'what could and couldn't work in our school with our pupils'. However, this is not always the case, in the current climate of strong, central direction of policy, there can sometimes be a sense of loss of autonomy: 'I think I find now that within the course of my week there are very few actual decisions that I make. Decisions are made for me and I become the implementer of those decisions. Sometimes I just feel like a workhorse really'.

Teachers in the project found that participation in the research process opened up the issues of accountability and autonomy for discussion and to some extent reduced their feelings of powerlessness. There was a feeling of being at 'a watershed', looking forward to the possibility of more self-evaluation in schools, of flexibility in the curriculum content and the valuing of children's learning rather than a narrow view of a 'set' curriculum. One participant talked about balance:

> ... there seemed to be too little, clear, analytical professional structure in the seventies but now there seems to be too much managerial prescription. We need to get a balance between providing a professional structure that people can see and one in which they can be flexible, and has a degree of freedom for professional autonomy.

There would appear to be a paradox in current notions of accountability where there is 'greater decentralisation of decision making and more collaboration, but within the context of increased state power over what goes on in local schools' (Carlson and Apple, 1998, p. 8) and which causes teachers to experience what Ruddock (1991) described as feeling 'like puppets on a string' with regard to ownership of changes and innovations. Graham (1999, p. 98) concludes that '... better results in raising standards, improving and motivating teachers are likely to be achieved by improving teachers' autonomy, not by diminishing it.' Looking to the future, these teachers have more knowledge of what works or what does not work in their own classrooms and schools and will be able to speak with confidence about raising achievement, developing their teaching and current research findings in their topic area. They will be more empowered in their own professional context.

There is no 'recipe' for teacher research. A wide variety of approaches must be available in order to allow teachers to identify their own focus and areas for improvement. The collaborative processes developed in the project were of great value to the teachers by providing support, challenge and different perspectives on their teaching. What is also clear is that in initiatives like this, aimed at involving more practitioners in research which is more meaningful to teachers and schools, the importance of the research process must not be forgotten. The process of formulating research questions, debating and discussing these questions and systematic inquiry alongside the interrogation and analysis of findings is complex and takes time. Teaching and learning are also complex activities, which involve thinking and discussing and emotional engagement.

Research, I would argue, is a powerful force for professional development with much potential for the improvement of practice. Care needs to be taken to protect the inquiry process, to encourage 'bottom up' issues to emerge on the research agenda, to look wider than test results and surface measures of pupil achievement.

Investigating the professional self is controversial as argued in this chapter, in the views and opinions of the participants, and in the relevant literature cited. The professional self will not be 'pushed under the carpet'. Teachers feel strongly, even passionately, about their ideas, beliefs and their teaching. This should be celebrated. Being passionate about your teaching can be good therapy as evidenced by the teachers in the project. If researching your own practice, collaborating with colleagues, improving your teaching and developing a professional language to talk about your teaching, is what research does for teachers then those experiences are no less therapeutic and, will arguably, be a powerful factor in the recruitment and retention of teachers.

References

Ball, S. and Goodson, I. (1985) *Teachers' Lives and Careers*. London: Falmer Press.

Bolam. R. (1999) The Emerging Conceptualisation of INSET: Does this constitute Professional Development? Paper presented at the *Annual Conference of the Standing Committee for the Education and Training of Teachers*, 26–28 November 1999, GEC Management College, Rugby.

Campbell, A. and Kane, I. (1998) *School-based Teacher Education: Telling Tales from a Fictional Primary School*. London: David Fulton.

Campbell, A. and Kane, I. (2000) Best of times, worst of times: the importance or otherwise of regular in-servicing. *Journal of Teacher Development*, 4(2): 293–302.

Carlson, D. and Apple, M.W. (1998) (eds) *Power/Knowledge/Pedagogy*. Boulder, CO: Westview Press.

Clandinin, D.J. and Connelly, F.M. (1996) Teachers: professional knowledge landscapes – teacher stories – stories of teachers – school stories – stories of schools. *Educational Researcher*, 25(3): 24–30.

Dadds, M. (1995) *Passionate Enquiry and School Development: a Story about Teacher Action Research*. London: Falmer Press.

Day, C. (1993) The importance of learning biography in supporting teacher development: an empirical study. In: Day, C., Calderhead, J. and Denicolo, P. (eds) *Research on Teacher Thinking: Understanding Professional Development*. London: Falmer Press, pp. 221–232.

Day, C. (1999) *Developing Teachers: the Challenges of Lifelong Learning*. London: Falmer Press.

Graham, J. (ed.) *Teacher Professionalism and the Challenge of Change*. Stoke: Trentham books.

Hargreaves, A. (1992) Cultures of teaching: a focus for change. In: Hargreaves, A. and Fullan, M.G. (eds) *Understanding Teacher Development*. New York: Teachers College Press.

Hargreaves, D. (1994) The new professionalism: the synthesis of professional and institutional development. *Teaching and Teacher Education*, 10(4): 423–438.

Holly, M.L. (1991) Personal and professional learning: on teaching and self knowledge. Paper presented to the Collaborative Action Research Network Conference, April 1991, University of Nottingham.

Hoyle, E. (1974) Professionality, professionalism and control in teaching. *London Education Review*, 3(2): 13–19.

Little, J.W. (1982) Norms of collegiality and experimentation: workplace conditions of school success, *American Educational Research Journal*, 19, 325–340.

Little, J. W. (1990) The persistence of privacy: autonomy and initiative in teachers' professional relations. *Teachers College Record*, 91, 509–556.

MacBeath, J. (1999) *Schools Must Speak for Themselves: the Case for School Self Evaluation*. London: Routledge.

Ruddock, J. (1991) *Innovation and Change*. Buckingham: Open University Press.

Smyth, J. (1991) *Teachers As Collaborative Learners*. Buckingham: Open University Press.

Thomas, D. (1995) (ed.) *Teachers' Stories*. Milton Keynes: Open University Press.

Whitty, G. (1999) Teacher professionalism in new times. Paper presented at the Annual conference of the Standing Committee for the Education and Training of Teachers, 26–28 November, GEC Management College, Rugby.

Chapter 3

Using videos to investigate speaking and listening

Liz Jones

Introduction

Our aim when working with videos was to focus on teacher talk, that is the ordinary and everyday language strategies that teachers adopt when they want children to listen so that they might learn. In addition, we also wanted to try to identify how teachers encourage children to speak so that children's implicit knowledge might be made explicit. Moreover, we wanted some appreciation of how to extend children's listening skills. Issues therefore included the quality of teacher explanations as well as the overall clarity and structure of their speech. A particular focus was on questioning style, including both the construction and use of questions. Finally, the development of speaking and listening skills is a cross-curricular requirement of the National Curriculum and it links with, and complements, the work of the National Literacy and Numeracy Strategies.

Video as a research tool

> ... the best way to improve practice lies not so much in trying to control people's behaviour as in helping them control their own by becoming aware of what they are doing
>
> (Elliott, 1977)

In general, there is agreement that video recordings of practice can promote critical reflection and can be instrumental in bringing about changes to practice. Hutchinson and Bryson (1997) maintain, for example, that video has the capacity to provide 'documentary material which can be later analysed in order to develop appreciations' (p. 285). The teachers within the consortium had a range of issues which they both wanted to analyse and appreciate. Temple School, for example, was developing strategies for improving mental maths. The teachers therefore wanted evidence whereby they could assess both their own questioning styles and the children's responses. Accordingly each of the teachers was filmed when undertaking a mental maths session. Time was then made available so that the three teachers involved in the project could work together in order to view and disseminate the recordings.

Many points were identified as a consequence of this shared process. Gary Gornell, for example, noted that some of the children were given insufficient time to think in order to develop an answer. From watching himself Gary gained a sense of being 'driven by the learning objectives of the session'. Through sharing his practice Gary not only identified an important issue but he could see possibilities of working on these issues in the classroom (Jaworski, 1990 p. 63).

Perhaps, however, one of the most crucial features to emerge from this joint viewing was a significant and positive improvement in perceptions of self (Tuttle, 1972). As one teacher noted:

> I was dreading watching my video with the group ... watching on my own I was too self-critical – but working together – you move from just focusing on the negative. The groups' comments and observations have made me realise how skilled and skilful I am. I think it's hard to see the good bits of your teaching ... you're too busy seeing the bad.

The process of disseminating the video recordings of the mental maths session had both 'acted as a catalyst to critical self-reflection' and 'a stimulus to appreciating different perspectives on actions which previously may have been taken for granted' (Hutchinson and Bryson, 1997, p. 290) or, as in the instance above, mainly interpreted in a critical way.

Unsystematic readings

As has been noted above, video recordings have the potential to capture some of the complexities of teaching and learning. However, there are certain problems and difficulties when working with the medium. For example, we found the task of watching, listening and making notes highly problematical. The act of writing took the eyes away from the screen and so inevitably something was missed. Moreover, classroom events, including actions such as the asking and answering of questions, occur quickly thus making any immediate reflections about such interactions difficult. Below are outlined two accounts which document some of the ways of working which have been developed since the inception of the consortium.

Anne-Marie's story

Anne-Marie was the first teacher of the group who subjected her practice to the scrutiny of the video camera. She wanted evidence of children's understandings and their knowledge of particular scientific concepts. As a consequence, Anne-Marie's HEI Link made a video of a science session and in addition a written transcript of the recording was made. Effectively, this gave us two sources of data which we could work with. The transcript would allow us to focus on the language that was used during the session. Meanwhile, we could return to the recording in order to pick up on all those other factors which are part and parcel of classroom talk and effective communication including the body language of both the teacher and the children, tone of voice, bored expressions and obvious involvement. Initially, we focused on the first page of the transcript. The topic was 'change of state' and the class were a Year 5 class of mainly lower ability.

Transcript of Anne-Marie's science lesson

AM: Put down your pencils and close your books. The first word (*referring to words on sheet*) was 'liquefy'. If you did 'liquefy', or you think you know what 'liquefy' means, put your hand up. Yes Tama?

Tama: Something very watery, like milk.

AM: Something watery, like milk. What do you mean by watery?

Tama: Something watery, that runs very fast.

AM: So, it's something that runs. Anyone else think of another meaning? ('runs' written on the board).

Steve: 'Liquefy' means something you can't squash.

AM: Martin, can you sit properly.

Sam: Miss, I've got another one.

AM: Yes, Sam?

Sam: 'Liquefy' means something's solid, and it can melt into liquid – that means 'liquefy'.

AM: So, you're turning a solid into a liquid. Is that right?

Sam: Yes, Miss.

AM: Alright. Let's look at the next word – 'condensation'. Did anyone do 'condensation'?

Sam: Miss, if there's a cold window and hot room, or a hot room and a cold window, then the window starts to have, starts to get condensation on it.

Our initial reading of this page bore more resemblance to a brainstorming of ideas rather than a systematic analysis of the data. Individuals offered ideas, interpretations and explanations which were rooted in their own experiences, knowledge and understandings of classroom events. It was noted, for example, that the transcript would suggest that there was a gender imbalance; other than one contribution from a girl, Tama, all other teacher talk is directed at and with boys. Altogether our readings of the transcript prompted a number of general questions:

- How can teachers develop situations so that teacher and child can work together at unravelling muddled thinking?
- In what ways can the structure of whole class teaching be managed to allow time for teachers to address the needs – particularly their speaking and listening needs – of all the children?
- Who speaks and who remains silent?

From dialogue to systematic perusal

So what was achieved by using the transcript as evidence? First, it provided a basis upon which and with which a group of teachers could generate a series of hypotheses and where certain basic yet crucial research questions could be asked: 'What is happening here?' 'Why is it happening?' and 'What are some of the causes?'. In trying to address these we brought, and as a consequence shared, those personal beliefs, ideals and assumptions that each of us hold about teaching and learning.

However, we did have certain worries about our way of working. Were we, for instance, being thoroughly systematic in our perusal of the evidence? Had we been sufficiently focused? In other words, had we used the evidence in order to further our understandings about speaking and listening? Or, had we allowed ourselves to become sidetracked with other issues? Thus despite having a wide-ranging discussion we were very aware that we had failed to fully address our topic. We had not, for example, discussed the questioning skills of the teacher. Nor did we comment on those ways she gave positive feedback and credence to the children's answers. In addition, scant attention had been paid to the children's responses. Take as an example Tama's definition of 'liquefy'. We did not discuss whether it was appropriate, nor did we reflect on the use that was made of detail and the way it had been incorporated in order to extend and illustrate the explanation: 'Something very watery, like milk'

We were also aware that we would have great difficulty in disseminating some of the ideas, thoughts and reflections which we had had so that they could be shared with and be of practical use to other teachers. Moreover, because so much time had been given to the transcript we had effectively chosen to ignore the video footage of the session. Overall, we were concerned that we had been:

- insufficiently focused on speaking and listening;
- insufficiently systematic in our analysis and so had missed vital characteristics, including for example the skill of the teacher in offering 'feedback' to the pupils;
- uncoordinated in our attempts at triangulation of evidence. The focus was on the transcript rather than being more directly linked to and substantiated by video evidence;
- insufficiently aware of the children's responses.

Although we had concerns about our way of working, what had been established among the group was a culture in which such enquiries could be undertaken. Such a culture has to exist so that critique can occur. However, while it was clear that videos allowed for an unpacking and unpicking of practice, it was evident that we needed ways of being more focused. Briefly, our task then was to develop a framework or a viewing guide which would help focus our attention on speaking and listening. When doing this we were able to call upon the expertise, knowledge and experience of a number of agencies and other researchers. For example, practical advice was offered by LEA colleagues. We were able to examine, scrutinise and experiment with examples of schedules that are used in Manchester schools when observing teachers in the classroom. In addition, we also revisited past research which had been undertaken, including that of Tharp and Gallimore (1998) and the work of the National Oracy Project (Norman, 1992). It was after considering theoretical and practical explorations that an analytical framework evolved (see Toolkit 5). The framework focused on five main areas (Box 3.1).

Analysing video clips

The creation of a framework was a significant step in developing more efficient ways of watching. Other measures which were aimed at maximising our concentration levels were also incorporated. For example, rather than watch videos of complete

Box 3.1 Guide to reflection

- teacher style of questioning;
- children's responses;
- inclusion strategies, e.g. teacher and pupil interactions;
- strategies for stimulating/encouraging listening;
- strategies for stimulating/encouraging speaking.

lessons we would select clips lasting no more than a few minutes. The use of short video clips is justified by Fanselow (1988), who noted that 5 minutes of classroom observation was sufficient to promote extended discussion. Jaworski (1990) also endorses this point. In her view, lengthy examples of video lose impact; short clips are more effective in maintaining viewer concentration.

Having taken steps to evolve more efficient ways of watching videos the teachers then had to make a number of decisions, including identifying a specific focus. Sue Jennings, for example, wanted to assess what kinds of strategies worked at enhancing children's listening skills. Meanwhile, Claire Van-Es had a number of wide-ranging concerns, including whether children were given sufficient answering time, whether they were posed questions which challenged their thinking and whether she had a propensity to direct questions at certain children. Similarly, Sarah Brealey was keen to establish more pupil-to-pupil interaction. Besides identifying a focus, the teachers were also in control of times and lengths of filming. Some, for example, were keen to have evidence of the beginning of a session whereas others wanted an overview and so were filmed for brief moments at the beginning, middle and end of a lesson.

As mentioned, our early attempts at working with videos centred on whole group discussion. This was immensely valuable, for it allowed each of us to gain some appreciation about each other's beliefs and philosophies. However, logistically this practice became unwieldy because there was insufficient time at the monthly consortium meetings to analyse the rapidly growing stock of video clips. Moreover, immediate feedback was essential. After all, one of the primary functions of the videos was to support the teacher's critical reflections so that transformations in practice could occur. As an alternative the strategy of working with a critical friend(s) was developed. Here the teacher worked in conjunction with myself, sometimes Olwen McNamara and on occasions with a colleague from school. Short extracts of video would be examined and then paused. The framework was then used as a means of keeping us focused. However, its 'looseness' still allowed for discussion and for alternative views and different perspectives to be offered.

Sue's story

Below is an example of reflections which centre on Sue Jennings and which were prompted by watching both a 5-minute video clip and by referring to the framework. The clip centred on an English session where the children had to make a question out of a statement.

Teacher's style of questioning

It was identified that the strategy of asking 'Who would like to have a go?' was being used. The notion of 'having a go' implies that there is room within this particular context for children to offer both a right and a wrong answer. In other words, they can risk making a mistake but in so doing there is still the opportunity to learn. Also, we noted that the practice of rephrasing a question was being used. Sue would first pose a question which incorporated more complex language. After a slight pause, she would then rephrase it by simplifying the language: 'Can anyone tell me why I am reluctant to use the black felt-tip on the board?'; 'Why don't I want to use the black pen?' This practice achieved a number of things. First, it allowed children thinking time. In addition, the more able children in the class were able to attend to the first question, whereas the second modified version included and accommodated the less able pupils.

Children's responses

We observed that Sue used prompts to extend a child's answer and that often it was a tactic adopted after a closed question had been posed:

Sue: Who has been to Wales? (some of the children raised a hand)
Sue: Adam, can you remember the journey ... how did you get to Wales?
Adam: We went on the bus...
Sue: ... on the bus ...
Adam: Yes, on the bus and it took a long time.

It is apparent from this example that Sue provides opportunities for children to demonstrate their knowledge and understanding and to offer contributions which include their own experiences of the world. Moreover, such responses provide evidence which can be used to assess a child's speaking and listening skills. The recording also highlighted that Sue repeated children's responses. This ensured that:

* the child's answer was audible to the whole group;
* the child's answer was given status;
* it created an opportunity for clarification to take place;
* it created an opportunity for an answer to be extended;
* it prevented the teacher's voice from dominating the lesson.

Inclusion strategies

The video identified that Sue used looks and other kinds of body language in order to manage the class so that space was created for individual children to speak. In addition, she gave status to the children's answers by repeating their words and by writing their responses on the board. Moreover, a number of manoeuvres were used which were aimed at keeping the group on task. For example, Sue would urge all the children to 'look at the board' and to 'look at the first example we did ... remember what we did here ...'. In addition, the word 'we' was used more or less constantly so that there was a sense that the task was one that was being tackled by both the teacher and the children.

Strategies for stimulating and encouraging listening

It was evident that the teacher's tone of voice was used to good effect. We noted that children who were in danger of becoming restless were re-engaged when Sue either raised or deliberately lowered the tone and pitch of her voice. Also, she injected drama into the proceedings by getting the children to act out a question and answer scenario.

Strategies for stimulating and encouraging speaking

The video clip highlighted how praise was used to good effect. Regular compliments, including 'you're a star', were paid to children. Such strategies contribute to developing an ethos where the children felt encouraged to 'have a go'.

Effectively, the video recording of an extract of practice enabled Sue to stand outside her practice so that she could take stock and review it. As Jaworski (1993) notes, it is this facility to be able to 'step outside' which is crucial to the reflective process. In my role as critical friend I was able to offer an outsider's perspective. The value of this position, we found, was that it worked at offsetting individuals' predispositions to perceive themselves negatively and their 'colouring' of events (Laycock and Bunnag, 1991). By adopting an ethnographic approach to the data we were able to 'open the world of the obvious and the routine for questioning why things had come to be the way they were, and for speculating on what they might become' (Hutchinson and Bryson, 1997, p. 290).

As Sue herself commented: 'Working in this way has allowed me to look at familiar and habitual aspects of practice in order to make them unfamiliar.'

In pragmatic terms what did such reflections achieve? For Sue, watching and analysing her practice was a means of reminding herself that she is a highly skilled practitioner. That said, however, the recording heightened Sue's awareness about two aspects of practice. First, while Sue was able to identify many exchanges between herself and the children, there was a lack of pupil-to-pupil interaction. She was therefore prompted to ask: 'In what ways can lessons be structured so that the children are both enabled and encouraged to talk with one another so that ideas can be discussed and information exchanged?' In addition, Sue was also able to reflect on the number of times that she had reiterated what the task was that the children had to complete. In part, Sue recognised that this strategy was frequently used because the children that she teaches all have varying degrees of learning difficulties. However, she also wondered whether it might be related to the children's listening skills. From this thought the following question emerged: 'How can we assess whether children are listening and comprehending?'

These two questions spawned a number of actions. For example, Sue began to develop a range of situations where her children had to talk to one another. For example, each child was encouraged to independently read a book. The books were specifically selected in that they were both brief and at a suitable reading level. The children then retold their stories to one another. In addition, the children were divided into groups of four. These groups were constructed so that there was a mix of children both in terms of gender and in terms of 'talkativeness'. The groups were given a poem which had to be first read and then discussed. Sue had provided each of the groups with a grid on which were written a series of prompts, for example 'This poem is funny because …' and 'A young child would like this poem because …' Shortly after this work was undertaken I returned to Sue's classroom in order to capture the work on video.

Assessing speaking and listening

Meanwhile, work was undertaken in order to develop a framework that would help us to both think about and assess children's speaking and listening skills. Our framework was abridged and developed from a combination of source materials: the Assessment of Achievement Programme, 1988; and the National Curriculum AT1: Speaking and Listening, 1988. We identified what we considered to be the most salient features of each and modified them for our purposes. A condensed version of the Framework for Assessing Speaking and Listening (the full framework can be found in Toolkit 4) is shown in Box 3.2.

The task of designing the assessment framework so that it could meet our needs was a collective one, and the experience was yet another way of both problematising and making ourselves conscious of those variables that were embedded within speaking and listening. In addition, we used the 'Listening and Speaking Assessment Framework' along with the analytical framework ('Guide to Reflection' Toolkit 5) when viewing video clips. It made us, for example, listen more closely to children's responses. Having listened we were then in a position to ask questions including 'If this child is operating at Level 1, what steps might be taken so that this child could extend his/her thinking a little more?'

Eliciting pupils' views

Our final move was to collectively design a pupil log. It was a data-gathering technique that the Northeast Consortium had used fruitfully and we had two purposes in mind when designing our questionnaire. First, it should be used as an awareness-raising exercise with the children such that they should become more alert to the value of contributing in lessons and listening to the contributions of others. Second, it should be used as a research instrument to augment the video evidence of classroom practices that we were in the process of collecting. The pupil log (Toolkit 6) covered areas such as listening, speaking, remembering, thinking and preferred learning styles. An extract is shown in Box 3.3.

Our intention was to use the log in conjunction with other data sources by way of triangulation, checking out, for example, our perspectives on the lessons that were videoed. As a general rule we asked children to complete their pupil log at the end of a lesson that was being videoed. In addition, there were other occasions when teachers were interested in collecting pupil perspectives on particular lessons. There were several ways in which the logs were used with pupils depending upon their age and ability levels. For example, if the children were able they completed the written questionnaire; sometimes the teacher would read out the questions and the children would either write or articulate their response. Occasionally someone else, such as a colleague from the HEI/LEA, would interview the children and tape or video their responses.

Box 3.2 Framework for assessing speaking and listening

Coherence in response – listening
Level 4: Ideas are clearly and logically expressed, in a range of different contexts, and through discussion lead to a logical and consistent conclusion.
Level 3: Ideas are clearly and logically expressed demonstrating understanding of the main points.
Level 2: As a result of listening more carefully the child selects appropriately from, and exploits, the ideas in the stimulus materials and others' contributions.
Level 1: The child makes occasional and appropriate reference to what has already been said but demonstrates no clear sequence.
Level 0: The child has failed to make use of the ideas in the stimulus materials in any relevant way.

Fluency in speaking
Level 4: The child accurately, fluently and confidently uses a range of appropriate vocabulary and speech style and demonstrates competence in grammar.
Level 3: The child uses confidently a wide range of accurate, consistent and fluent vocabulary in different contexts. Use of stress, intonation and tone is appropriate.
Level 2: The child rarely has difficulty in making herself understood and attempts to use a range of vocabulary and syntax but these are not always accurate.
Level 1: The child generally speaks audibly and is comprehensible, though vocabulary and syntax are limited.
Level 0: The child fails to make herself understood, even in a very limited way.

Interaction in the classroom
Level 4: The child takes account of the needs of others and builds on their contributions. Eye contact and body language are used effectively.
Level 3: The child takes an active part in discussion provided that the audience is supportive. Eye contact and body language indicates readiness to communicate.
Level 2: The child contributes to discussion if prompted but shows limited awareness of audience.
Level 1: The child responds when spoken to but is very reluctant to initiate or sustain speech without frequent prompting. Eye contact and gesture are minimal.
Level 0: The child is extremely reluctant to take part in any sort of exchange.

The primary function of the pupil log was to identify those aspects of a session where children had been attentive and/or had actively engaged in the lesson. The logs then supplemented other data and contributed to our knowledge and understanding of an important part of children's learning. For instance, we now have some insight into how children feel when they are able to correctly answer a question. Such responses include:

- If I got it right I will try again (Year 6).
- It shows people what you know (Year 5).

Box 3.3 Pupil log

Thinking about speaking
- How many questions did you *answer* in the lesson today?
- Do you like *answering* questions in lessons?
- What feels good about *answering* questions?
- What feels bad about *answering* questions?

Thinking about listening
- Are you a good listener?
- What makes listening hard?
- What makes listening easy?

- It makes me feel good (Year 3).
- I feel brave and it makes you want to learn (Year 6).
- I feel confident (Year 4).

Meanwhile, getting the answer wrong elicited the following replies:

- You feel embarrassed (Year 6).
- People laugh (Year 5).
- You sometimes get it wrong and feel ashamed (Year 6).
- If you put your hand up and get the answer wrong you get upset (Year 4).

As teachers we need to have such glimpses into children's thinking. They serve to remind us that effective pedagogy is both about teaching and learning. In more recent times there has perhaps been an overemphasis on the technical, 'means-ends' of teaching, where as a consequence the voice of the child as 'learner' has been missed. Both the logs and the videos ensure that the voice of the child is neither lost nor ignored.

Reflections

The task of trying to describe all our experiences of working with videos would have been impossible. We soon established that simply watching a video unaided was an unwieldy method for accessing information. The use of a viewing and reflection framework enabled us to be more proficient and more economical in terms of time. It enabled us to perceive more clearly what was occurring during the lesson. The use of videos in conjunction with the framework enabled each of the teachers to evaluate aspects of practice before moving to make changes to practice. By highlighting certain instances we have sought to emphasise a number of strengths of the medium. Videos have:

- contributed to and sustained the process of critical reflection;
- supported processes of change;
- helped to identify an issue which could be explored;

- rendered the familiar unfamiliar, thereby allowing a reconsideration of habitual ways of doing and being;
- provided evidence of practice from which we could identify our strengths;
- provided the basis for nurturing and developing a partnership between teachers;
- become part of and contributed to a sense of openness between the teachers;
- facilitated discussions between teachers in the consortium, consortium schools, groups at a distance when they have been a central feature of conference presentations.

Finally, clips of the videos are now being assembled into a CD Rom. We perceive this to be a means of extending the work of the consortium such that other teachers, like ourselves, can begin to develop and share conversations about their practice. It is our firm conviction that videos have contributed to the development of greater self-knowledge and have confirmed Elliott's (1994 p. 105) view that:

> ... teacher knowledge is embedded in concrete practices. Teachers may be unaware of the action and their beliefs and assumptions which underpin them. Understanding comes through the analysis of evidence about practice and the generation of new knowledge comes via the formulation and testing of action hypotheses in the light of such analyses.

References

Elliott, J. (1977) Conceptualising relations between research/evaluation procedures and in-service teacher education. *British Journal of In-service Education*, 4(1/2).

Elliott, J. (1994). Research on teachers' knowledge and action research. *Educational Action Research*, 2: 102–105.

Fanselow, J. (1988) Let's see!: contrasting conversations about the classroom. *TESOL Quarterly*, 22(1): 113–130.

Harvard, G., Day, M. and Dunne, R. (1994) Eliciting and developing students' schema of classroom practice using video-disc system. *British Journal of Educational Technology*, 25(1): 4–18.

Hutchinson, B. and Bryson, P. (1997) Video, reflection and transformation: action research in vocational education and training in an European context. *Educational Action Research*, 5(2): 283–303.

Jaworski, B. (1990) Video as a tool for teachers' professional development. *British Journal of In-service Education*, 16: 60–65.

Jaworski, B. (1993) The professional development of teachers – the potential of critical reflection. *British Journal of In-service Education*, 19(3): 37–42.

Laycock, J. and Bunnag, B. (1991) Developing teacher self-awareness: feedback and the use of video. *ELT Journal*, 45(1): 43–53.

Tharp, R and Gallimore, R (1988) *Rousing Minds to Life: Teaching, Learning and Schooling in Social Context.* Cambridge: Cambridge University Press.

Tuttle, R. (1972) The effects of video-tape self-analysis on teacher self-concept effectiveness and perception of students. *Dissertation Abstracts International* 33: 1577A.

Part 2

Insights into teacher research

Chapter 4

Happily ever after

Plotting effective narrative writing with
10-year-old children

Gudrun Heatley and Ian Stronach

Introduction

This piece of research aimed to improve narrative writing in Year 6 and to help boost National Test scores from a rather low 42 per cent at Level 4 and above (against a national target of 80 per cent). The school had identified narrative writing as a particular focus for improvement. It is hoped that this account, jointly produced by the teacher and the researcher, will make the findings accessible to other teachers and researchers, exemplifying both the innovation and the research, and helping to inform other teachers' judgements. It is, of course, a small-scale study. Its ambition is to provoke discussion about good teaching, and not to offer prescriptions for practice. Equally, it is only one kind of teacher research, involving the teacher in systematically engaging *with* rather than *in* research.

What was the problem?

Teachers at the school generally believed that narrative writing was poor because the school was an inner-city school with a catchment that was quite deprived and contained a large proportion of pupils with English as an additional language. To begin with, the class teacher, Gudrun Heatley, felt the main problem was that the pupils lacked the ideas in the first place, not having the variety of experiences and levels of parental support that more advantaged pupils often experienced. We decided to explore this by analysing a set of essays written at the beginning of the school year: our aim was to find out the different ways the pupils went about the business of creating stories, and the cultural resources on which they seemed to draw. This would also give us a baseline for the year, and we would try to measure progress by comparing the pupils' performance with later essays and National Test results.

What was the solution?

The research was carried out by the teacher, Gudrun Heatley, and the researcher, Ian Stronach. In this case, demands on the teacher's time meant that, although the research direction was determined by the teacher, most of the research itself was carried out by the researcher. The aim of the research was to establish the baseline mentioned above, and also to evaluate a new approach to narrative writing (*First Steps: Writing Developmental Continuum*, 1994) that Gudrun had introduced. That model is explained and illustrated in the Note at the end of this chapter: it involved teaching pupils how stories were framed, in a largely behavioural specification of stages and criteria. As she later said:

> My interest in the project stemmed from some 'research' which I'd undertaken with my Year 6 class in 1996/97, when I had thoroughly overhauled my teaching of non-fiction writing. The subsequent results, in raised pupil confidence, in teacher assessments, endorsed by significantly improved SATs results [for the class], encouraged me to question whether a transfer of similar teaching strategies would work in the teaching of fiction writing.

Baseline data analysis: narrative writing

The children were following a new structured narrative writing scheme. Prior to that, they had been given an essay to write in September 1997. The following is an attempt to analyse the children's stories written on that occasion with a view to identifying the narrative strategies that they seemed to adopt prior to the change in their curriculum. The essay was entitled 'Help!' The children were given the first sentence: 'The mouse ran across my feet'. Seventeen story strategies were identified (listed below).

Tom and Jerry

> ... and the house cat called tom was chasing him. The mouse was called Jerry.

> Jerry jumped in the flour sack next to the door he came out white he jumped of the shellf. Tom caught him But threw him in to the sinck. But the waiter wasth the flour off ...

These seemed to be among the least successful stories, with the author trapped in a this-happened-and-then-that-happened mode of narrating, even when introduced with a little irony:

> The cat was £50. I named it Tom to my surprisment the mouse was called Jerry.

My friend the mouse

> Then we went into the front room and wathed it got to bed time the mouse went into the hole and I went to bed ... so the mouse said lets play into the garden so we went into the garden the mouse swang on the washing line I swang on the swing.

In another instance the mouse is christened 'Shu' after the girl's grandmother and becomes a sister to the author. The storyline then becomes a succession of everyday events like playing, shopping, etc.

Kill off the mouse and write what you like

This was the favoured strategy for a group of boys. They could not wait to bump off the mouse, as in the start of the following essay:

> The mouse ran across my feet and It went under the bed and I got my stick and when the mouse came out I hit it. I picked the mouse up ffrom it's tail and chucked It in the bin.

With the mouse out of the way they could get on with something more interesting.

> So they burried in Helton park ... the noise was A Voice. It said 'your house is built ON a SeMatry theN it all went quite.

> The ghost was talking very weard you shall die it was so white you wouldn't bare to look at it ...

What they really wanted to write about turned out to be either computers, horror movies, space aliens, or playground football.

> Now it was play time ... by the time it timup time the skor was 1. 2.

One achieved a remarkable recovery which we could label 'The Mouse from Outer Space', sloping off to the favoured terrain and then brilliantly reinstating the mouse:

> 'your father killed our only way back to our world' 'you mean that mouse was the only way out of our world' 'affirmative' replied the figure.

Woman makes fuss over a mouse

> 'Ah Ah there is a mouse in the hotel Ah!' The lady in room eighteen was making a big fuss over nothing.

> Oh my god Ahhhhh mice, mice, MICE!

> ... then My Mum said 'if I see another mouse I moving' then she saw another mouse 'That's it I'm moving' said My Mum a week later were in are new house.

This strategy seemed more favoured by the girls, and tended to fit with the three-times-and-you're-dead plot.

Pied piper

> The attendant's could not get rid of the mice but one day a man came no one moved because they did not know him so people steared at the stranger and then just like that all the mice followed him.

Casualty/animal hospital

and got run over ... and took it to the animal hospital

I can call farida and sadaf they'll help me fix the mouses bones ...

The mouse is injured in the first paragraph, accidentally or otherwise, but sympathy intervenes:

I kicked it because I thought it was a ball and then I saw the mouses tail and them I took the mouse to the vets and my friend the vet called Sleena said it is badly ingerd So I said what shall I do

The mouse on the moon

... and I opened my eyes and I sawed mouse was green with red eyes. Then I screamed and the mice ran my hands was sinking I looked I was sitting on the moon because on the side of me it said THE MOON!

Kill the bloody thing (at the third attempt)

The next day they put another mouse trap but it still did'nt work they kept on trying.

The cat was called fluffy there is a nice mouse in the friDge go and gobble it up. fluffy had sharp claws and sharp teeth.

She turned her head and slivered under the bed we herd chrunch tigger had gulped the mouse.

the butcher saw the mouse and got his chopper and tryed to kill it so we went home.

Luckly he had a rope he tied the rope around the mouses feet and killed the mouse and that was the end of the mouse. The next day the mouse was not there he had gone It was his feunral.

The more successful versions aimed for a dramatic crescendo, each incident surpassing the last in terms of some kind of extreme behaviour (e.g. mousetrap/tied up/ripped apart).

Frankenstein mouse

I asked Rizwan that can you make this mouse back to life Rizwan said to me in a very confidence voice yes, but! but what I said to Rizwan in a loud voice. But it will be human size.

Mouse and man reconciled

In this kind of story initial violence or hurt is followed by reconciliation: the mouse becomes one of the family. Either the mouse is adopted, or is given a name, or has babies and is forgiven everything. Sometimes, it seemed to depend on who was supposed to have spoken the title of the essay – if it was the mouse that said 'help' its chances of adoption seemed to improve:

> The mouse said 'some ones trying to kill me please help me please' So I said '.o.k. but claem down'

Fable: the mouse that nearly froze the world

> The golden frozen moving mouse ran and ran and ran. One day there was a baker puting out some cheese he was a meen old brown eyed fat baker.
>
> I need food 50 piece's of food so one person sneced her 50 pice's of cheese then she ran to the hot's pool in the world and put 50 pieces of cheese ledding into the hoted pool in the world then the mouse ran and ran a ran flowing the cheese ...

It was common for writers in this genre to use the fable's repetitions (ran and ran and ran) in telling their story.

Fairy tale: the princess and the frog/mouse

> I ran to her and told to 'tell me what happed to the ugly lady?' 'It was me. A wich put a spell on me.'

An everyday story of pet-owning folk: pet escapes and is recaptured

> When I got back I put the old food and water bowls into the cage and placed the tunnels in very carefully.

Pet mouse in domestic farce

> my cat rushed past my feet I fallen over in a wahing basket 'Ahhhh!' Bang!

Mouse turns nasty

> Now I am scrad with mouse it look like it gone Eat me and I called the cat and I said Get that Moues alt of my home
>
> I said hey he speces this mouse is not dagres mouse then I was happy. but it was a dagres mouse then I ran out side then I said help me save me.

As the above quote suggests mice that spoke were generally deemed to be OK, at least at first.

But it was all a dream!

Arh, Help, 'I was in a cage full of mouses. 'Help, Help get me out! 'Wake up, Wake up' I woke up and found out that it was a dream

Humour in mousieform

Michael Cheese was scared of mice.

And this amazingly good comic description of the audience at a scary film *Mice in the Underground*:

As the film went on there was popcorn shaking all over the place. people leaped from the back row to the front row. Some jumped up and banged their heads on the ceiling. Some just quietly and surprisingly fell asleep.

Discussion I

We talked over a number of issues, noting the following:

There are a number of kinds of stories in there. There is realist narrative, the depiction of a mouse that escapes, is carefully recaptured and expensively rehoused. There is Science Fiction. There is Fable and Fairy Tail. There is Cartoon. And there is Drama. Each of these genres requires a different kind of story-telling. Like the last one requires a crescendo of failed attempts to catch the mouse followed by a successful denouement. Others – like fantasy – require less linear telling. They can jump from one plane of reality to another etc.

This raised the question: 'What would a single structural aid to narrative writing do to such a variety of story-telling? Is it/can it be used flexibly by the children?' In general, we were both struck by the surprising range of strategies that the pupils seemed to use. It did not really fit with the notion that they lacked cultural resources in terms of a range of possible story-telling strategies. Gudrun's feeling was that perhaps the *First Steps* narrative writing structure would concentrate minds and help the children to structure their stories, of whatever kind, more successfully. At the same time, we had been interviewing the children in small groups and that allowed us to explore their motives and thinking when it came to writing essays, and how they reacted to different teaching approaches.

The pupil evidence

In the first set of interviews 2 months into the study, the pupils said that they liked writing essays better than any other kind of writing, although it could be tiring ('your hand hurts'; 'facts writing is just boring'). It was a kind of freedom: 'you can write anything you like'; 'exciting'; 'if you do your own story you can put your own feelings a bit more you know'; 'you can use your imagination like Aliens and stuff'.

Some wanted even more ownership: 'She chooses the titles, not like 'Terry meets Ryan Giggs'. Instructions from the teacher on length, form and accuracy were occasionally regretted: 'keep on writing keep on writing no full stops no nothing'. There seemed, therefore, a difficulty for the pupils in simultaneously expressing themselves freely, and writing cautiously.

The interview data suggested that at this stage the pupils had identified six ways in which the teacher helped them:

- giving ideas;
- prescribing or proscribing approaches (e.g. not starting with 'One day ...' using adjectives and different verbs);
- starting them off with a few sentences;
- getting them to read each others' stories;
- getting advice from an author who visited them in school;
- giving them 'planning sheets.'

Opinion was divided on the last of these. One group found them helpful because it asked more questions of them than the beginning-middle-and-end approach that they had used in Year 5. The other group was critical: '... 's rubbish. We get this big piece of paper and we've got t-h-e be-ginn-ing, the mid-dle [they're in sing-song chorus by this point] the end, the init-iating event, the prob-lem, how the characters solve the problem, resolution'. And it got in the way of the 'brilliant ideas' that occur when you're writing the story down.

Discussion 2

We decided that the next step was for Gudrun to talk over the children's reservations with them. She subsequently reported that 'the discussion we had was much more in-depth than we had before' and the pupils' contributions were 'very very useful'. The research seemed to have allowed the teacher to have a different kind of discussion with the pupils, encouraging them to reflect on how they were taught as well as what they felt they had learned. The children were supportive, seeking even to reassure ('please miss we do think you're a good teacher'). Despite their reservations, she felt that the *First Steps* structures were helping them in ways that were hard for them to appreciate at this early stage – it was like learning to drive. Once 'mirror-signal-manoeuvre' had been internalised, they would be better able to combine story structure and creativity. To help with that process, she had introduced the '5-minute story': the pupils now had 5 minutes to sketch out their story, taking into account the *First Steps* 'narrative plan', which she felt that some at least were beginning to internalise. Part of the remaining problem was that they were poor at self-criticism: they were beginning to see what was good about stories in books, and what was either good or bad about their classmates' stories when they were read out, but it was still another thing applying that to their own stories.

By this time (month 6 of the project) we were interested in seeing what effects the teaching seemed to have had on the pupils' narrative writing. There were no credible tests that would 'objectively' measure these differences, and so we decided on a number of different approaches. First, we decided to compare a recent essay with the earlier 'baseline' one. We would then compare that latter test with their actual performance in the subsequent National Test. Second, we would interview the same groups of children to see to what extent their account of their learning in this area reflected the teacher's intentions. Finally, we would look at all the evidence, including the actual National Test results themselves, and try to see whether we could come to any conclusions.

More pupil evidence: talking a good story

There was pretty clear evidence from the second set of interviews that the children knew considerably more about narrative writing strategies.

The groups spontaneously identified the following:

- Plan your story. They knew different ideas for planning and seemed to feel that the '5-minute story' approach was the best.
- Stories need a beginning, a middle and an end.
- It was important not to go on and on – 'some stories just keep on going and going and going'. 'On and on' by this time had become a coded reference to a number of things, such as not using 'then' or 'suddenly' all the time, or having a succession of events rather than a plot.
- Use different beginnings, such as starting with direct speech, or something 'exciting'. Never start 'One day …'.
- Realise that 'a good story likes to catch the reader'.
- Think of 'good words'. They contrasted the virtues of 'good' and 'excellent', 'exclaimed' and 'said'. 'Said is a bad word'.
- Think of a good ending. It was bad if you 'come to the end and nothing happens'. And whatever you do, don't end with 'then I woke up and it was a dream'.
- Describe people, 'like what they look like, the colour and everything'. 'It's just boring if you say Terry was happy. I want to know why he is happy and who he is with and what happens in the park' (sometimes you hear the echo of the teacher's voice pretty clearly in the children's accounts).
- Read more books and you will get 'more ideas'.
- Listen to other people's stories and remember the good bits.
- Take care with punctuation, and always check your essay when you have finished.

The above list covers most of the writing strategies promoted by Gudrun, although it is interesting that the labels were no longer referred to. Perhaps they had been 'internalised' as had been anticipated earlier. So the first part of our aim had been realised: the children had learned the narrative strategies. They could now talk a good story. The question was: could they write one?

Comparing the earlier and later essays

For most of the class there seemed four clear differences in the approaches they made to writing.

1   They had learned how to create more interesting introductions using a variety of strategies, such as direct speech, a dramatic event or an introduction that implied an earlier story that might be later unravelled. For example, a September offering: 'I screamed aloud as a giant'. The same pupil the following January: 'In the year

3002 two astronauts went to Pluto for the second time'. Or: 'I started to chase the mouse but it ran into a hole' [along with the story], as opposed to the later beginning 'There was a big bang it sounded like thunder …'

2   Descriptive writing in the later essays was more complex and vivid in its vocabulary (e.g. 'automatic'/'unbelievable'/'facilities'/'shuffled') and the verbs 'say', 'do' and 'go' were less overworked. The message of the 'good word' had sunk home. For many of them it still seemed easy to spot where they had consciously tried to use a strategy (i.e. not fully internalised it?), but for some their fluency made that a difficult business.

3   There was more use of simile: for example, the alien spacecraft had moved from 'shiny' to 'like a bowl of spaghetti inside'. The aliens were developed in more telling imagery – 'it felt like raw meat'.

4   There was generally a clearer sense of character (age/description/motivation) and plot (rather than the 'Suddenly … Suddenly' device for moving on to the next event).

Overall, quite a few in the class (and not just those with the most accurate English) had an idea of the 'shape' of stories and how they could be started, plotted and ended. Beginning: 'The reconstrucksion work was going on in Woolworths. It was the last thew days before it colsed down to be rebuilt'. Ending: 'And if you should ever go up in space yourself you will probably see a great big purple dog floating around whilst doing sums in his head'.

So far, so good. It seemed that the pupils could both talk and write better stories. The question now was: Would they reproduce that improvement under exam conditions?

Story writing in the national tests

It is in the nature of unseen examinations that unpleasant surprises appear. For the first time, the essay choices included a wider choice, including two writing-for-communication options. Gudrun believed that this increased the chances of the pupils making inappropriate choices. But seventeen of the class chose 'You're in Charge', which was the kind of question for which they had been best prepared. One chose 'Changes' (another imaginative essay) while eight opted to write a 'School Newsletter' and four wrote an 'Interview'.

The impact of the narrative strategies teaching was again clear in a number of ways.

1   Most had a beginning strategy of one kind or another, and the stories generally had a form to them, ending with some sort of resolution. It was noteworthy that the first verb deployed by the pupils tended to be a 'good' one (like 'exclaimed'/'concluded'). They also tried hard to write descriptively and to characterise the people in their story, with mixed results (e.g. 'my large gigantic bed'; a 'hunched backed, old, crouched, ugly old crouch').

2   It seemed to be the case that as the story hotted up, caution was thrown to the wind, along with much punctuation, and there was a tendency to push the text towards cartoon formats (e.g. 'EArthquaKE' or artistically rendered BANGs or

'alien' talk written at a slant to depict its otherworldliness). Most stories ended in a worse condition than they had begun.

3   It was clear that the writing under exam conditions was not as good as it had been in classroom essay-writing. The January essays seemed to be more imaginative, had better narrative structures and were probably more accurate.

Reflections

1   The National Test score in English had been 42 per cent, achieving Level 4 plus in 1997. The target set by the school was a 5 per cent improvement. The result was 77 per cent achieving Level 4 plus. Gudrun felt that, quite apart from the new writing strategy, the main factors in that success included additional homework and a rather different spread of ability: teachers in the school perceived a larger 'middle' in that year group, giving them a better chance to make big improvements in the Level 4 plus percentage. Had both teaching and researching been skewed towards results? Certainly that had been a teaching aim, but we had discussed the complex nature of such compromises: *First Steps* had offered a way forward that Gudrun's professional intuition had favoured in any case.

2   It can only be a professional judgement that the *First Steps*/5-minute story made a difference to the National Test results: there is no way of proving it through this sort of small-scale research. Nevertheless, that would be our conclusion, given that we think that we know that the pupils had both internalised the method and applied it in practice both in classroom essays and, to a lesser extent, in the National Test exam. It was clear from the interviews that they regarded the '5 minute' plan as a good way of structuring their essays.

3   The research process had given the teacher feedback from the pupils that she could not receive directly herself. It had prompted a different kind of discussion between the teacher and the pupil about the 'narrative plan' and how it worked. The pupils had (unusually) been involved in discussing the pedagogical strategy, and thus how they themselves believed that they learned best. Their own learning was made more explicit to them. This may be an important consideration, as research literature elsewhere has suggested (Hall, 1998, personal communication). In addition, the analysis – as opposed to the 'marking' – of pupil essays was not something that teachers had either the time or the experience to carry out.

4   How had that analysis changed things? The first explanation, accounting for poor narrative writing, was cultural; the pupils, it will be recalled, were felt to 'lack good ideas'. Cultural explanations are contextual, and because of that they are also implicitly passive in terms of what teachers can do. They say that is their problem, not mine. However, the analysis of the baseline essays suggested that the pupils had a wealth of ideas, even if they were not always good ideas – they did not always choose wisely in terms of which genre to use, or how to tell the story within a given style. The analysis confirmed that the problem was an organisational rather than a cultural one. Such an understanding is active rather than passive. It then became a question of finding out what kinds of pedagogic changes might make a difference.

5   The next stage of the action involved implementing an initially fairly rigid version of the narrative writing scheme in *First Steps*. The pupils were divided over this:

some liked the structure, others mourned their loss of freedom. The teacher, deploying the mirror-signal-manoeuvre metaphor of learning to drive a car, used her professional judgement to reject that initial feedback on the grounds that the pupils would internalise the schema and could then employ it more flexibly. She then offered a more open 5-minute-story approach as a final structuring strategy. Research evidence supported her claims to 'internalisation', and to inform conversations between teachers and pupils about what seemed to work and why. The result seemed to be improvements in subsequent writing. It is significant that the research could not tell the teacher what to do: it was not 'evidence-based' but 'evidence-informed' professional practice. Nor could the narrative writing scheme tell the teacher what to do, professional judgement played a considerable part in its implementation, since it was adapted and subsequently treated as a stage of learning rather than a formula for writing. Success, if it was based on these processes of reflection at all, depended on two forms of professional discretion: what the research evidence might imply, and what the responses of the pupils implied for an evolving teacher strategy. The issue boiled down not to writing schemes, research models or evidence, but to the quality of professional discretion. Presumably, that is what we want this sort of reporting to inform.

6 Initially, the process of research was supposed to be teacher-led. It was, in the sense that the teacher decided on the focus of the research, while the researcher looked for practical and economical ways of addressing the teachers' concerns. The researcher, Ian Stronach, concluded that the process, as opposed to the focus, was researcher-led: Gudrun Heatley simply did not have the time to engage in research processes in a more active way. Her conclusion was that such work was 'massive' and unrealistic to expect from the majority of teachers. Was it research? A critic suggested to us that it was not: it was 'a new version of the old teacher/ researcher separation.' Our confession would be that we had no 'model' of research in mind. We simply took the limits of time, resource and energy available to us to shape enough space for research to 'happen'. Probably, it is not so much the 'old' teacher/researcher separation. More likely the intensification both of primary teaching and HEI researching led us to play this 'speeded-up' game of inquiry and action (Stronach et al., 1996).

7 Ideally, the teacher and the researcher would have liked to continue the experiment by offering an abridged version of this report to other teachers at the school. This proved impossible because Gudrun was promoted and left the school, and the school subsequently withdrew from the consortium (but not because of the project). The next step – which will have to be taken by others – would be to take these findings, relate them to the research literature that directly addresses this sort of writing and consider what conclusions or further hypotheses can be drawn in relation to 'research-based' approaches to professional practice. But it is likely that we should be looking to educate our professional uncertainties rather than to proclaim evidence-based discoveries.

Acknowledgement

An earlier version (Heatley and Stronach, 2000) of this chapter appeared in *Educational Action Research*, 8 (3): 403–417, 2000.

References

Beard, R. (Standards and Effectiveness Unit) (1998) *National Literacy Strategy: Review of Research and other Related Evidence*. London: DfEE.

Education Department of Western Australia (1994) *First Steps. Writing Developmental Continuum*. Melbourne: Longman.

Hall, N. (1998) Personal communication to the authors in response to the 'Base-line data analysis'.

Heatley, G. and Stronach, I. (2000) Plotting effective narrative writing with 10-year-old children: an action research study. *Educational Action Research*, 8(3): 403–417.

Stronach, I., Allan, J., Morris, B. (1996) Can the mothers of invention make virtue out of necessity? An optimistic deconstruction of research compromises in contract research and evaluation. *British Educational Research Journal*, 22(4): 493–509.

Note

The innovation was *First Steps. Writing Developmental Continuum*, which was researched and developed by the Education Department of Western Australia and published there by Longman (1994). Gudrun Heatley adapted and simplified some of its content. *First Steps* is a highly structured approach to creative writing. It proposes a sequence of stages that pupils should learn in order to structure their essay construction (as the parroting of the children shows in the article). Planning sheets provide pupils with the opportunity to organise their writing according to some fairly prescriptive guidelines. It has been described as a behaviourist approach to 'creative' writing, although that is a fairly extreme representation. Gudrun Healey's approach to *First Steps* was to take bits from it that seemed to fit the situation her children were in, and then to adapt it, softening it into a much less prescriptive '5-minute' story. The innovation was used, therefore, as a stage towards a more 'free' pattern of writing.

Chapter 5

Helping weak readers up the reading ladder

Sue Jennings

Introduction

What do you do about 10-year-olds who are approaching the end of Year 5 and still have reading ages that stick stubbornly somewhere between 8 and 9 years? Their National Tests loom ahead, with demands that cannot be adequately met from such a reading base, and beyond that the secondary curriculum awaits them, with high demands for independent reading. Whatever the reasons for this delayed reading progress, it is important to identify efficient and effective methods of enabling these children to close the gap between their chronological ages and their reading ages, if at all possible. By this stage the children usually have a reasonable grasp of basic phonics, and even where this knowledge has areas of uncertainty, going over this ground for the umpteenth time does little to increase their reading ages, for it is not a better grasp of basic phonics that enables a reader to move further up the reading progress ladder.

Do they simply need more reading practice, more opportunity to develop and consolidate reading skills that are already there in rough and ready form and that just need refining? It is certainly true that these children need to practise their reading and equally that a lack of reading practice is often a contributory factor to their current situation. But they cannot practise skills that they have not yet acquired using knowledge that they do not yet possess. So what particular knowledge, skill or understanding does a child with a reading age (RA) of 9 years 6 months have that a child with a RA of 8 years and 6 months does not? How can you find that out, if you do not know?

There are numerous published schemes supporting the teaching of the initial stages of reading. Key Stage 1 teachers and others working with beginning readers can be confident about what to teach – the sounds of the letters, the recognition of initial/final/medial sounds in words, the skills of building and blending consonant-vowel-consonant (c-v-c) words (e.g. run, bag, hit, mop), etc. But these schemes tend to end at the point where basic phonic knowledge (the forty-four phonemes of English and their spelling variations) has been grasped. That will bring the child to a RA around 7 years and 6 months to 8 years. In terms of decoding skills the child is now about halfway to becoming a competent adult reader. This led me to ask:

- What lies on the other half of this journey?
- What skills does the child need?
- What resources are available for the teacher?
- Why do I not recognise this as part of the Key Stage 2 teacher's repertoire?

- How do children become competent adult readers if they are not taught the second half of the necessary knowledge base?

These questions are of real importance in my own school, where around half of the children in a typical Year 5 class have reading ages below their chronological ages and where even this apparently unsatisfactory level of reading skill has only been reached with a great deal of effort on the part of both children and teachers. Our school is situated in an inner-city 'pocket' in Salford where the statistics on crime, health, economic deprivation and social disadvantage all tend towards the extreme. Many of our children have never known anyone in their family to have a job. Discontent with local levels of crime and nuisance behaviour leads to many families repeatedly moving from one council estate to another. Every year we lose several children from each class and take in more newcomers who have typically attended two, three or even four other primary schools already (sometimes they are familiar faces who are returning to us for the second or third time). Our free school meals level is approximately 65 per cent and approximately 45 per cent of the children are on the Special Needs Register. Although small – one-form entry – the school has for the last 5 years employed me as a full-time specialist literacy support teacher.

The issue

There is nowadays strong support for the idea, exemplified in the National Literacy Strategy Framework (NLS) for teaching, that beginner readers need a structured phonics input in order to make progress in reading (DfEE, 1998). Much research has been carried out around the question of how best to teach this basic phonic knowledge to particular groups of children at particular stages, but mostly in Key Stage 1. I would recommend Byrne (1998) and McGuiness (1998), a much more vivid and personal account but equally well researched, to anyone with an interest in the teaching of the early stages of reading. Both books illuminate the subject of just what connections the child has to make in order to understand the reading process.

Towards the end of Key Stage 1 I find that many children – the good readers – begin to 'take off' with their reading. Their reading progress outstrips the phonics input that they are receiving in class, often considerably. They achieve reading ages of 9 or 10; yet we have not 'taught' them phonics at this level. They seem to reach a critical point where their knowledge and understanding of the reading process enables them gradually to fill in the remaining gaps, albeit generally with the assistance of someone hearing them read regularly and correcting mistakes. Thus good readers in Key Stage 2 do not require any phonics instruction. They somehow complete the second half of their phonics education by themselves.

Poor readers reach Key Stage 2 with much of the phonic input from Key Stage 1 still unlearned, so this material must be repeated if they are to make any progress. The Additional Literacy Support materials provided by the DfEE in 1999 are designed to provide the necessary support, offering extra basic level phonics teaching in Years 3 and 4 to those who need it. Once the poor readers have had a re-run of basic phonics it might be expected that they would be ready to 'take off' with their reading, having reached the point where good readers begin to make their own independent progress with little need of further specific teaching. But this is not what happens.

Poor readers continue to struggle. Stanovich (1986) demonstrated that in the reading game the rich get richer but the poor get poorer. Good readers broaden their knowledge and vocabulary through reading, which makes further reading easier, creating an upward spiral. Failing readers continue to fail. In our school such children frequently lack many of the skills and strategies which good readers bring to the task of reading. Typically their skills of analysis, analogy, memory and deduction are poor. Sometimes, despite the level of teacher input, their decoding skills are still poor. A major problem, well explained by Stanovich and Stanovich (1995), is that poor readers need to develop many different skills and combine them effectively.

Further phonics input for the whole class does not usually stop in Key Stage 2, but as exemplified in the NLS it has no particular sequence or structure. It is not directed towards helping children decode words for reading but towards helping them encode words accurately for spelling. In fact, such teaching is not truly phonic any more, as phonics relates to sounds, whereas spelling is to do with letter order, primarily a visual skill. The NLS recognises this shift in emphasis in the headings for its plans for the different terms: Key Stage 1 has the category 'Phonological awareness, phonics and spelling', whereas Key Stage 2 has similar word level targets, but categorised as 'Spelling strategies', or 'Spelling conventions and rules' (DfEE, 1998).

The change in emphasis between say '-ight' taught as visual-pattern-for-spelling, as opposed to phonics-for-reading can be a handicap to poorer readers, many of whom do not readily generalise their learning. When meeting a new '-ight' word in a reading context some days later they may recognise that they have worked on this letter string but are unable to remember the sound that it makes. The NLS targets some highly useful areas for further phonics teaching in Key Stage 2, but under the banner of spelling. For example:

> to explore the occurrence of certain letters, e.g. v and k and letter strings, e.g. wa (swat, water), wo (worship, won) and ss (goodness, hiss and missile) within words: deduce some of the conventions for using them at the beginnings, middles and endings of words
>
> (DfEE, 1998, Year 4, Term 3, Word Level objective 5)

A detail of objective 5 is shown in Box 5.1 and might help to highlight the difference between a spelling (letter string) approach and a phonics approach.

Many good readers are oblivious of the rules shown in Box 5.1. They internalise and use them without being consciously aware, and certainly without being taught or practising them. But poor readers do not seem to make the necessary connections and repeatedly stumble when required to decode these words. They really need to be taught these rules and patterns as part of an ongoing Key Stage 2 phonics programme.

Our starting point

The central focus of our School Development Plan at the time we joined the consortium was raising standards in literacy at Key Stage 2. (This was in 1997, before the advent of the National Literacy Strategy.) As part of this I wanted to expand the teaching of phonics beyond the basic level, to poor readers in Key Stage 2. Our school was inducted rather hurriedly into the consortium during the second round of bidding, when two

Box 5.1 Detail from Word Level objective 5

At Key Stage 1 children meet the words 'was', 'want' and 'what', which are treated as phonically irregular words and learned as such. But they are not irregular, they obey the regular phonic rule that:

- 'Wa/wha' is pronounced as *wo*: wasp, wallet, wander, watch, wash, waddle, waft.
- The irregular ones are wag, waggle and wham (also wobble and whopper – why are they not spelled wabble and whapper?).
- The rule is maintained with consonant blends 'sw' and 'tw': swan, swallow, swamp, swap, swab, swastika, swaddle, twaddle.
- Irregular ones: swag, swagger, swam (will the children notice the connection with the irregular ones above?), swot – as opposed to swat.

We find also that:

- 'war/whar' is pronounced as *w* + *or* (not *w* + *are*): wart, wharf, warp, reward, dwarf, swarm, swarthy, thwart.

The following important extension will only be explored when working from the starting point of *sounds*, rather than letter strings.

The 'wa'-sounds-like-*wo* rule also applies with letter 'q', which has the sound *kw*, i.e. it contains a *w* sound. So:

- 'qua' is pronounced as *kwo*, and 'quar' as *kwor*: quality, quadrilateral, quantity, squander, squash, quarrel, quarter.

This point would be missed in the NLS exploration, which deals with the letter string 'wa' (which has no particular connection with letter string 'qua') rather than the sound wo (which forms part of the sound kwo). Also, working from the sounds wo and wor makes the exploration much simpler and clearer, as it removes the need to discuss words such as wait, wake, way, wall, wary, which introduce a large number of other spelling/phonic rules into any exploration of the letter string 'wa'.

of the original schools had to drop out. During the summer, before the consortium met for the first time in the autumn term, our school received notification of an OfSTED inspection taking place in January 1998. In a school like ours, where children start from such a low baseline, we are all too aware of how poor our results look when seen simply as raw scores rather than as a measure of added value. As a school we are proud of the results our children achieve, but we are not naïve about how other people might view those same results when not fully aware of all relevant aspects of context.

The pre-inspection term was therefore an anxious and very busy time, and I wondered what on earth I was doing getting myself simultaneously involved in a research project. Incidentally, if you are interested in the idea of participating in research, do not wait for the time to be right, just go ahead and do it. It is nice to think that there might come a time in one's life as a teacher when one might actually have a bit of breathing space for things like research. This is definitely a pipe dream!

Our inspection report was very positive, which made all the preparatory work seem worthwhile, but the post-OfSTED Action Plan unavoidably required some rethinking of my research design. At this stage I was very glad of support from Olwen McNamara, my HEI link person/mentor/friend/(therapist!), who was able to suggest alternative methods and ideas when I was stuck. I also benefited from having observed the development of the research foci of other members of the consortium, which inevitably helped develop my own ideas.

I was already teaching the phonics work described above throughout Key Stage 2, but felt that by Year 5 the children needed something slightly more advanced, something that might constitute the next step. What was the next step? I was not sure, so I started by looking at the reading test used by the school, the Salford Sentence Reading Test (SSRT), which tests children's decoding ability (not comprehension) from RA 6 years to RA 10 years 6 months.

I used this test to identify:

- the phonic level at which the children were sticking;
- the phonic content of the sentences beyond that point;
- the knowledge/skill embodied in the higher level sentences;
- the bits of this further knowledge/skill that the children lacked.

By looking at the SSRT in this way it was obvious to me that our poor readers in Year 5 lacked the knowledge and skills necessary to read polysyllabic words, such as invitation, electricity, dangerous, excitement. Similar information could be obtained using a different reading test.

At this point these children's standard reading strategy (apart from just guessing) was to decode words letter by letter. This strategy is ineffective with words of more than six or seven letters because the average short-term memory can only hold six or seven newly presented items (Buzan, 1990). To decode longer words we need to group the individual letters together into syllables as we go. This involves some understanding of what a syllable is. Polysyllabic words also contain new phonic information, particularly in their endings.

The research and intervention programme

Thus it was that I decided, as a research focus, to explore effective strategies for the teaching of polysyllabic words to try to boost reading levels of poor readers in Year 5.

Establishing a baseline

The reading ages of all children in the school aged 6 or over are assessed in January and July every year using the SSRT. This test is administered one-to-one, the child reading aloud up to the point where s/he has made six errors. There are three versions of the test card, A, B and C, which are used in rotation so that children do not become over-familiar with the test material. Sixteen out of thirty-four children in the Year 5 class had reading ages below their chronological ages in January 1998, ranging from RA 6 years 5 months to RA 10 years. These sixteen children were identified as the target group for research purposes and were split into two groups of eight of mixed ability according to reading age for the teaching of a twenty lesson programme. Parents were informed of the programme and its aims, with an outline of what the children would be doing, and a request that they support their child in practising spelling, re-reading word lists and practising poetry.

The establishment of baseline data for the school was an overall objective of the research, particularly in respect of the use of standardised tests to establish the extent of phonological and general learning difficulties, and levels of self-esteem. The whole target group had a baseline RA assessment just before the beginning of the programme and in addition an NFER Non-verbal Reasoning Test (N-VR) was administered to all the children in Year 5 before the beginning of the programme to provide a measure of general ability. The TTA funding paid for a research assistant to help with the testing, which would have taken a great deal of teacher time, and with marking and collating the results.

The N-VR test forms part of the NFER's full scale Cognitive Abilities Tests, which also include a verbal test and a quantitative test. The three tests together give a rounded picture of the child's abilities, and are commonly used at secondary level. However, at primary level the verbal and quantitative tests, though useful diagnostically, are considered to be less reliable as the children can have considerable difficulty in dealing with the structure of the test. Most of our target children for example would have been unable to read the verbal test and would therefore have achieved a 'no score', which would have told us nothing new and would have made an aggregate score from all three tests unreliable. The NFER recommended the use of the Non-verbal Reasoning test on its own as a more reliable measure of the primary child's general ability.

The whole class also took the Harter Self-Esteem Measures, in which the child assesses how she/he views her/himself in five areas: social acceptance, scholastic performance, athletic competence, behaviour and physical appearance. This test was administered informally in very small groups to try to eliminate peer pressure; with the lowest ability children it was administered one-to-one.

Finally, the phonological awareness of the target children was tested using the NFER PhAB test (Phonological Awareness Battery). This gives a range of eight oral tests administered one-to-one, assessing basic phonological awareness, such as recognition of initial and final sounds, recognition of rhyme, ability to create spoonerisms, etc. Each test has a critical score level below which the child is considered to be having difficulty in that area. Scores cannot be aggregated to form an overall measure because the test is designed to be used diagnostically.

The teaching programme

The target groups each had a daily 50-minute lesson for 4 weeks, all taught by myself. The lessons had a set structure:

- Groups of polysyllabic words with similar endings were decoded and discussed.

- The children made up sentences which included the target words.
- Some of the words were practised as spellings.
- Poems (one per week) that contained some of the new words were read and practised.

In addition there was a spelling test and a poetry performance to an appropriate class once a week.

Three separate strands of phonics teaching ran through the programme:

1   The first (and not truly phonics) was the identification of syllables by their vowels. All found the word 'syllable' difficult to remember and hard to pronounce, so we called them 'chunks' instead. We practised reading some words that were long but phonically simple, e.g. superintendent, in order to demonstrate how reading a syllable at a time made a long word much simpler to decode. One problem I had not envisaged was that some of the children's decoding was so slow, and their auditory short-term memory so poor, that by the time they reached the end of the word they had forgotten the first syllables. It sometimes took several slow, repeated readings before the reader could 'hear' the whole word (the rest of the group meanwhile just bursting with delight that they knew the answer, and sometimes unable to stop themselves saying the word out loud).

2   The second strand of phonics was the rules governing soft 'c' and 'g' ('c' making an s-sound, 'g' making a j-sound, e.g. recent, regent). Many polysyllabic words have come into English from Latin, often via French, from which the soft 'c' and 'g' rules originate, so the problem crops up constantly and it is important that the rules are understood.

3   The main bulk of the programme was devoted to the new phonic material contained in the word endings. Words were introduced in groups with the same or similar endings, with a different focus each week, as outlined in Boxes 5.2–5.5.

Note that the material in Box 5.2 would normally be taught in Year 5 as spelling. But as spelling it is a nightmare of complexity. How do you decide whether a word that ends in the sound *ur* is spelled -er, -or, -ar or -our? When taught as phonics it is simplicity itself: it does not matter what the vowel is, the sound you read is always the same. That we were not decoding separate letters but reading the ending as a chunk that says *ur* or *yur* needed constant repetition and stressing.

By week 2, the children were already improving at reading in syllables and enjoyed the challenge of the more difficult words. They competed to be allowed to tackle the longer words, and the focus of their attention on the word lists was strong. It had begun to dawn on them that these words could be read once the *sh* rule and the unstressed vowel rule were remembered, and the strategies for reading syllables were employed.

When putting together this programme I had to compile word lists for myself. Nowadays the NLS Spelling Bank for Key Stage 2 provides some useful lists.

You will find my word lists in Toolkit 3, plus some extra lists that I have used since, as I know how time-consuming and difficult it is to find twelve words that end in '-icity' or '-tial', or whatever. A sample of words ending in '-ous' with 'ci', 'sci', 'ti' and 'xi' is given in Box 5.6. I tried to stick to words that a lower ability 10-year-old could

Box 5.2 Week 1

Week 1 of the programme began with an easy group: unstressed vowels with letter 'r', noticing that it did not matter which vowel(s) was used, from the reader's viewpoint they all made the same sound *ur*, register, inspector, calendar, splendour, and that if letter 'i' appeared in front of the other vowel(s) the sound was *yur*: familiar, behaviour.

Box 5.3 Week 2

In Week 2 we covered endings that say *us*: cactus, tremendous.

Here we learned an essential rule of advanced phonics. The letters 'ci', 'si', 'ti', 'xi', 'ssi' and 'sci' all make the sound *sh* when at the beginning of a final syllable: precious, superstitious, anxious, conscious: ancient, patient; inertia, Patricia; nation, mansion, impression; special, impartial, controversial, etc.

We also looked at endings with unstressed '-ent', which is pronounced *unt* whether the ending is '-ent', '-cent', '-scent', '-cient', '-tient' or '-ment', and also at words ending in '-al', '-ical', '-tial', '-cial', and '-sial', again noting the unstressed vowel and the *sh* sound.

Box 5.4 Week 3

In Week 3 we read words with endings that say *un*: darken, cousin, human, foreign, potion, extension, procession. This brought more practice of the *sh* rule.

Box 5.5 Week 4

In Week 4, as our poem for the week was *Macavity, the Mystery Cat* (T.S. Eliot), we looked at endings with '-y': '-ly', '-ity', '-vity', '-inity', '-acity', '-arity', '-ility', '-ality'. We also revised all the previous work covered.

Box 5.6 Words ending in '-ous' with 'ci', 'sci', 'ti' and 'xi

precious	delicious	luscious	cautious	obnoxious
gracious	suspicious	conscious	infectious	anxious
spacious	officious	unconscious	nutritious	
atrocious			ambitious	
ferocious			superstitious	
vicious			conscientious	

relate to, omitting ones such as contentious, precocious, audacious, which are part of a more adult vocabulary.

The work was nearly all collaborative and oral. Each day, twenty or thirty new target words with the same ending were read aloud by individual children, helped by other children as necessary. Word meanings were discussed, and sentences including the target words were made up orally. Each child then wrote down three of these sentences. Three of the target words were added to the week's spelling list, which was then practised using the 'Look, Cover, Write, Check' method.

The children liked making up sentences, especially silly ones: 'My soup is nutritious and delicious'; 'Mrs Jennings is ancient but decent and intelligent'; 'Paul's feet are odorous'. They competed to write sentences containing the greatest number of target words. A very high proportion of the words we read were completely new vocabulary for all or nearly all the children. Writing the sentences helped to give a context for remembering the meaning, as did the poems.

Poetry

I wanted the children to have some practice of reading polysyllabic words in context, to reinforce their new decoding skills, to practise saying these longer words and to reinforce meanings. I decided to choose poetry texts, a decision which proved successful in a multitude of ways. I read a great many poems searching for polysyllabic words combined with humour, with a strong rhythm and rhyme, which would appeal to lower-ability 10-year-olds. Examples were hard to find and resulted in some compromise. We started with one of Tony Mitton's Big Bad Raps (fairy tales with a big bad character, retold as rap poems): one group read *Huff Puff Houses*, the other *Beans Talk*. These poems were for fun and confidence building, easy to read and with a very strong rhythm. Both groups then read *The Shark* by Lord Alfred Douglas, a very short poem with much more subtle humour and some difficult vocabulary, e.g. demeanour, treacherous. Then we tackled Sections I and III of *Night Mail* by W.H. Auden, a real challenge, which the children responded to well. Finally, we read *Macavity, the Mystery Cat* by T.S. Eliot.

Poetry, when matched for age and interests, is an enjoyable form of text. For poor readers it is manageable in size, the layout makes it easy to find and keep your place when reading, the lines are encouragingly short and unlike narrative text it begs repeated re-reading. The words the children were trying to master stretched their reading skills to the very limits both in terms of comprehension and of decoding. Repeated re-reading was both essential and beneficial. By the end of each week we had read the current poem at least fifty times in class, plus further readings at home, yet no-one showed any signs of boredom at the thought of reading it again. The children were going to be performing in front of another class, and of course wanted to be fluent. Some parts of the poems were read in chorus, some in pairs and some individually, according to each child's choice. But as well as enjoying reading their own sections, they also frequently wanted to read each other's or they all read the whole poem.

Performance was a very important aspect of the programme. It encouraged them to try to learn their particular lines of the poem by heart. Many of them had poor memory skills and never succeeded in fully learning their lines. No-one was criticised for needing their script when performing. As is often the case in a group performance, they frequently ended up knowing each other's lines better than their own, and thus were able to prompt each other when necessary, and take over the lines of anyone absent on performance day. This put them in charge of their own performance, removing any reliance on me.

The fun aspects of language are very evident in poetry, not just rhyme and rhythm but also alliteration, onomatopoeia, word play, etc. Not only is fun a great motivator and an excellent support to memory (Buzan, 1990), but it also plays an important role in language development. Playing with words is not a mindless activity but a way of exploring and understanding language (Crystal, 1996, 1998). Although the children found the polysyllabic words difficult to pronounce, even after considerable practice, they were not in the least put off, merely demanding more practice and delighting in their increasing fluency. They liked these new words and could be heard at other times of the day declaiming them sonorously, sometimes with exaggerated pronunciation or strange intonation, sometimes incorrectly, but obviously deeply engaged with these new combinations of sounds. Year 5's class teacher mentioned a similar delight among her more able group – the other half of the same Year 5 class – reading non-fiction text about fungi and revelling in all the unfamiliar Latin names.

Many of our children have a very poor sense of rhythm and we frequently clapped the rhythm as we read – or tried to clap it! It was illuminating to see how many of them would automatically stop clapping when it was their turn to read, unable to cope with simultaneous reading and clapping, despite the fact that the one was supposed to support the other. The poetry became a very significant part of the daily routine, much looked forward to as it always came at the end of each lesson. The children often wanted to continue after the bell and could frequently be heard reciting their lines in time with their feet as they stomped down the wooden staircase leading from our room.

The one non-humorous poem we studied was *Night Mail* by W.H. Auden (Sections I and III), which contains a wealth of polysyllabic words and consequently a challenging vocabulary level. The children were concerned that their audience might fail to understand or appreciate this poem, which describes a wide variety of different types of letters in the mail. We interpreted it in the light of the children's own experience, and they made visual aids to hold up during the performance, e.g. a large Valentine for 'timid lovers' declarations,' and a letter announcing a Lottery win for 'news financial.' This both reinforced their own understanding and made the poem more accessible to their audience.

The results

The results in terms of raised reading ages (SSRT) were pleasing. The average child makes reading progress that matches his chronological growth. Poor readers make slower progress, gaining perhaps only half a month's reading skill in a calendar month, and sometimes achieving a negative score by losing progress previously made. In the 3 months preceding the programme the sixteen children made an average gain of three-tenths of a month per month, i.e. they were progressing at about one-third of the speed of the average child. At the end of the programme, which took 1 month to deliver to the first group and 2 months to the second group, as a result of interruptions in the timetable, they were tested again. Both groups had made the same average rate of gain of 4 months per month (range −3 months to +14 months). This is four times the rate of the average child, a truly remarkable achievement for these children (see Tables 5.1 and 5.2).

Individual children's results were very varied and some seem very erratic (e.g. DH), but to me this is part and parcel of working with disadvantaged children: they lead difficult lives and are not always in a position to give their full attention to learning. PE for example (Table 5.2) had been brought up by his grandmother since infancy. She had died of cancer the term before and other relatives were disputing who should take care of him. So it was hardly surprising that he made no reading progress between January and May of that year. SH (Table 5.1) had an RA that very nearly matched his chronological age in January, having made a big leap forward in the previous 6 months despite having a below average N-VR score. The material in the programme was aimed at giving children the knowledge and skills to move from around RA 8 years 6

Table 5.1 Results of N-VR test and reading tests for Group A

Group A name	N-VR April 98	RA Jan 98	Change in RA in 3 months Jan to April	Change in RA during May programme
SC	97	9.0	+4 months	+14 months
DH	92	7.6	+2 months	−3 months
SH	85	10.0	0	0
LZ	74	6.5	−1 months	+4 months
LB	94	8.3	0	+7 months
AH	88	9.2	+2 months	+4 months
NT	89	9.0	+4 months	+4 months
MW	95	8.2	0	+2 months
Average monthly change per pupil			Up 0.5 month per month	Up 4 months per month

Note
All reading ages (RAs) are given in years and months, e.g. 7.10 means 7 years 10 months.
N-VR scores range from 70 to 140 with the average child scoring 100.

Table 5.2 Results of N-VR test and reading tests for Group B

Group B name	N-VR April 98	RA Jan 98	Change in RA in 4 months Jan to May	Change in RA during June/July programme
SB	86	8.4	+3 months	+7 months
PE	80	9.0	0	+6 months
RB	94	8.3	−4 months	+12 months
DC	N/S	9.0	0	+6 months
LE	80	8.1	−1 months	+9 months
KF	80	8.1	+4 months	+8 months
NG	N/S	9.8	+2 months	+8 months
LR	N/S	8.1	+1 months	+9 months
Average monthly change per pupil			Up 0.2 month per month	Up 4 months per month

N/S, no score, i.e. below 70.

months to around RA 9 years 6 months and did not contain material that would help him to move on beyond RA 10 years, so I was not surprised that he made no further progress. He was included in the programme because his spelling was very weak and we thought he would benefit in that area, which he did.

One interesting aspect is that the second group, who took twice as long to complete the programme, made twice the average progress of the first group, i.e. the first group took 1 month to complete the programme and made an average of 4 months' reading progress whereas the second group took 2 months to complete the same programme and made an average of 8 months' reading progress (range +6 months to +12 months). This seems to imply that a slower delivery was beneficial. Two of the sixteen children left the school between July and the following January, when they had their mid-year reading test. The remaining fourteen made average gains of three-tenths of a month per month during that time. They had retained the improvement they had made and continued to progress at their usual rate.

Spelling attempts improved during the programme, with fewer mistakes per word, a greater awareness of syllables and more phonic accuracy, e.g. for the word suspicious, early attempts were 'surpises' and 'surpsous', later attempts were 'suspisions' and 'suspicous'. The idea of including spelling was not that the children should end up mastering the spelling of these (to them) very difficult words, but that attempting to spell them would reinforce the phonics work we were doing.

The results of the other tests carried out provided useful baseline data upon which to interpret other findings. The N-VR test, accepted as a good measure of a child's general ability at primary level, demonstrated that the high level of poor readers in this class was not surprising, with twenty-six children scoring below 100 (the average score) and only seven scoring above (see Table 5.3). It was reassuring for the class teacher to note that all the children with reading ages below average (the project children) had below average N-VR scores, whereas ten further children with N-VR scores below 100 had nonetheless achieved above-average reading ages (non-project children).

These scores are standardised, ranging from 70 to 140, with the average score being 100. Children scoring below 70 are given a no score mark.

Several of the target children were thought by their class teachers and by myself to have considerable difficulties with phonological awareness, including four whom we believed to have mild to moderate specific learning difficulties. Our school has a higher than normal proportion of children with specific learning difficulties and many staff have a degree of skill in both recognising and remediating such difficulties and I have a Diploma in Teaching for Specific Learning Difficulties. These weaknesses did not show up on the NFER Phonological Awareness Battery (PhAB) perhaps because of the phonological awareness training that formed a regular part of their normal literacy lessons. These four children (SC, RB, DH, MW, see Tables 5.1 and 5.2) all scored considerably better on the N-VR test than on their reading tests, which is consistent with them having a specific difficulty. The two children who did score significantly on the PhAB test (one of whom immediately left and does not appear in the statistics) were both of very low ability, one having a Statement for Learning Difficulties and N-VR score of 74.

Table 5.3. Results of N-VR tests for Year 5, showing difference in range of project children (RA below chronological age) and non-project children (RA at or above CA)

N-VR score	Project children	Non-project children
No score	3	1
74–79	1	0
80–84	3	1
85–98	4	2
90–94	3	5
95–99	2	1
100–104	0	2
105–109	0	1
110–114	0	2
115–119	0	2
120–124	0	0
125–129	0	0
130–134	0	0
135–140	0	0

The results from the Harter Self-Esteem Measures were of particular interest to the rest of the teaching staff and provoked a great deal of discussion, a lot of which centred on the validity and reliability of the measures in the context in which we had used them. Despite the informality of the setting and the high level of adult support, some children persisted in viewing it as a 'test' and were anxious to get the 'right' answer, either putting the same answer as they thought their neighbour had or the answer which they thought was 'good', rather than the answer that represented their feelings. After the sessions, one or two children asked questions such as, 'Miss, what did I get in that test? Did I get a good mark?' The staff felt that the reliability of the results was very much tied to the ability of the children to understand the purpose of the activity, and their willingness to cooperate with those aims. It was felt that more preparatory work should have been done with the children to familiarise them with the whole concept of measuring self-esteem. Most of the children however did seem to engage appropriately with the descriptors. The overall picture showed the boys as having lower than average self-esteem, and lower than the girls. This stimulated a lot of interest, for this is the reverse of what one would expect from observing the children's behaviour.

Our discussions led us to question whether the children had been adequately prepared for the other tests, and whether they had fully engaged with them. We felt that any test relies on the child being willing to do his/her best, and that 'doing one's best in a test' is an attitude not shared by all our children, some of whom come from disaffected home backgrounds. Staff felt that they would like to try using the self-esteem measures again after carrying out a considerable amount of introductory work with the children. The N-VR test is now used routinely towards the end of Year 3, when all the children in that year are old enough to come well within the age band covered by the test. Subsequent new arrivals in Key Stage 2 are tested upon entry. We have not reused the PhAB tests.

Children's and parents' perceptions

The children were interviewed by Olwen McNamara at the end of the programme. Interviews were semi-structured, in small groups. To the children she was a familiar face from several visits, but an outsider with whom they might risk more honesty than with a teacher. Most of the children had enjoyed the work, and found it challenging, and felt that they had coped and had learned. Their favourite bits were the poetry and making up sentences, the humorous bits.

> I thought we was going to do it like sit at a table and all the way through work, work, work, but it's been great.

> Now I'm not nervous going into Year 6 'cause I was nervous of all my SATs and everything but now I know all my words I'm not nervous.

> [The class teacher] gives us dead hard words but I think I'll be able to handle them because I learned how to split them up.

> Some of the words we get stuck on we just do them in chunks.

The performance aspect had been enjoyed by most because the audience 'clap and laugh at the end of it', although some had felt 'embarrassed' or 'nervous'. Some experiences in class had nevertheless been missed. For the first group it was science lessons: 'We've been missing our experiments cause we are doing volcanoes and we are going to make them erupt!! I wanted to do it ... but I guess my spelling is more important.'

During the programme several parents expressed interest in the new activities and became very involved in helping their child. These parents were eager to hear what progress their child had made. Other parents showed no interest and offered no support. It has to be borne in mind that some of our parents have lower levels of literacy than their children. At the end of the programme parents were informed of how many months reading progress their child had made during the programme, along with our appreciation of how hard the children had worked, and thanks for any support that they had given their child. Some parents expressed delight at the results and thanked the school. Some mentioned how much their child had enjoyed the programme. Some asked if their child could have more of the same at a future date. Some gave no response. There was no negative feedback.

Reflections

I look back and see how much work this all took – finding a focus, devising the programme, searching for poems, writing word lists, finding the right tests. Then staying with the focus and not being distracted when 'real life' created difficulties, collecting all the data I said I would, and ensuring that the research remained within the school's priorities as well as my own. I remember the steepness and the apparent never-endingness of the research learning curve in that first year as both an attraction and a challenge. Also, the enormous pleasure of achieving results, both answers to original questions and unexpected results, and then the burden of trying to communicate them to others. I am aware of the support that came from being part of a consortium and of the personal and professional growth that it engendered. And this work was just the first year of three! Engaging in research is not for the faint hearted, but it is hugely rewarding to have created some evidence that what you believe in actually works.

Acknowledgement

This chapter is based on an earlier paper by Jennings (2000) published in *English in Education.*

References

Buzan, T. (1990) *Use Your Memory*. London: BBC Books.

Byrne, B. (1998) *The Foundations of Literacy: The Child's Acquisition of the Alphabetic Principle*. Hove: Psychology Press.

Crystal, D. (1996) Language play and linguistic intervention. *Child Language Teaching and Therapy*, 12(3): 328–344.

Crystal, D. (1998) *Language Play*. London: Penguin.

Jennings, S. (2000) Advanced phonics: teaching strategies for poor readers at Key Stage 2. *English in Education*, 34(3): 31–40.

Literacy Task Force (1998) *The National Literacy Strategy: A Framework for Teaching*. London: DfEE.

McGuinness, D. (1998) *Why Children Can't Read*. London: Penguin.

Stanovich, K.E. (1986) Matthew effects in reading: some consequences in individual differences in reading in the acquisition of literacy. *Reading Research Quarterly*, 21: 360–406.

Stanovich, K.E. and P. J. (1995) How research might inform the debate about early reading acquisition. *Journal of Research in Reading*, 18, 2, 87–105. Reprinted in Oakhill, J. and Beard, R. (eds.) (1999) *Reading Development and the Teaching of Reading: A Psychological Perspective*. Oxford: Basil Blackwell.

Chapter 6

One mouth, two ears

Seeking ways to make children and teachers effective speakers and listeners

Sarah Brealey and Claire Van-Es

Introduction

This chapter focuses on our first experience of the research world. Since qualifying 4 years ago, Claire has been teaching a Year 3 class at St Malachy's and is responsible for the administration of the annual sacramental programme and also coordinates ICT (information and communications technology) and art. Sarah has been teaching for 3 years; she teaches a Year 2 class at St Malachy's and, as such, is responsible for the execution of the Key Stage 1 National Tests; her other responsibilities are science, music and health education. In addition, both are involved in extra-curricular activities, invaluable for providing contact with children as they move up the school. In Sarah's case this involves running a number of music sessions, and Claire is the school netball coach.

St Malachy's is a one-form entry, voluntary-aided, Roman Catholic primary school situated in Collyhurst, north Manchester, an area of high socio-economic deprivation. The school has close links within the local church community, and the spiritual welfare of the children is central to its ethos. The school has been with the consortium since the beginning, although we were not the original researcher coordinators but took on the role when our predecessor was appointed to a Deputy headship elsewhere. Thus, the project described in this chapter was the result of only 1 year's involvement with the Manchester and Salford Schools Consortium. The focus of the initial school project was science, but in Phase 2, when we became involved, the project focused upon what we came to see as the impoverished speaking and listening skills of the children. Throughout the project our main source of evidence was video recorded episodes of classroom practice. This use of video was only made possible by the ongoing support of Liz Jones from Manchester Metropolitan University. The support not only provided us with the equipment necessary but also with the human resources to make video-recording a practical option.

Our story

> The new climate must encourage teachers to review their teaching techniques in the light of evidence about effective classroom practice and how well the pupils are making progress.
>
> (DES, 1992, Paragraph 118)

Our initial aim was to ascertain whether the children's abilities to engage with science were being hampered, not because of their understanding of the concepts but because they struggled with the vocabulary and with articulating their ideas. Our ambition was to improve the speaking and listening skills of both children and teachers. Using evidence from video recordings of classroom practice, investigations were undertaken in order to gain an understanding of the factors affecting the speaking and listening skills of the children. This chapter gives an account of how, together with a colleague, Julie, we subjected ourselves to critique in order to have more awareness of children's talk and teacher's talk. In this way we hoped to gain an appreciation of some of the gaps in the children's understanding and also to reveal how we ourselves might at times be complicit in hindering the children from learning, through, for example, our use of inappropriate questioning techniques. The exploration also raised a concern about the children's ability to talk within groups, with or without the teacher. Two members of the Key Stage 2 staff, Claire and Julie, initially undertook this investigation and their experiences have acted as a catalyst for change within their own Key Stage and later in Key Stage 1.

Year 3

Video 1 (whole class science lesson)

The following account centres on Claire and her class of Year 3 children. She hoped that by engaging with video evidence she could examine how both she and the children used language and, in addition, whether it was possible to identify specific strategies that encouraged children to listen attentively and purposefully and talk fluently and coherently. The context for the first video was a science lesson in which the topic was 'food'. The focus of the video was the introduction to the lesson and the plenary session. The video camera, in this case, was static and focussed on the whole class. During the introduction the children were sitting on the carpet, and this new topic was introduced in the style of a brainstorm. The children were given the opportunity to share all their previous knowledge of 'food'. Claire then led them in a question and answer session.

A pattern for watching and analysing both this and subsequent videos was developed with colleagues from the Manchester Metropolitan University. Information on the video evidence and the framework we used to aid analysis was given in Chapter 3. Briefly, the video was allowed to run for approximately 5 minutes before being paused and a brainstorming session then occurred between the teachers and, often, a colleague from the university. Using the evidence from the video and our knowledge of the children, we were able to assess a number of factors. These included establishing a baseline from which we could set realistic targets aimed at improving speaking and listening skills. As a consortium we had developed a set of criteria (see Toolkit 4) for assessing pupils' speaking, listening and interactive skills. The consortium had also developed over a period of time, as a result of working with videos, an analytical framework (see Toolkit 5 for full version). Thus, our brainstorming sessions were not random, rather they were guided and shaped by this framework which focused on five main areas:

- the teacher's questioning style;
- the children's responses;
- issues relating to inclusion, e.g. teacher and child interactions;
- the teacher's strategies for stimulating listening;
- the teacher's strategies for stimulating speaking.

By watching short excerpts from the video and by basing our discussions on the framework, we were able to remain focused yet our talk was rich and detailed. We noted, for example, that Claire encouraged the children to formulate their own questions with regard to food. Further, by asking 'What do you want to know about food?' the children were encouraged to draw on their own knowledge and understanding. Moreover, these strategies encouraged thinking. We observed that individual children were given time to think, and there were occasions when they were encouraged to extend and elaborate upon their answers. Sometimes, however, it seemed that children were unable to fully articulate their responses because of the overarching pressure to maintain the lesson's momentum and pace. In one instance, for example, the video captures a boy who was still speaking as Claire turned her attention to another child. For Claire, however, one of the most significant features to emerge from the video was how much she herself dominated the session. As she put it: 'I talk far too much and I don't allow the children the opportunity to talk between themselves; there's no discussion.' We discussed this issue at great length and concluded that the lack of open discussion was due to the children's past experience and the 'schooling' of carpet etiquette. While sitting on the carpet the children had, over the years, learnt that the teacher talks and they listen and learn. We had not previously been conscious that we would have to overcome this barrier, or that it even existed.

After watching the first video we concluded that the children showed a lack of varied and interesting scientific vocabulary. They found it difficult to formulate a specific question and were unable to clarify its meaning. For example, one child formulated the question 'Where does food come from?' This gave Claire the opportunity to encourage the child to develop the question, 'What do you mean? Where we get food from or, where does it actually come from?' We wondered if the lack of clarity of expression and impoverished vocabulary was evident across the curriculum and this prompted us to wonder how we could encourage more pupil talk and ask:

- Does the context of whole class teaching inevitably exclude pupil-to-pupil interaction?

And if it does:

- Can we encourage pupil-to-pupil interaction in a whole class situation?

And if not:

- What kinds of situations would encourage and facilitate pupil talk?

Video 2 (first step to group discussion)

As a consequence of these deliberations, Claire decided that she would plan to incorporate small group discussions at various points during the coming weeks. We also felt that we needed to video one of these groups at an early stage in the proceedings so that we would then have a benchmark against which we could make subsequent comparisons. Accordingly a group of four children were filmed. They had the task of comparing and contrasting two recently read books. They were asked to discuss the content of the books and identify any similarities and differences. Their final task was to write some of their findings on a sheet of paper that had been divided into specific columns.

In very many ways the session was not the success that we had hoped. The children did not really engage in any discussion. Instead, they very quickly moved into the writing aspect of the task. As a consequence, the talk became a matter of simply reading out loud what they had written. However, although the session did not achieve its intended aim, the video became a fertile source for stimulating reflections. We concluded from our discussion that the lack of success may have been due in some degree to any or all of the following:

- The task set was over-ambitious.
- The children were unaware that the discussion was the main focus of the task.
- The writing detracted from the overall intention of the task.
- The teacher's instructions were not clear.
- The children were camera shy.
- There mix of children was wrong.
- The group was too big.

> If you don't know where you are going, it is difficult to select a suitable means of getting there.
>
> Mager (1962)

In the light of our analysis, we decided on a number of actions that we felt would benefit the children so that they were more able to participate in group discussions. The QCA *Teaching Speaking and Listening in Key Stage One and Two* (DfEE, 1998) was a very useful resource when planning the lesson. We studied in detail the Year 3 framework for planning and drew out a number of objectives for discussion and group interaction. Our choice of objectives was guided by the viewing of the previous video. These objectives included:

- ensuring that the planning was sufficiently detailed;
- making the instructions clear to ensure that the children were aware of the teacher's expectations;
- negotiating ground rules for interaction with the children.

The children started to work in pairs, in which they had to share ideas and collaborate so that they could decide how to undertake and complete certain tasks. Following on from this, the pairs of children were then merged into groups of four.

These groups were not arbitrary, however; we had planned that there would be a mix of both gender and ability levels. Also, certain ground rules were set, including an understanding that each group member must contribute at least one statement. Claire also established some rules for herself in her role as teacher. One, for example, was to give the children a variety of information including strategies and structures that would assist them in group interaction. Hence, a number of discussions took place in the preliminary stages of the work in which Claire and the children discussed the importance of 'talk': 'Why talk?' Claire used these discussion to raise questions that she hoped would cause the children to think and clarify their ideas. These were:

- Can talking take a variety of forms?
- Are questioning, discussing and listening all valid skills?
- Does/how does talk provide a method of learning?
- Does talk require rules of behaviour, about interrupting, dominating, valuing contributions, etc.?

Subsequently another video was made which focused on a small group discussion. In order to assess whether any developmental shifts had occurred, attention was focused on the same children who had featured in the previous video.

The task, which formed the basis for the discussion, was concerned with writing a collective story, which would then be recorded on to a cassette tape so that other children could listen to it. Before doing any writing, however, the children had a brief brainstorming session with the teacher to establish effective ways of working. A number of issues were identified. These included deciding where the best place was to write the story (e.g. classroom, home, library, etc.); who was going to take responsibility for writing; and what kind of story to write (e.g. mystery, horror, adventure, etc.). Claire then left the children to discuss these and other issues that they felt were important. The video subsequently concentrated on both the brainstorming session and the children's discussion.

Video 3 (success at last)

It was evident from the video that the preparatory work which had been undertaken had been effective. The children, for example, were able to offer both reasons and justifications for certain choices: 'the library would be best [to write the story] it's quiet'. In addition, they were prepared both to listen to one another and, importantly, to encourage each other to speak. They could also manage some of the dynamics that are a key feature of any group; for example, a somewhat forceful boy was reminded 'we've got to listen to everyone's ideas, not just yours'. It was clearly evident that even during this relatively short story-writing activity the children were continuing to acquire the necessary skills to work as a group. After detailed viewing of the video it became obvious that one particular child had changed his use of language when contributing to the discussion. He no longer used 'I' and now used 'we'. This we saw as success. Moreover, the children settled and resolved issues; they were now able to use key language to take the group forward, having learnt negotiating and brainstorming techniques.

In his teaching the wise man guides his students but does not pull them along; he urges them to go forward and does not suppress them; he opens the way but does not take them to the place;… if his students are encouraged to think for themselves we may call the man a good teacher.

(Confucius, cited in Brown and Wragg)

Year 6 analysis

Video 1 (whole class science lesson)

Other staff within the school became interested in our ways of working, and Julie, our newly appointed Deputy and Year 6 teacher, was interested in looking at her teaching practice using video. We planned to look in detail at the speaking and listening techniques of both Julie and the children in Year 6 and decided that the first video should be filmed when Julie introduced the new topic 'micro-organisms'. The first lesson was planned in the same format as the Year 3 whole class teaching question and answer session. The introduction of a new topic made it necessary to have a longer session on the carpet than usual. Julie used a wide variety of resources. These included posters, science vocabulary, big books, white board and a selection of food. The use of these resources enabled Julie to maintain the children's attention and interest during the question and answer session for a longer period of time than would have been usual.

Subsequent analysis of the video, using the analytical framework (Toolkit 5), allowed us to highlight a number of issues within the class. For example, the number of boys answering questions far outweighed the number of girls. This became a central concern for Julie and encouraged us ask:

- Why were the boys offering proportionally more answers than the girls?
- Did the high number of boys within the class intimidate the girls?
- Do the girls prefer a more practical science lessons?
- Did Year 6 girls perceive science to be a boys' subject?

After lengthy discussions with the class teacher we concluded that the most likely cause of this gender inequality was the relatively high ratio of boys to girls. Throughout the hour-long question and answer session only three girls volunteered answers. We concluded that the girls in the class possibly felt excluded and were almost completely marginalised from the discussion. In addition, the seating arrangement was such that whereas the girls were on the carpet the boys were seated on tables behind, and hence were more in eye contact with the teacher. We then wondered whether the girls would be more willing to play an active part within a single-sex discussion group.

The whole of teaching and learning is shot through with the art of questioning.

(Hamilton, cited in Brown and Wragg)

Video 2 (can the girls discuss better in single-sex groups?)

Julie planned a group task in which she would place the children in single-sex groups and video the group of girls. The focus of this task was for the group to discuss in detail any changes they felt would have occurred by the year 3000. This was to be an independent task and Julie supplied an instruction sheet which contained questions for the children to discuss and answer. In later analysis of the video evidence, it was obvious that during the discussion all the girls took part but two were dominant. Unfortunately, the children appeared to have read and disregarded the sheet, which made their discussion blinkered and static. They found it difficult to extend their thinking, and thus their discussion, past their own everyday experiences. For example, they talked about food, time machines and cartoons. One child's idea was to have an endless supply of chocolate: 'I've got an idea, when you've got a chocolate bar and you eat it and it grows and you eat it and it grows...'

When Julie entered the discussion, she posed the question 'What will be the most important change?' The answer given was about the environment. For example, the group shared their thoughts on pollution and food chains. This gave Julie the illusion that the group had spent a great deal of time discussing environmental issues, where in fact they had only briefly touched upon them. When viewing the video, Julie was amazed to see that the answer she received was not at all related to the children's previous discussion. Was this because:

- the children were aware of the teacher's expectations;
- the children did not refer to the instruction sheet and related questions;
- there were too many instructions upon the sheet;
- the instructions given were too vague;
- the children needed a more focused question.

It was also very interesting to see the change of roles among the girls when Julie entered the group. Out of the six girls, the quieter two stopped interacting altogether, the dominant two took a more passive role and the remaining two became the main speakers when presented with questions from Julie. This made us aware of the personality differences and dynamics within the group: some of the children were more confident when conversing with an adult than with their peers.

We discussed this video at great length, which enabled us to plan the next step. We felt that the girls did not struggle when talking within a single-sex group. However, the quality of the discussion then became our main concern. Once again we consulted the QCA *Teaching Speaking and Listening in Key Stage One and Two*. Using the Year 6 framework for planning enabled us to construct a lesson using step-by-step instructions. Our aims were to:

- improve the *quality* of discussion;
- ensure that all children were involved in the discussion;
- observe the roles adopted within the girls' group and see whether changes were evident when the teacher intervened;
- observe the group dynamics within the boys' group.

Video 3 (success at last)

The pupils, working in single sex groups of between four and six, were asked:

> Using the time-line provided, decide individually what changes may occur to clothes over the next 50 years. As a group talk about your answers. Using everyone's ideas, can you design an outfit of the future?

The children were given a number of pictures that they had to place on a time-line in appropriate places. To assist the children to stay on task, they were provided with three instructions on separate cards. They were to complete each task before starting the next one. The cards read:

1   Look at the pictures on the table. Place them on the time-line in the position you feel is appropriate.
2   Can you predict any changes that might occur over the next 50 years? Write any ideas you have on the post-it notes and place them on the timeline. PLEASE WORK ALONE.
3   Read and discuss everyone's ideas in turn. Consider them all and then design a final outfit together.

After viewing this video it was evident that the extensive preparation and planning for this session had been valuable. Each group was able to complete the task. They were able to share their ideas and discuss their reasoning. Overall, we felt that the quality of the discussion was superior. There were a number of explanations for this success. By setting a time limit, of 10 minutes, it focused the children so that they did not have the opportunity to stray from the task. We also gave the group a smaller number of instructions which did not overwhelm them, rather it encouraged the children to move smoothly through the short activities. This was a dramatic improvement from previous attempts at discussion.

As previously mentioned, we were also interested to ascertain whether the role changes recorded during the girls' discussion would recur. We thought that we had adopted a number of strategies to ensure a more inclusive discussion. The inclusion of an activity where the children worked independently of each other allowed even the most isolated child to participate. As a result, the children had a more equal role to play, which avoided the possibility of a dominant party emerging. Julie also adopted a passive role when she joined the group for the plenary session. This was to encourage the children to share their findings and conclusions. Julie became the listener, allowing the children ownership of their valuable discussion. After viewing the video it was evident that the previously observed role changes from dominant to passive did not occur, in either the boys' or the girls' groups. We felt that this was due in part to the employment of the above strategies.

Year 2 analysis

After reflecting upon all the videos, in both Year 3 and Year 6, we thought it would be interesting to see whether techniques adopted and developed by Julie and Claire could be adapted for working with younger children. We were curious to see whether it was possible to use the strategies developed within Key Stage 2 to assist a Key Stage 1 teacher when planning a speaking and listening activity. In the light of the success that Claire and Julie had achieved, it was not difficult to persuade Sarah to implement a similar approach with a Year 2 class. We decided that the focus for the video should be a mixture of whole class teaching and collaborative group work within literacy. We were interested to see whether the ways of working and vocabulary developed in a whole class teaching situation would transfer to the group session.

Can the strategies developed be adapted in Key Stage 1?

The lesson began with the children on the carpet, with Sarah questioning them on their preconceived ideas of group work. 'What do I mean when I say work as a group?' Sarah felt that this was necessary as she hoped that it would clarify the importance of discussion within the activity. One boy's understanding was, 'When you don't argue and you don't go, "I want my stuff and now you do your stuff". You share.' Sarah thought that this showed excellent insight about how to approach group work. By sharing his thoughts, this allowed the rest of the children to have a clear understanding of group work and elaborate upon what they felt was expected of them when working in a group.

> Teachers should have the opportunity to interact with their pupils, offer explanations which develop thinking, encourage speculation and hypothesis through sensitive questioning, create a climate of interest and purpose.
>
> (DES, 1992, Paragraph 105)

The object of the lesson was to examine how authors describe characters and set scenes. This was introduced by using an extract of 'familiar text', in this case *The Rainbow Fish*; the children were asked whether they could identify the adjectives within it. As each word was highlighted the children were asked to close their eyes and picture the scene. As more and more adjectives were identified the children were able to complete the full picture. They then discussed the importance of these words, and the children acknowledged that without adjectives it would be difficult for us all to have the same image. Once again, this carpet session was controlled and the discussion was structured by the teacher. A necessary aspect of carpet work is for the teacher to facilitate and guide the talk, ensuring that all the children are active in both listening and speaking (in turn).

Analysis of whole class discussion in previous videos had led us to believe that when planning a group discussion in Key Stage 1 the strategy of introducing the task to the children would be different. The children would need much more guidance about the task and were obviously unable to follow written instructions because of their level of reading. This made it necessary for Sarah to use the carpet time to demonstrate how to approach the group activity without the teacher being present. Sarah planned to approach this problem by demonstrating the task in the form of a 'human sentence'. This involved writing out a simple sentence with each word on a separate piece of paper. The children stood in a line, each holding one of the words.

The object of this practical approach to sentence work was that the children became very aware of how sentences were formed, i.e. a capital letter at the front, full stop at the end. By using this method with this task it allowed the children to participate and visualise the process of extending a simple sentence.

Each group was given an envelope containing:

1 a picture of a character for the children to describe;
2 a simple sentence;
3 paper on which the children could write additional words.

Sarah explained the contents of the envelope and how the children were to utilise them. They were instructed to look in detail at the picture and make a collection of adjectives that helped them describe the character as demonstrated during the carpet session. Using these words, the children were then asked to construct a description, building on the given simple sentence. The aim of the group discussion was to reinforce the work on adjectives carried out during the carpet session.

One group of five children was videoed attempting to complete the given task. It was a mixed-ability and mixed-sex group. It was interesting to observe that the brainstorming session that had been demonstrated during the carpet session did not take place, rather the children immediately entered into the writing aspect of the task. They did, however, share their ideas by taking it in turns to write adjectives and place them in the appropriate part of the sentence. Although the group did not complete the task in the way it had been rehearsed on the carpet, they did achieve the intended goal. By sharing their ideas they bypassed the need for a brainstorming session and successfully found their own means to complete the given task. It was refreshing to see how they rallied around to assist the less able children with their writing and spelling. At one point a word was placed in an inappropriate position; rather than pointing this out as a mistake, the group read the sentence aloud. This enabled the child to identify her own mistake and correct it.

After completing the task the children assembled on the carpet. They were asked to share their new, extended 'human' sentences with their fellow classmates. One such example was: 'There was an old man with grey hair and wrinkles. He was a granddad and came from Africa. He was kind and gentle.' Each of the character pictures was put on display; the children were then invited to point out the character being described. The children always chose the appropriate character for each sentence, thus giving each group a sense of achievement.

Teachers need to be able to give precise instructions, to explain ideas clearly, to demonstrate practical activities, to pose different kinds of questions and to help pupils understand how well they have done.

(DES, 1992, Paragraph 103)

We felt that the children successfully completed the task, with the use of rich and varied talk. We especially liked the manner in which the children placed their own identity on the task. It was evident to all involved that the strategies developed in Key Stage 2 could be integrated with ease into a Key Stage 1 classroom.

Reflections

Our aim was to improve the speaking and listening skills of both the children and the teachers at St Malachy's. A particular intention was to ascertain whether the children's ability to engage with science was being hampered because they struggled with the vocabulary. As the research progressed, the focus moved naturally from science to literacy, because the problem was seen to be impoverished linguistic skills in general rather than simply a lack of scientific vocabulary. We hoped that by developing the pupils' listening and speaking skills we would also see an improvement in other areas of the curriculum. The children involved in the research showed a remarkable improvement in a short time span in their ability to discuss and share ideas. The video recordings provided us with evidence that the research enhanced our own classroom practice, and this success acted as an incentive for at least one other teacher to become involved. Encouraging the further participation of our colleagues will be a long process, yet we now see our task as involving other staff in using the video evidence we have collected. Our success will depend on the strategies being seen as part of an ongoing whole school venture – an approach to developing effective speaking and listening skills in both children and teachers.

For the teachers who took part, the experience of subjecting ourselves to the scrutiny of the video camera was painful but fruitful. Painful, because such close scrutiny at times made us feel vulnerable. Fruitful, because the videos were testimonies of our professional growth and development. By engaging with video evidence we developed fresh understandings of our practice, and it was from these that we were able to perceive new directions. As critical friends, we have learnt through, and with, each other, using insights derived from the discussions of our own classroom practice. We also felt we were able to help each other by identifying aspects of 'good practice' so easily overlooked; each of us was very quick to see the faults in our own classroom practice. In addition, by engaging in such discussions all of us acquired new skills of analysis, reflection, feeding back, etc., and we learnt to manage challenging moments in interpersonal relations by being objective. We also greatly appreciated the rewarding moments of working and talking together with a few of our colleagues in the school and particularly with our colleague Terry Stringer from Salford LEA, who has supported the school throughout all the stages of its involvement in the project. And we are also grateful to Liz Jones, an HEI colleague, who acted as a valuable catalyst to critical reflection and at times helped us to keep on task and focused in our viewing of the video evidence.

The other major benefit that the medium of video offered was the potential to communicate vivid insights derived from authentic representations of classroom practice to the wider teaching community. The next stage of the process involved the other consortium teachers joining with us to watch selected episodes from the classroom videos. They welcomed the opportunity of entering a colleague's classroom and questioning and discussing behaviour and actions similar to, and different from, things they do habitually and instinctively when teaching.

References

Brown, G. and Wragg, E.C. (1993) *Questioning*. London: Routledge.

Department of Education and Science (1992) *Curriculum Organisation and Classroom Practice in Primary Schools*. A discussion paper. London: DES.

Department of Education and Employment (1998) *Teaching Speaking and Listening in Key Stage One and Two*. DfEE: London.

Mager (1962) *Preparing Instructional Objectives*. Palo Alto: Fearon.

Chapter 7

'Not only, but also ...'

'Hard' and 'soft' research stories

Mandy Walsh and Dave Hustler

Introduction

There are always different ways of reporting on a research project, different stories which might be told. In this case study we present at least two stories, one of which might be termed the 'hard' version and the other the 'soft' – or at least this is how we have come to think of them. For us the more important, and lasting, story is the soft version, and we will spend the bulk of the chapter on this, not least because our feeling is that this is where the more interesting messages are for others. Readers might prefer to start with what is for us the more interesting 'soft' story, which begins later (pp. 99–101). Clearly, any account of a research project involves a selection from a broader or more complete picture, and certainly any attempt to provide a full picture here would fill a book, let alone a brief chapter. However, the way we have chosen to present these two stories should not be viewed as just two differing selections from the 'full picture'. For us, both stories provided some answers regarding what the school gained from the research, both stories are interdependent and developed from the same initial focus and both stories could be regarded as honest accounts. Our interest here is in how, through their differences, they connect with the ways in which different views emerged in the school regarding the nature, relevance and possibilities of research. In brief, the two stories we have constructed capture some crucial issues to do with how some colleagues in one school experienced research, and its relevance to them and us as professionals. We will return to these issues in our concluding discussion. Now, let us turn to the 'hard' story, and in doing this we will need to outline what that 'initial focus' was, together with some brief comments on the school.

The 'hard' story

This Catholic Primary School is in the north of Manchester drawing from a mixed area of better-off families in employment and owner occupation and poorer families in low-paid and no employment. There are 330 pupils, about 30 per cent of whom are entitled to free school meals. Although the area is ethnically diverse, the school population is primarily white, baptised Catholics.

Our initial research focus for the project relates to the children, and to how their skills developed in a particular area: their understanding of both inferential and literal meanings within the context of literacy. Here was an area where we felt that the children at our school seemed relatively weak when we considered the standards achieved in reading and language work in the early years. An analysis of the National Test results at the end of Key Stage 2 showed that the children were achieving a high standard, but there was room for improvement at the upper end of the attainment scale. Although the number of children reaching Level 4 was as expected, many were missing out on the higher levels by a few marks. It was felt that these higher marks were achievable when looking at the type of questions the children had answered and the way in which they had answered them. Many of the inferential questions were misinterpreted and more literal answers were given. We had arrived then at our, still somewhat general, research focus: to review teaching strategies at Key Stage 2 in both oral and written comprehension with a view to improving skills and attainment in literal, inferential and appreciative responses to comprehension.

It should be noted that initial staff involvement was limited, with the head, Dave and Mandy (Literacy Coordinator in Key Stage 2) working to put the project together. However, all Key Stage 2 staff agreed to the focus, and also agreed to provide some of the data requested and participate in the project as it unfolded. We will have more to say about staff perspectives on research generally (and on the project specifically) later (pp. 95–99). What we can note here is that our initial outline of the methods to be adopted and the data to be gathered clearly fitted with understandings in the school regarding what the research was about. Judith Bell (1999), in her very useful book *Doing Your Research Project*, has some introductory comments about conventional perspectives on research, and refers in particular to Howard and Sharp's (1983, p. 6) observation that 'Most people associate the word "research" with activities which are substantially removed from day-to-day life ...'

In brief, we made use of pupil and staff interviews (see pp. 96–99); then a number of Key Stage 2 teachers applied an agreed pedagogic framework, followed by a consideration of how this seemed to affect the children's understandings and skills as measured using standardised tests. This then approximated to an input/output model of research. First came the assessment of where the children, or rather the sample of children, were to begin with in terms of attitude, as well as attainment according to various measures, and teacher views. Then came the application of an agreed pedagogic intervention in terms of the teaching format. Then we needed to see where the children were in terms of attitudes and attainment. For most colleagues in the school, and perhaps for most readers, this was what research should be about. The project could almost be characterised as a small experiment and more details are given below.

For the sample, each class teacher was asked to choose a representative group of children who were above average ability, working at average ability and below average ability (excluding extremes). Six children were identified, three boys and three girls, from Years 3, 4 and 5. The children would be tracked until they sat the National Tests at the end of Year 6. The Key Stage 1 results were used to help identify those pupils who fell into the groups we needed in Year 3. For the children in Years 4 and 5 we used the QCA test results and the knowledge of the class teacher to acquire an understanding of the individual pupils and their literacy performance. Each class teacher was asked to write a brief pen-portrait for each child they had chosen. This was done at the beginning of the project and again in the final stages. The use of brief child pen-portraits was very illuminating and useful at various stages of the research. They were not demanding on staff time; ours were about half a page long, with staff giving a description of a particular child's literacy performance and attitude within the class, and anything else that might be relevant to gain a sense of the child. It was often fascinating and very instructive to compare earlier portraits with later portraits of the same child.

We had a sample of children, selected according to roughly common criteria, and in retrospect we were right to limit the sample size. This was not just to do with the manageability of a small project and the potential the small sample had for allowing us to focus in more depth on the children. It also related to initial staff discussions about research and the extent to which we were presuming upon hard-working colleagues to become involved in providing data, given their uneasiness at this stage about the possible relevance of the research to their professional activities (p. 95).

Once the groups were established, all the children were interviewed by a post-graduate student to establish their views on language and where they felt their strengths and weaknesses lay. The student was familiar with the children from previous meetings. We felt justified in using a semi-outsider for the additional degree of independence he brought to bear. However, we did not accept the argument that involving colleagues in researching their own circumstances is not appropriate because it undermines 'objectivity' or 'independence'. For information about involving 'critical friends' in research see McNiff *et al.* (1999, pp. 84–86).

Interviews with staff (some early ones conducted by Mandy and then a later set conducted by Dave) helped flesh out the pen-portraits of the sample children. The interviews also generated information on colleagues' differing teaching approaches in the delivery of the text level work during the Literacy Hour, and this provided a basis for staff discussions on agreeing a common approach or format. This format subsequently emerged from a staff meeting where we agreed that it would be useful to adhere to a standardised approach: we felt it would benefit the children and make the analysis of colleagues' ways of working and their impact more manageable and 'scientific'. Although the National Literacy Strategy had not been implemented at the time, Literacy Hour procedures were emerging on the educational scene, so the format we adopted will be familiar:

1   reading through the text by selected children;
2   teacher reading;
3   discussion and question/answer, e.g. vocabulary, meanings of words/other usage in context, characters/children's own experiences, leading to 'How would you answer this question?';
4   teacher picking up on queries/questions/problems/misunderstandings;
5   individual work;
6   extension work to be put on the board, with the teacher's preference of when this should be; and
7   plenary session, e.g. drawing on the children's answers and involving the whole class in an analysis of their answers, and use of modelling to identify strengths.

With the format agreed, a time-frame was worked out for all teachers to deliver the text in this way. We also made arrangements together to review the work done and to discuss refining and improving the way of working.

This, then, was the core of our methodology, though there were other sources of data that we drew on (e.g. at a later date the children were given logs to complete in an effort to gather data about their views on certain lessons and their own performance within that lesson). In some ways, it might be suggested that the Literacy Hour is a form of national experiment, in which National Tests are the key measure for judging success. In a sense our approach could be viewed as a small-scale, local, version of this experiment.

We have of course analysed what has emerged in some detail in terms of overall cohort results and in relation to test scores of sample children as well. In general terms, looking at the results the children have achieved, the first thing we noticed was a steady improvement, even if this was sometimes only within the same level. The results of the sample children in each year group showed that all had made substantial improvements in all areas, particularly in reading comprehension (see Table 7.1). Some of the children scored at the upper end of the next level, with one child going from Level 1 to Level 3c in under 2 years. We will focus now on the sample of six pupils in one particular year group, showing their progress through the project.

Mary and Lucy were chosen to represent the upper end of the group. They both had very highly developed oral and written vocabularies. Both children were widely read, having read both fiction and non-fiction; they showed good understanding of the text level, offering detailed answers during the Literacy Hour. They displayed a particular strength when looking at the richer text incorporating inferential elements. Both scored Level 3 at the end of Key Stage 1. By the end of Key Stage 2 both achieved Level 5 in the National Tests. During the interim years, they had made steady progress in this area, which the QCA tests show.

Paul and Tina were chosen to represent the middle range of the same group, for although their language development was good they lacked the vocabulary and level of development to put them in the same group as Mary. Both were highly skilled in literal comprehension, but inferential meaning often escaped their understanding. These children made steady progress during the 2 years that they were tracked. They had achieved Level 3 at Key Stage 1, and by the end of Key Stage 2 Tina had achieved Level 5 and Paul had achieved Level 4, with both children displaying a good

Table 7.1 Results for reading comprehension

Name	1996*	1998†	1999†	2000‡
Lucy	3	(t)4	4a	5
Mary	3	(t)4	4a	5
Tina	3	(t)4	4c	5
Paul	3	3a	4a	4
Tim	2c	3b	Absent	3
Joseph	1	3c	3b	4

*Key Stage 1 national test.
†QCA tests.
‡Key Stage 2 national test.

Note
For the QCA test results for 1998 and 1999 the grading within a level is indicated by c, b, a (a being the highest). (t) indicates that the child is working towards that particular level, for example, Lucy in 1998 achieved a (t)4 meaning that she was higher than a 3a but had not yet achieved level 4c .

understanding of the text and answering well orally and in written work. The difference in attainment at the end of Key Stage Two 2 was because Paul's answers were always shorter and lacked the fine detail of his partner. (This last statement on the depth of Paul's writing relates to discussions of 'boys' writing', a research project in itself and an issue that connected with some other materials in our data.)

Of the last pair of children, Joseph made the most progress. Joseph and Tim were both underachievers in language. They were slow to develop their phonic ear in reading and spelling and had a limited vocabulary, which compounded their lack of progress. Both children found it difficult to answer evaluative questions, had difficulty grasping the full meaning of the text and failed to answer inferential questions appropriately. Their grasp of content was poor. At Key Stage 1 Tim scored Level 2c and Joseph Level 1. By the end of Key Stage 2, Tim had achieved Level 3 and Joseph Level 4.

In the school we would argue that that our data overall does point to quite an improvement in achievement in the areas on which we focused. We have attempted to analyse 'case studies' of particular children in more detail, using materials such as interview data, log materials, and pen-portraits from different teachers. These materials have been helpful in understanding some of the shifts and developments in their National Tests and QCA results.

One of the great benefits of using a mixture of methods is that it allows a picture of a child to be built using different sets of data. One set of data can illuminate another, and sometimes raise some interesting questions which can help to shape future research directions. Some people argue that the strength of using a variety of methods is that the results from one method can be cross-checked for accuracy against another. This may be true, but it is the potential for raising new questions and opening up new understandings which we value.

However, we will close this section with a brief aside on how our approach, as presented so far, might be judged. We recognise that there are many difficulties attributing the sources of such changes in this sort of research model. There are a variety of arguments and positions regarding what constitutes the most appropriate methodologies for educational research. A number of textbooks on research methodology outline these (see especially Pollard, 1996; Bell, 1999). Our research might be criticised because of, for example, the absence of control groups or problems with the sample; the ways in which the 'agreed format' we adopted varied in practice (so it seems difficult to suggest that any improvements could be put down to the particular teaching approach intervention); the multitude of other possible explanations for improvement, such as literacy being in the air anyway; a group of staff becoming more motivated and energised after the traditional post-OfSTED blues syndrome; the Headteacher's interest in, and support for, the project; the lively personality of the Literacy Coordinator, etc.). So, the basic judgement about our research project, as presented so far, could be that it has some interesting bits and pieces to it, but that it is really a failure, because as a project designed to investigate what works, it is methodologically flawed. In brief, we have not shown that there is any reason to believe that the teaching approach intervention we introduced has had any effect on the children's achievement. This might, for example, be the verdict of researchers such as Croll and Hastings (1997). We would accept some aspects of the assessment of this the 'hard' version of our research work, but there is another way of describing the research.

The 'soft' story

We have chosen the term 'hard' for the first story, because the research project as presented so far connects with the notions of 'hard' evidence, samples, measurable effects and the language of 'semi-experiments', objectivity and being (or attempting to be) scientific. There is no doubt that this is the notion of research that most colleagues at the school had at the outset. At the beginning of the project colleagues answered a questionnaire on research and evidence-based approaches and what these might have to do with being a professional and the potential for improving practice. The questionnaire was discussed at a staff meeting during which some staff attitudes became apparent:

- Research brought with it the dangers of additional paperwork.
- Research was carried out by strange people from the academic world.
- Research had little to say of relevance to the day-to-day business of working with children in the classroom.
- Research often came clothed in messages about what teachers were doing wrong and added to the sense of external agendas and multiple external innovations imposed on an undervalued and overcriticised profession. (*Testing Teachers*, by Bob Jeffrey and Peter Woods, gives a very powerful and readable account of these issues.)

We also need to take note of other, often neglected, aspects of the local context for the project in its first year. The school had experienced an OfSTED inspection, and although it emerged with a very sound report, most colleagues felt completely drained by the experience and somewhat reinforced in their negative views about the relevance of 'outsiders' to their professional practice. Added to this, during the early period of the project there was a good deal of anger about particular external initiatives such as the Literacy Strategy. The anger was fuelled by a belief that colleagues had for a long time, and with some success, been teaching in ways which approximated pretty closely to Literacy Hour guidelines, albeit not dressed up in what one teacher interviewed called the 'newly fashionable vocabularies associated with the Literacy Strategy'. The importance of local school cultures and people's associated perceptions on standardised external initiatives is discussed by Cochran-Smith and Lytle (1999).

We need to 'come clean' now about how our initial thinking and planning for our research had to take account of colleagues' perspectives. The 'soft' story is almost a mirror image of our 'hard' version. It relates what we left out of that story, and the central theme here concerns how staff gradually became involved in the project, and how it became a school project. If the 'hard' story was more about the impact on children of certain teaching strategies, the 'soft' story is primarily about the staff; we characterise it as 'soft' because it focuses on how people talked about and seemed to feel about the project. It is concerned with the parts often left out in an account of a research project, for us this 'but also' is an important element. 'Coming clean' is to do with our view that we had to set up a project which tied in with colleagues' notions of what a research project should look like. One aspect of this is that, although they were willing to provide some data, it could hardly be a project which presumed strong staff involvement from the beginning. It was to be a project conducted mainly by the designated school research coordinator collaborating with the university and the Headteacher. We hoped that in setting up this 'hard' version we would also build in the resources for gradually engaging more colleagues. If we were unsuccessful then, hopefully, the project would still be of some worth. Now to more detail on the 'soft' version, and we start with another way of characterising the school.

The school, as we have noted, is relatively successful in terms of both recognised 'league table' measures and the sense which insiders and outsiders have of a caring and supportive staff operating with what some would regard, and appreciate, as traditional pedagogic strategies. There has been little turnover of staff, and a flavour of stability characterises the school. Staff get on well socially, and, in common with many primary schools of this sort, staff at the outset of the project felt that they did a good professional job in their own classrooms but knew very little about the details of how their colleagues operated as teachers. Talk about pedagogy as such was not a common feature of staff room discussions or staff meetings, nor was there any good reason to think it should be more prevalent. As we have noted above (p.95) there was a collective sense of teachers being unjustifiably under fire and imposed upon, so there was a natural professional defensiveness about one's own professional domain in the classroom. There is no doubt that this culture has changed in some significant ways. How has this come about? We will point to some elements of the research project that might have effected this change.

It is worthwhile trying to establish what potential participants in such research think about research and how perceptions here can be associated with other issues. For most colleagues, research was clearly viewed as something that other people did, and it also seemed to be associated with yet more criticism of teachers. The link between research and the outsiders doing it also seemed to be associated with other observers such as OfSTED. Impressions such as these definitely slowed down any early involvement of our colleagues in the project, and we needed to know about these suspicions in order to make progress.

Talking about the children

What probably had a crucial initial impact in terms of discussion in the staff room and at staff meetings were some of the particular comments children had made in their interviews and in some of their pupil logs (see Toolkit 6). One child said that non-fiction stories appealed more 'because it happened in the past and you look back at it like storms and look back and know it happened in real life.' Another said:

> I am all right (at comprehensions) but sometimes if you have to do a whole sentence I try and cut it short and get it wrong. If I write the whole sentence I get it right, but if Miss said I can draw a picture after the work I rush to get it finished so I can do a picture.

Another child asked the teacher if she was going to be reading her log (a real sign of teacher trust and involvement was that teachers had agreed that they would pass the pupil logs straight on to Mandy). Another, when asked what sort of books she liked, said, 'short ones'. None of these comments alone was particularly newsworthy, but they got us talking, sometimes quite heatedly, about matters such as:

- gender and fiction/non-fiction preferences (children's *and* teachers' preferences);
- what sort of motivation strategies occasionally led to errors, and associated judgements about children's capacities;
- ethical issues to do with whether or not pupil logs should be read, and associated matters to do with whether or not everything a child produces in the classroom should be looked at by the teacher and the impact of different sorts of audiences;
- what makes us laugh about what children say and do, and the possible impact of this on children and what it says about our understanding of children.

It is not surprising that quite a few researchers have discovered that what engages teachers, sooner rather than later, is what the children themselves are saying, and this certainly seemed to work in our context. We also found that various colleagues were struck by how the positioning of the children in the sample groups by the original criteria seemed to have changed as they moved across teachers and through the school. This involved us in discussions about whether the children had changed and/or whether the teachers' judgements about the children were different. Lots of discussion then developed focusing on individual children who staff knew from the past (including references to family background and other sharing of knowledge), plus some interesting comparisons of progress in maths with progress in English. Materials from different teachers' pen-portraits of the same child stimulated discussion as well; for example, at the end of Year 4 Joseph 'would not attempt any independent writing without the help of a group situation or the assistance of the class teacher.' By the end of Year 6 the class teacher wrote of his independent writing, 'he is capable of lengthy stories, but lacks punctuation.' At the end of Key Stage 1 he scored a Level 1, but by the end of Key Stage 2 he achieved a Level 4 in reading comprehension.

The relatively small sample size meant that at times we became involved in how particular children seemed to relate to specific pedagogic strategies in this or that way; in doing this, staff were sharing and exchanging information about their own teaching approaches at quite a detailed level. Having what some people refer to as the 'rich data' of a case study can make research material more accessible, more interesting and more relevant to the 'real' nature of day-to-day classroom life.

Talking about each other's teaching strategies

Perhaps the sharing which developed from discussing the data about and from the children laid some foundations for talking about each other's teaching approaches, but there were two aspects of the project which really took this much further. The first was to do with the agreed standardised teaching format referred to earlier. The second was the series of interviews with individual members of staff. The additional data we draw on below comes primarily from staff meetings. It was very helpful that staff agreed that illustrative individual comments from the interviews could be fed back into staff meetings. It was apparent from the discussions leading to the agreed format, and the discussions and interviews reviewing the experience, that staff were varying the format in all sorts of interesting ways, and several staff were trying out practices which other colleagues had found 'worked for them'. There are a host of very specific minor pedagogic strategies which we could illustrate, but we will focus here on some of the more general comments from the interviews which led to extensive discussion.

> You have to vary things.... It's a matter of professional judgement ... experienced intuition ... discretion. It depends on all sorts of things: the text, the weather, how the children are...

> I like the way we have been able to discuss it with each other because it has given me ideas...I am really against having some overriding formula.

Comments such as these led us into all sorts of issues to do with the influence of context and of 'experienced intuition'.

> 'I altered it when I got fed up with it.' The point the teacher went on to discuss was that what bores teachers will often bore children.

> 'I tried reading the questions ... they liked it and said it was better.' As the teacher remarked later, the explicit attempts to get feedback from the children on pedagogic strategies they found better, or not so good, were quite illuminating.

> 'I found I was always choosing the same children.' As has often been the case, when some systematic classroom observation takes place there can emerge a lot of food for thought, and occasionally considerable surprise, regarding how a teacher involves children and who is involved more or less.

> 'They like it when I tell them how many marks are with the question, so that they can give themselves a little score and I find that they are much more forthcoming and get more involved in the plenary.'

> 'But ... sometimes reading the questions first is better than reading the text ... it depends.' And just what it depends on, in a particular instance, can provide some very helpful insights into the nature of teachers' experienced intuition.

Lots of discussion focused on what seemed to motivate the children (or the teacher!), on how a particular variation led to this or that, or on what had now been noticed but had not been thought about before.

Other comments led to very extensive and more general debates, for example how we categorise children ('The poor children I have are very sensible poor children') or literacy across the curriculum ('You have to do a lot of literacy in science'). Perhaps the comment that led to the most interesting debate about general responsibilities as a teacher was 'I do always bear in mind that I would not put a child under pressure'. This led into a lively debate about the relationship between teachers being under pressure and putting children under pressure, as well as the view that teaching and schooling should be, in part, about putting pressure on children.

Once again, our point is not that any one of these discussions was especially earth shattering. The point is that the discussions became increasingly informed by the evidence from the research project, in a way which suggested that the project had increasingly become seen as *our* project, drawing on and examining and sharing *our* professional experience in *this* school with *these* children. Curiosity had initially been fuelled and gradually more and more colleagues became actively involved in the discussions focusing on pedagogy, but no longer with the sense that such discussions were imposed on staff. One key point here is that the staff meetings and staff discussions should be regarded as part of the data. These discussions were summarised and fed back to colleagues.

John Elliott (1991), in Chapter 2 of *Action Research for Educational Change*, discusses with reference to case studies some of the ways in which research initiatives can be 'owned' by the school, rather than hijacked by outsiders (no matter how well-meaning these outsiders might be).

Engaging in peer observations

Finally, we can just touch on a development which we could not have envisaged in this school at the beginning of the project. Two colleagues agreed to engage in some peer observation, focusing on teacher strategies to encourage participation and variation in types of teacher questions and types of pupil engagement. Detailed observations were made of the project sample. At a staff meeting the two teachers involved reported on the experience to colleagues, focusing on how interested they had become in how the pace of their lessons varied, on lots of little differences in teaching style, on matters relating to the capabilities of different age groups and on how unexpectedly enjoyable it had been!

Some lessons were learnt here about not trying to have too complex an observation schedule, and also how any schedule is both a way of looking and a way of not looking. We found it crucial to have a discussion very soon after the observation in order to be able to discuss some of the passing impressions which were not part of the schedule. Even more important was to allow teachers to negotiate schedules which related to their interests and which were about informing rather than criticising.

From this small beginning other colleagues made arrangements to do peer observations, having negotiated areas for special attention and having picked up on some of the 'dos and don'ts' from the colleagues who did it first. This developed into a series of observations and discussions of those observations with teachers looking at differing age ranges in Key Stage 2.

Such developments may not be of much consequence in some schools used to such work, but we had moved a long way from the almost total absence of discussion about pedagogic matters relating to what was going on in each other's classrooms. Approaches such as peer observation (which in our case built on the research project) require resources and support and we were fortunate to have a Headteacher committed to the project, and more importantly committed to generating an atmosphere in the school which allowed the increasing participation in professional discussions of this sort.

What is perhaps the most important indicator of where we have got to is that staff are now in the process of discussing a project focus on writing, using some of the methods of data gathering which proved useful to us earlier. Partly because of the comprehension research process, some staff asked other colleagues to look in similar ways at fiction and non-fiction writing. We are also using methods that we are now familiar with to collect data through assessment and to 'target set' in a more evidence-informed way.

Reflection

As a result of this project we have learned that you cannot predetermine where a research project is going and where it might lead. In terms of crude numbers of colleagues involved in any strong sense, this project started with two school staff, then four, then all staff were and are actively participating. Certainly, given our ambitions that more and more staff would gradually become involved, the project has had considerable success. This is particularly striking when we consider that being 'actively involved' does not just mean 'helping to gather data' or 'taking account of some results'. In this case the data and associated discussion increasingly became focused, directly or indirectly, on colleagues' own classroom pedagogic practices and associated professional assumptions and beliefs.

Many commentators have talked about the importance of groups of colleagues in schools developing their professional voice, one grounded in evidence. Some talk, at times it seems in somewhat idealistic terms, of the need to create 'professional learning communities' and of the importance here of 'a sense of ownership and responsibility' (see, for example, Earl *et al.*, 2000, p. 10). Certainly, at the school level, a professional learning community does seem to have developed more fully. Staff regularly, and with enthusiasm, discuss pedagogic strategies; several are involved in peer observations; there is an interest in grounding discussions in evidence, and, as we have noted, a wish to do some research work together again on another area of language. This is really quite a stark contrast with what most colleagues thought initially about research in terms of its practical possibilities, relevance and potential for improving classroom practices, as we noted at the beginning of this chapter.

What, then, are the key reasons for this change? Along the way, we did touch on some ways in which a piece of information, or part of the research project, seemed to be particularly beneficial in terms of involving colleagues. However, in retrospect, we think there are more general features which were important. First of all, the whole process moved slowly and we did not attempt to rush things; gradually staff curiosity was fuelled and we were fortunate in having an overall project time scale which did not require immediate results and which allowed things to grow and take account of other events and activities on the school agenda. Second, staff came to feel that this project, and research more generally, could be a natural and positive part of the life of the school and not solely serving the interests of outsiders. In brief, the project gradually became disassociated from the general antipathy to multiple externally imposed initiatives and requirements – it became the *school's* project.

The third feature builds on the first two and in our view is crucial. From the comments colleagues have made, in the interview context and in discussion, the project has, in a strange way, allowed for a renewed sense of professionalism and self-worth. This seems to have come about in a variety of ways. Teachers have felt that their 'experienced intuition' as professionals has been valued; that they have had some choice on which aspects of their teaching to focus; that they have been able to choose the evidence that might be worth gathering; and that as the project developed they have had a stake in how the overall project shaped up. Very importantly, the project did not develop as yet one more 'stick to beat teachers with'. There seem then to be some messages we have learnt in the school context about motivating professionals under fire. It may even be that what really helped the project to get going, was that the research helped colleagues to reassert their professionalism.

References

Bell, J. (1999) *Doing Your Research Project*. Buckingham: Open University.

Cochran-Smith, M. and Lytle, S. (1999) The teacher research movement: a decade later. *Educational Researcher*, 28(7): 14–25.

Croll, P. and Hastings, N. (eds) (1997) *Effective Primary Teaching: Research Based Classroom Strategies*. London: David Fulton.

Earl, L., Fullan, M., Leithwood, K., Watson, N. *et al.* (2000) *Watching and Learning: OISE/ UT Evaluation of the Implementation of the National Literacy and Numeracy Strategies*. Ontario Institute for Studies in Education, University of Toronto: Toronto.

Elliott, J. (1991) *Action Research for Educational Change*. Buckingham: Open University Press.

Howard, K. and Sharp, J. A. (1983) *The Management of a Student Research Project*. Aldershot: Gower.

Jeffrey, B. and Woods, P. (1998) *Testing Teachers: the Effect of School Inspections on Primary Teachers*. London: Falmer Press.

McNiff, J. Lomax, P. and Whitehead, J. (1996) *You and Your Action Research Project*. London: Routledge.

Pollard, A. (1996) *Reflective Teaching in the Primary School*. London: Cassell.

Chapter 8

Temple goes mental

Researching the learning and teaching of mental arithmetic

Gary Gornell and Rob Halsall

Introduction

Temple Primary School emerged from the amalgamation in 1997 of two very separate Infant and Junior schools. There are about 460 pupils, including nursery children, twenty full-time staff and a large team of part-time teachers, language support staff, nursery nurses and classroom assistants. They work in old buildings that are rapidly disintegrating; however, a new building is planned to open in 2001. Ninety-five per cent of the pupils speak English as an additional language. The majority are of Islamic-Pakistani descent, but there are usually fifteen to twenty nationalities and even more languages represented at any one time. Another key feature of the pupil population is the very high level of pupil turnover. Before 1998, Key Stage 2 National Curriculum National Test results had been consistently below national averages, and the raising of standards in the core subjects was the main issue addressed by the Headteacher upon amalgamation.

When the school was invited to participate in the Manchester and Salford Schools Consortium, the Headteacher viewed it as, at least, another opportunity to engage staff in debating approaches to teaching and learning, especially in respect of numeracy. Literacy was receiving additional money, in-service opportunities and monitoring time, and the Headteacher, other members of the senior management team, governors and the maths coordinator were raising concerns about maths curriculum development falling behind that in literacy. This was shown to be the case when the pilot testing of the Key Stage 2 mental arithmetic tests revealed obvious shortcomings in the children's abilities to use mental strategies to solve mathematical problems.

The pedagogy underpinning the teaching of maths in the school was being seriously questioned by several teachers. An expensive commercial scheme had been introduced prior to amalgamation, but its implementation had not been adequately coordinated, and there had been no accompanying staff development or monitoring regarding its use. In many classrooms the teaching of maths consisted of short expositions followed by long periods in which the children proceeded through text book exercises, many of which failed to address their needs. Differentiation consisted of simply handing out text books aimed at different ability levels and the learning of mental arithmetic depended almost entirely on the recall of facts in the four rules, with occasional tables-testing. Participation in the Manchester and Salford Schools Consortium was seen, therefore, as an opportunity to experiment with different pedagogical approaches in Key Stage 2, to focus staff attention on the teaching and learning of mental maths with regard to performance in maths generally and to use the research data and processes to assist the general drive in the school to raise standards. What we present in this chapter is:

- an account of the changes made to the teaching and learning of mental maths in respect of one cohort of pupils as they progressed from Year 4 through to Year 6, 1997–2000;
- an account of the research into the impact of these changes;
- the research findings relating to the above;
- a discussion of the 'lessons learned' about both effective pedagogy and engagement in the research process.

Phase I

Pedagogic change: Year 4 pupils 1997–98

The first phase of the project involved three Year 4 teachers (who between them shared the teaching of two mixed-ability classes, 4B and 4K) in moving away from considerable reliance on the published maths scheme by way of greater use of whole class teaching, involving more active forms of learning (including greater use of maths games and of class/group discussion work). The first step taken was to undertake background reading on the effective teaching of numeracy (e.g. Askew *et al.*, 1997). There were also plans to investigate 'good practice' in a number of local schools. When the project effectively began, the intended pedagogic changes included many features of the National Numeracy Strategy (still 2 years away from its implementation):

- more detailed weekly and daily planning;
- at least one full hour per week given over to mental arithmetic;
- 5-minute game to start each number lesson;
- 15–20 minute teacher-led introduction;
- 20-minute individual practice for pupils on a specific skill which was the learning objective of the lesson;
- a plenary session to check pupil understanding followed by another short mental maths game to encourage flexibility of strategies when dealing with number problems;
- employment of more games and investigations;
- encouragement of more pattern spotting;
- banks of vocabulary, signs and symbols to be built up in each class and changed with the topic;
- more time for discussion about numbers;
- utilisation of cultural differences in learning; talk and sharing of alternative strategies to solve problems;
- raising of self-esteem and enjoyment of maths.

Time to plan, monitor and review the project was allocated between February and July 1998. However, there were some inherent problems:

1   The organisation of the teaching was complicated: 4K had two members of staff

teaching maths over a 5-day week in a ratio of 3:2 days per teacher, whereas 4B
had just the one teacher.

2   An OfSTED inspection was announced for the spring term and interest by the
three teachers involved was reduced as other issues were prioritised. The inspection
took up disproportionate amounts of time and energy prior to the visit and left a
demoralised, demotivated and exhausted staff.

3   The project coordinator was not one of the directly involved teachers and so
project monitoring and guidance became difficult. This was compounded by high
levels of long-term absence of staff, which resulted in reduced availability of staff
cover to allow the coordinator to organise the project.

4   There were marked differences in teacher enthusiasm and capacity to engage in
the project: one teacher was about to go on maternity leave; and another was a
Deputy Head who had significant responsibilities regarding the inspection. In
addition, 4B's teacher was so enthusiastic that he altered his pedagogy prior to
the start of the research project 'proper', thus complicating the research design
and analysis.

As a result of the above, there was less data collection than planned, especially
regarding lesson observations, staff discussions and recording of significant incidents
and of progress. However, the planned changes to pedagogy *were* instituted, helped
by the fact that the teachers of 4K proposed that they would take on some of the 4B
teacher's English work while he taught mental arithmetic in their classroom. As a
consequence, there was consistency of methodology and approach in teaching, although
the pedagogic changes occurred for 4B before they did for 4K, some 10 weeks before
administering the mental arithmetic baseline test (see next section). There were also
other very positive aspects of participation in the consortium, including professional
discussions with other school project coordinators, LEA personnel and HEI colleagues;
the sharing of published research findings; support for the school in data collection,
data analysis and report-writing; and the availability of additional funds to buy any
teaching resources necessary to implement the changed pedagogy. In addition, pre-
and post-test data were collected, along with data from interviews with all pupils.

The research: Year 4 pupils 1997–98

The purpose of the research was, quite simply, to ascertain the extent of improvement
in pupils' age-standardised mental arithmetic scores, February–May 1998, and to
explore the reasons which might have accounted for any improvement, including the
impact of the changed pedagogy. The key research questions were:

- What is the baseline (early February 1998) performance in mental arithmetic of
the Year 4 pupils?
- What is the performance following two half-terms of changed classroom practice?
- What factors appear to have affected progress?

The (optional) Year 4 national test in mental arithmetic, made available to schools
by the QCA, was adopted in order to ascertain mental arithmetic performance. This
was administered to the year group (to those present) in February and June 1998,
leading to pre- and post-test data for thirty-four of the fifty-four children. In relation

to exploring factors possibly bearing on pre- and post-test performance, we collected Stages of English Language Acquisition (SELA) scores and attendance rates; gathered teachers' perceptions on changes in, and effects of, teaching methods and on the response of the pupils to the work in class; interviewed every pupil individually, exploring their attitude (and any shifts in this) to number work and to teaching methods, and taking the opportunity to assess the extent to which they did extra work at home, whether this was on their own initiative and whether they received support in such work.

Outline findings

In exploring possible factors impinging on progress we recognised that we were dealing with small numbers but hoped, nevertheless, that at the very least the analysis would generate further questions to explore. In terms of the four subgroups of children in Table 8.1, we could find no apparent association between progress and:

- attendance;
- SELA scores;
- whether children remarked on liking/not liking number work;
- whether children reported that they undertook additional number work outside of school;
- whether the children particularly mentioned liking the more 'active' learning methods used in class.

However, there were some discernible associations, in particular:

- More marked progress was made in class 4K than in class 4B.
- Lower achievers on the initial test (score < 90) improved more than higher achievers (initial score 110+) and other children (initial score 90–109).
- The children whose improvement was as high as 9 per cent plus reported the greatest incidence of receiving support at home in undertaking additional number work.

Discussion

The improvement overall in age-standardised scores was quite considerable, but particularly so for 4K, whose results were probably influenced by the fact that this class contained the highest percentage of initial lower achievers. This might suggest that for many pupils progress might have had little to do with a differing approach to number work – if one assumes that the greatest gains would likely come from the lower achievers anyway. However, it was the case that gains were made in 4B and

Table 8.1 Changes in age-standardised mental arithmetic scores (n = 34)

Change (%)	No. of pupils
Increase of 9+	9
Increase of 5.8–7.9	4
Increase of 1.8–4.7	16
Reduction of 1.2–9.4	5

with pupils, across both classes, other than low achievers (60 per cent of the initial lower achievers improving by 5.8 per cent plus, but still a fairly high 24 per cent of other pupils). *We believed, then, that the data suggested that changes in the teaching methods had some beneficial impact.*

First, whereas the teaching approach changed in 4B, it changed even more in 4K. As explained earlier, 4B's teacher had changed his pedagogy some time before the pre-test date. In contrast, change only occurred in 4K's lessons after this date. Second, the teachers' perceptions were that many pupils showed greater enthusiasm in class when the changes to teaching and learning were introduced; that poorer readers improved when the maths scheme was discarded, or supplemented by a more teacher-led approach; that the more varied lessons retained pupil attention and concentration better; that whole class activities which did involve each child allowed teachers to spot better children who were having difficulty coping. Third, although the pupil interviews did not evidence a clear preference for the more active learning activities, most of the pupils did comment or imply that they enjoyed the greater variety of provision.

However, we remained unsure of what factors were of particular significance in the overall improvement of performance. Was it the fact that *any* classroom intervention would have had a favourable impact? Was it simply the use of a greater variety of activities? Was it the fundamental shift from a scheme-based to a much more teacher-led approach? Was it the greater emphasis on whole class interactive teaching? Or was it something else altogether? For example, something to do with home support. And was it the same thing for all the pupils? Indeed, what about those pupils who had not improved their age-standardised scores? Clearly, there was much that we were uncertain of. However, the work in the first phase of the project at least served to make us aware of the strong possibility that the changes we had begun to implement might be having a positive impact on pupil progress.

Phase 2

Pedagogic change: Year 5 pupils 1998–99

Unfortunately, the reformulation of project goals and action for 1998–99 was sidelined until other developments in the organisation of teaching in Key Stage 2 were implemented in the light of the school's post-OfSTED Action Plan. As a result, the project lost momentum until the school had adjusted to, and 'recovered' from, the inspection. In fact, the most immediate decision made as a result of the Phase 1 experience was that the project coordinator would have to be placed as a Year 5 teacher in order to steer and monitor the project better. Independent of the Phase 1 experience, it was also decided, as a result of a school policy decision, that Year 5 and Year 6 classes would be divided into three ability groups by age-standardised scores (based on QCA tests 1997).

The eventual decision about the precise focus was made collaboratively between the Headteacher, the project coordinator, the two other participating class teachers and the school's maths coordinator. It was made in the light of reflection on Phase 1 and further reading and discussion of research into the teaching of Mental Arithmetic, especially in the context of the introduction of the National Numeracy Strategy. We were particularly intrigued by Swan's (1997) work, which explored how reflective activities can transform the classroom atmosphere, so that passive inactivity is replaced by vigorous discussion on the meanings of concepts. This helped to prompt our realisation that our pupils were not doing enough speaking and listening in maths lessons, that their learning was often 'passive' and that we teachers had an opportunity to explore our questioning techniques in greater depth. We also thought that, in preparation for the introduction of the National Numeracy Strategy in September 1999, we could practise using a shared structure to our lessons, especially in the warm up/exposition and plenary stages. The plan was to split the cohort into three groups of roughly equal size by mathematical ability; continue to deliver mental arithmetic teaching via the pedagogic changes introduced in the previous year; and, in addition, teach through more reflective activities identified as possibly important for raising attainment. Weekly planning included reflective activities such as:

- more classroom discussion about pupils' misconceptions and mistakes;
- pupils inventing their own problems involving the four rules of number;
- building up of mathematical dictionaries, word or idea books which explain important concepts or strategies;
- oral reviews of children's perceptions of the purpose of some or all lessons;
- pupils to prepare worksheets for peers;
- pupil–pupil interviews on what had been learned at the end of a topic;
- tests constructed by pupils at the end of a sequence of lessons;
- occasionally plan how they would teach a topic to other pupils;
- conduct mini debates on general learning issues, such as 'do we learn more from working on a few hard problems or from working on lots of short exercises?'
- pupils to assess their own progress against given criteria.

Unfortunately, the project was then further delayed because of the long-term illness of the member of staff teaching the set of higher-attaining pupils. Therefore, it was decided that a short-term, highly focussed version of the proposal would be attempted upon her return. It would still include exploration of some of Swan's ideas on reflective teaching methods, but would also incorporate some of Lee's (1997) ideas on effective communication, Straker's (1993) ideas on talk and Kerry's (1982) identification of 'the right sort of question'. To this end, the new, 'slimmed-down' approach would have a sharper focus. There would be a 3-week intensive project. Question and answer techniques would be employed during a 20-minute 'carpet time' introductory section of each mental maths lesson. There were to be 5 days of lessons in mental addition/ subtraction strategies using reflective teaching methods and more focussed questioning. This was to be followed by 5 days of lessons in mental multiplication/division strategies using reflective teaching methods and more focussed questioning; all of the approaches listed above were incorporated.

The research: Year 5 pupils 1998–99

The key research questions remained essentially the same as in Phase 1. Our expected outcomes were that we would be able to measure individual and group progress in mental arithmetic; obtain positive teacher responses and develop teacher learning about the teaching and learning of mental maths; develop a clearer understanding of factors affecting pupil progress and of the directions we needed to take in classroom practice (Table 8.2).

Table 8.2 Pre- and post-test, age-standardised mental arithmetic scores for forty-six children

	Whole cohort (n = 46)	Set 1 (n = 17)	Set 2 (n = 17)	Set 3 (n = 12)
Average increase (%)	7.08	13	3.34	3.94
No. of pupils improving by 10%+	13	9	2	2

Data collected comprised:

- lessons plans and evaluations;
- QCA maths and mental arithmetic age-standardised scores;
- teacher interview data (perceptions of pedagogic strategies adopted, together with attitudes, beliefs and opinions of teachers' delivery of maths teaching);
- pupil interview data (exploring understanding of the four rules of number);
- pupil's classwork (completed during reflective/interactive activities);
- video-recordings of a sample of maths lessons and recordings of staff discussions of these;
- lesson observation sheets (each teacher was to be given the opportunity to observe and share practice with the other teachers using an observation sheet adapted from Straker's (1993) work (see Toolkit 7);
- teacher diaries;
- attendance figures and SELA scores.

Key findings: pupil attainment

The data raised a number of questions; in particular:

1 Why was there an even greater improvement in Year 5 than in Year 4? Was it, for example, because of the introduction of setting; the further changes to classroom practice; the adoption of a short, intensive experience; closer pre- and post-testing; variations in the tests; the involvement of different teachers?
2 Why was the improvement so much greater for set one? Was it, for example, because setting favoured set 1 more than it did the others; the pedagogy favoured set 1 more than it did others; the tests were introduced and briefed differently for different sets; the set 1 teacher was 'better' than the others?

Quite simply we cannot offer definitive answers to these questions. In fact, the data prompted yet other questions: Are improved results maintained? How did performance on the mental arithmetic tests compare with performance on other maths tests? What of the children who did not evidence progress? Here, we noted the following:

- Although some Year 5 children did make big gains in mental arithmetic scores, we realised that these might not be sustained – some had also made gains in Year 4 but dropped back again between the Year 4 post-test and the Year 5 pre-test. This might raise doubts about the long-term impact of the initiatives (at least for some children). It certainly raised the issue of 'playing safe': should the school prioritise project activity immediately before the National Test exams?

- There was not always consistency in the gains made on different tests. Although all but two of the thirteen major 'improvers' on the mental maths tests made big gains on a more general maths test, a considerable number who did not made gains on the latter.
- Of the thirty-four children for whom we had pre- and post-test scores for Years 4 and 5, eighteen made no significant gains in their mental maths scores in either year, so whereas project activity in either or both years made a considerable impact on the scores for just about half the children, it had little impact for the other half (who were mainly set 2 and 3 children).
- Some, but far from most, of the 'non-improvers' had poor attendance records. The closest correlation observed, however, was between mental arithmetic (and general maths) improvement and SELA grades (which overlap closely with sets). Clearly, there might be an issue here in that the changes in classroom practice (more language-based) might have favoured those children who are most proficient in the English language.

Key findings: teachers' learning about teaching and learning

We present here the key outcomes of discussions held by the teachers participating in Phase 2, all of whom commented favourably about being 'shown respect' by having extra non-contact time to plan, to observe each other's lessons and video-recordings of lessons and to reflect: 'being given mind space to think about what was and what was not proving effective in lessons'.

1   *Planning.* We discovered that, as Watson and Mason (1994) point out, 'A skilful teacher may appear to pluck questions out of thin air. The reality is probably that a good deal of preparatory thought has been given to finding key questions which, in sequence, will lead pupils on to explore new thoughts and avenues of approach'. However, we had to spend much longer planning lessons in order to properly sequence our questions and to be able to satisfactorily pursue a train of thought when modifying our questions in the light of responses to the previous question. At times, each lesson was taking 1.5–2 hours to plan, totally impractical to sustain in the 'real world' of primary teaching.

2   *Pupil engagement.* Observations of each other's and of our own lessons demonstrated that in the less successful passages of lessons, marked for example by a relatively high incidence of negative use of contingency management, children were in passive roles, there was a high level of teacher modelling and instruction and a lack of pupil feedback. In contrast, the more successful passages of lessons had more well-paced sequencing of questions, with children fully engaged and focussed on their activities and tasks. In such lessons there was also evidence of high teacher expectations and of 'challenge', especially as evidenced through the use of open-ended questions. Crucially, giving the children an opportunity to create and explain their own methods of mathematical calculation prompted most interest and enthusiasm for the pupils. There was almost a mutiny at the end of one particularly successful lesson, which comprised a judge, prosecution, defence and jury arguing over the truth or otherwise of a series of presented mathematical

true or false statements. Arguments and evidence had to be discussed using mathematical vocabulary and terminology only. The particular teacher who conducted this lesson brought to mind an HMI (1990) statement, that:

> Successful teaching, whether with the whole class, smaller groups or individuals, depends on certain essential factors. These include the quality of the teacher's explanation, clarity and structure of speech, the skilled construction and use of questions and the ability to engage children in intensive discussion of increasingly complex ideas.

Certainly, the pupils' opportunities to create and explain their own methods of mathematical calculation prompted most enthusiasm on their part and, significantly, were related to score gains in post-testing.

3   *Learning theory.* We came to recognise that there are similarities between successful teaching of mental arithmetic and the learning theory underpinning the National Literacy Strategy, emphasising the interactive process of teaching and learning and particularly the 'social discourse, collaborative learning and the joint construction of knowledge' (Corden, 1999). There are further parallels to be drawn between the successful lessons in this project and what Askew *et al.* (1997) identify as the 'connectionist' belief orientation of certain highly effective teachers of numeracy. They found that teachers with 'connectionist' orientations were more likely to have classes that made greater gains than teachers with strong 'discovery' or 'transmission' orientations. They also argue that connectionist orientated teachers view mental mathematics as going beyond this recall of number facts: mental mathematics does not involve simply knowing number bonds but having a conscious awareness of connections and relationships to develop mental agility, and that 'This mental agility meant that for the connectionist teachers mental mathematics also involved the development of flexible mental strategies to handle efficiently number calculations.' Working on mental strategies, they believe, lays foundations that extend the pupils' levels of competency: developing confidence in flexible methods means that pupils would be able to tackle calculations for which methods had not been taught.

4   *Self and peer observation.* The three teachers who conducted observations in Phase 2 were so convinced of the positive benefits and usefulness of sharing practice in this way that class swaps were arranged between colleagues in all year groups in numeracy the following term. Moreover, the availability of video evidence of lessons where pupils were provided with opportunities to 'visualise' and where the use of correct mathematical vocabulary was given the highest value was important research evidence for teachers unconvinced of the research base of the National Numeracy Strategy. Staff who had yet to implement the National Numeracy Strategy and were unconvinced by its methods could watch good practice in their own environment with pupils whom they all knew. They could see the effective use of open-ended questioning, of effective prompting such as 'How do you know?', 'How could it help you?', 'How could you use the knowledge that 7 + 9 = 16 to help you solve 700 + 900?', 'What if ... ?' questions, as well as

'How have you got there?' and the constant refrain of 'You've got to give me your method.' All the above formed just a fraction of one excellent 30-minute recording of a participating colleague.

5   *The most successful methods.* Not all of the reflective methods that were originally planned for were tried out. However, there was particular success in:

- the building of mathematical dictionaries and word books;
- oral and written reviews of the purpose of some or all lessons;
- pupils constructing test questions at the end of a topic;
- mini debates on general learning issues such as 'Do we learn more from working on a few hard problems or from working on a lot of short exercises?'

The positive experience of non-threatening, developmental observations and feedback, coupled with encouraging test score gains, provided a solid foundation for both the next phase of the project and the introduction of the National Numeracy Strategy. Teacher expertise and confidence had increased alongside pupils' flexibility of approach to problem solving. A sense of the school's ownership of the research had also developed alongside a shift from negative feelings towards research and 'innovation overload' which had been evident in the staff room. During Phase 1 we had been unsure of what small-scale research actually meant, whether it could impact on attainment and whether staff could fit it into their already busy lives. Hence, it was essential in the second phase that the project's purpose was seen to be effective in helping to raise standards in pupil performance and in increasing teachers' knowledge and self-esteem. It was successful on both of these fronts and so we were confident about moving in to Phase 3, which would represent the final test of the project's usefulness, certainly from the point of view of raising attainment: the year of the Key Stage 2 National Tests for our cohort.

Phase 3

Pedagogic change: Year 6 pupils 1999–2000

The final phase of the project began with yet more problems! Two of the Year 6 teachers left for promoted posts during the autumn term and so the project could not re-commence until they were replaced. However, the school project team agreed that, whatever the eventual focus, the project would:

- further pupil's knowledge of mathematical vocabulary (important in coping with Key Stage 2 mental arithmetic tests) and improve their problem-solving skills (important on the written maths papers);
- continue the pattern of the previous short-term, sharply focused inputs which had proved to be both effective and manageable, and which would fit in with the overall revision scheme planned for Year 6;
- continue the practice of peer observation of lessons and discussion of lesson video-recordings, which had been so valuable in developing our own learning.

Once the two new staff were in place, all three classroom teachers analysed previous test papers undertaken by the children. What emerged was a consensus that the pupil's explanations were mathematically inaccurate and lacked the necessary vocabulary, and that they needed to engage in greater discussion of maths problems and the application of problem-solving strategies. They then set about some background reading around the general theme of explanations/explaining before determining the precise focus of, and methodology for, Phase 3. We had previously explored more interactive, whole class and reflective approaches. Now we wanted to give the pupils more opportunities to discuss their learning in mathematics and to practice applying it. As Barnes (1992) points out:

> Whatever teaching methods a teacher chooses – question and answer, guided discover, demonstration, or another – it will always be the pupil who has to do the learning. He or she will make sense of the lessons only by using the new ideas, experiences, or ways of thinking in order to reorganise his or her existing pictures of the world and how they can be acted upon. It is useful to think about this aspect of learning as a matter of the learner 'working on understanding' ... The readiest way of working on understanding is often through talk, because the flexibility of speech makes it easy for us to try out new ways of arranging what we know and easy too to change them if they seem inadequate.

Mercer (1991) adds weight to this argument in his reference to Vygotsky (1978, p. 26), which we felt had particular relevance to Temple Primary School: 'Children solve practical tasks with the help of their speech, as well as their eyes and hands'. Some of the most profound kinds of learning take place when people share, in words, their experiences of activities and events. For children, this could mean discovering, through talking with their teacher or friends, the purpose of a classroom activity and what they are expected to achieve. Bilingual children may gain particular benefit from being able to tackle problems and share understanding through another language as well as English. Learning through talk can also mean children sharing knowledge with other children so that the shared understanding they achieve is more than the sum of the parts they each contributed. There is also another exciting aspect to this new conception of the role of talking in learning. It is basically the idea that knowledge may itself be inseparable from language, that in communicating ideas we come to understand them better.

Now, the National Curriculum requires that certain aspects of mathematical explanation should be included explicitly in the curriculum. For example, at Key Stage 2 it is specified that 'Pupils should be taught to ... explain their reasoning'. The preliminary report of the Numeracy Task Force (DfEE 1998) also suggests that, 'numerate pupils should explain their methods and reasoning and teachers should collect information about ... the clarity of explanations given in oral and written responses'. The links between the notions of 'communication', 'understanding' and 'reasoning' are all complex and 'explanation' involves aspects of all three. As a result of our reading and analysis of pupil test performance, then, we finally arrived at a focus for Phase 3: pupil's explanations of mental calculation strategies employed to solve multi-part problems in addition, subtraction, multiplication and division. The desired outcome was that children would employ more specifically mathematical explanations of the strategies adopted in problem solving and that they would improve their ability to identify the knowledge needed for solving problems.

The children were still set in three ability groups with some overlap between sets one and two. Set 1 were pupils working roughly between National Tests Levels 3a to 5a; set 2 were pupils working at Levels 3c to 4c; and set 3 included pupils working at 3c and below. The classroom intervention spanned 3 weeks in April/early May 2000, utilising 10 hours of maths lessons using the following methods:

- provision of ready-made poster lists of relevant vocabulary for each day's problems;
- 10-minute introduction of focused, rapid response questioning, each pupil's response requiring further explanation by a peer about what strategies were employed – known facts, halving, doubling, partitioning, place value, etc;
- relevant vocabulary was also reinforced through being used in homework tasks in dictionary work and preparation for spelling tests;
- pupils were split into groups of three or four, some groupings being mixed ability (within the set), some based on language (e.g. Arabic- and Malay-speaking pupils were kept together when no language support was available);
- each group was given different multi-part problems involving whole numbers, fractions, decimals and measures and had 20 minutes to discuss their problems and:

1   list key words/phrases;
2   list what they needed to know (mathematical concepts);
3   make a rough estimate (and explain on what grounds it was made);
4   identify the strategies employed for calculation;
5   record the explanation (using words, signs, numbers, pictures, whatever helped) of how they approached and solved the problem;
6   take turns to report back and present their explanations to the rest of the class. The children were encouraged to share different strategies and methods and to challenge at the end of an explanation. The importance of taking turns and listening to the speaker were stressed throughout. The aim of focusing on explanation and method rather than 'getting the right answers' was stressed, as was the use of appropriate and unambiguous vocabulary.

Year 6: the research 1999–2000

The data collected included lesson plans, observation sheets and evaluations; classwork samples; video- and audio-recordings of lessons; teacher diaries; attendance figures and SELA grades; and children's descriptions about what knowledge is needed in solving problems involving arithmetic. Finally, the data also included test results. Pre-testing (31 March 2000) was via the 1999 Key Stage 1 National Tests Maths Paper B and the Mental Arithmetic Paper, whereas post-testing was based on the 2000 Key Stage 2 papers – the ultimate test of the project from its outset.

Key findings: pupil and teacher response

In terms of *the pupils*, from both the teacher and pupil data, it was felt that and it appeared to be the case that:

- the pupils' interest, motivation and rate of learning improved as they were encouraged to create and then describe their own methods and solutions to mental maths problems;
- the pupils persevered and concentrated on problems and showed great satisfaction when a problem was solved by the group;
- a reduced number of problems being explored in greater detail seemed to be of far greater benefit in developing pupil understanding (especially when examining alternative explanations in the plenary stage of the lesson); this being especially – but not solely – the case for lower attaining pupils;
- by underlining key parts of problems the pupils looked at problems more closely and recognised the operations involved far more quickly. Again, this was especially the case for lower-attaining pupils;
- the provision of vocabulary posters (specific to the area of numeracy being covered), alongside precise mathematics terms, proved most helpful to the pupils in explaining their own strategies and alternatives;
- less able pupils benefited most from direct teacher instruction and teacher (or able pupil) modelling (i.e. explaining using examples);
- pupil enjoyment of the lessons and a feeling that they were progressing served to help develop self-esteem and self confidence in maths (a very important factor in successful teaching and learning in our school);
- the mental maths lessons in particular were carefully planned with regard to sequence, balance and pace. This together with the factors in the preceding point were key in leading to a situation where the need for behaviour management was drastically reduced (in fact, virtually non-existent);
- lessons with few (one or two specific) learning objectives were found to be the most successful, especially for the less able pupils;
- Malay and Arabic pupils suffered from lack of language support more so than did other groups, and Malay and Arabic girls tended to work better in all-girl groups (especially in set 1 where they 'allowed' boys to dominate them more so than did girls of other ethnic groups).

In terms of the teachers, the key findings were that:

- once again, the opportunity to view and discuss, through the video-recordings, their own performance and the pupils' interactions was seen as being of immense benefit to them in evaluating teaching and learning and then planning future lessons;
- the quality of their questioning was recognised as having a significant impact upon the pupils' responses and attitudes to learning.

Key findings: pupil attainment

Ideally, we would have analysed the 2000 National Tests results in relation to previous years' results utilising a value-added methodology, but this was not possible because of the data that had previously been gathered. However, in terms of the cohort's Key Stage 2 National Tests results (mid-May 2000), we were hoping to see an improvement in the overall maths results in relation to those of the previous 2 years. Within this we

Table 8.3 Mental arithmetic (MA) scores and Paper B

	Year group	Set 1	Set 2	Set 3
Av. Increase* (%)	9.48 (n = 44)	8.5 (n = 20)	7.14 (n = 19)	37.5 (n = 5)
Av. Increase† (%)	48 (n = 46)	35 (n = 21)	65 (n = 18)	69 (n = 7)

*MA scores.
†Paper B scores.

hoped to see both National Tests Mental Arithmetic scores and Paper B scores exceeding those obtained for the mental arithmetic and Paper B pre-tests (Table 8.3). However, mindful of the overall improvements in mental arithmetic age-standardised scores since the outset of the project, up to the March 2000 pre-test, we did anticipate that there would be greater improvement in Paper B scores than in Mental Arithmetic (although we recognised that the classroom intervention during Phase 2 in particular should have had some positive impact on pre-test Paper B scores). Also, given that set 1 children had improved their mental arithmetic performance more so than had others up to Phase 3, we were anticipating that they might have less scope for further improvement.

In short, the overall results were most pleasing, with continued improvement in mental arithmetic performance and excellent improvement in Paper B between the pre-test and the actual National Test papers. (Note that the results for Paper A were very similar to those for Paper B). Moreover, the 2000 maths results at Level 4+ represented a considerable improvement on 1998 and 1999, having moved from 49 per cent to 45 per cent to 58 per cent. There was also success in relative terms: the differential between the school's and the national maths results narrowed significantly – in 1999 the gap was 24 per cent, in 2000 it was only 14 per cent – and the improvement in maths was substantially greater than it was in English.

Reflections

At the outset of the project we thought that we would be able to institute a classroom intervention programme, assess whether it had led to improved pupil performance and determine what it was about the programme that had affected this – although we never for one moment believed that we could come up with findings that would be generalisable beyond our school. It did not take us long, however, to realise the problems involved. First, there were those that affected the timing of the intended intervention, not least such things as the interruptions occasioned by an OfSTED inspection, staff absences and staff departures. Second, there were problems that affected research design and analysis. These included different teachers taking the cohort through Years 4–6; arriving at performance results on the basis of different tests year upon year; dealing with a changing cohort year upon year; the coexistence of other developments such as the National Literacy and Numeracy Strategy, the school's National Tests revision programme and the introduction of setting part-way through the project; and so on. Any quantitative analysis of pupil performance and any assessment of factors influencing success became highly questionable. For this reason, we tried our utmost to treat performance data as indicative material rather than as anything conclusive, and we recognised throughout that the factors which contributed most significantly to any success are difficult to pinpoint. In fact, we realise, at the end of the day, that we cannot say with great confidence that the nature of the classroom intervention itself was the most crucial factor in explaining what success we had in raising pupil performance. Rather, the key factor might simply be that involvement in the project brought about an intensified and focused effort on a highly defined objective. Nevertheless, there is much in our findings that relates to those from the evaluation of the Gatsby Primary Mathematics Enhancement Programme. In particular:

> ... whole-class teaching creates the conditions for effective teaching to occur ... More whole-class teaching allows teachers to be effective in a way that individualised approaches do not ... [and, moreover] The importance of engaging with students at a cognitively higher as well as lower level is clear from the inclusion of items such as asking open questions, allowing multiple answers etc.
>
> (Muijs and Reynolds, 2000, pp. 298–299)

So, has the project been worthwhile, and if so, for whom? We think it has been worthwhile and has been so for different parties. In particular:

- Although we cannot be sure about causal factors, and although we cannot know whether those pupils who made particularly great gains in their results did so as a result of project activity, nevertheless a not inconsiderable number of pupils *did* progress more than we think would otherwise have been the case.
- The majority of pupils responded to the changes in classroom practice very positively, expressing and exhibiting greater enjoyment of their work and greater self-confidence in undertaking it. There was also a much reduced incidence of poor and inappropriate classroom behaviour.
- Engagement in the project stimulated extensive discussion of approaches to teaching and learning and led to the far greater use of a shared vocabulary – much more so than anything else had ever done. Discussions around the peer observations of lessons and the video-recorded lessons were particularly powerful here, but so too was the background reading of literature on teaching and learning, something that the project stimulated better than anything previously. It was, then, a profitable professional development experience – although we recognise that the expanded 'mind space' it relied upon was very dependent on both the Headteacher's support and the additional resources provided by the project.
- Moreover, this experience had concrete outcomes in terms of actual classroom practice, not something which can always be claimed as a result of other forms of professional development activity. In particular, the questioning and explanations we used with this cohort has become more widely adopted in the school; more generally, we are emphasising the role of 'pupil modelling' much more and making direct teaching less a feature of our work. We have found ourselves now to be much more in line with Wheeler's (1970) stance concerning the role of the maths teacher:

> He will consciously withdraw as much of himself as possible so that he will not be an interference to the activity he wants to promote. In not drawing

attention to himself but to the tasks on hand he can be an impartial observer of their actions as they tackle them. Because he knows what the children are able to achieve by working at tasks themselves his judgement of their capabilities and attainments will be more reliable than anyone else's and he will reject external assessments if they conflict with his own ... He must use every means he can to focus the attention of the children on the problem, and this means he must efface himself of their attention. On the other hand, the children will be at the centre of his attention because he must study them to know how to help them keep to their task.

- The HEI link person found the experience beneficial in several ways. For example, it helped him understand better the changing and expanding role of teachers and Headteachers; it helped him keep up to date with National Curriculum developments and with such things as school development planning; it provided insights into the ways in which staff and pupil turnover affects schools; it developed his own skills in supporting teachers in doing and using research; and not least it served to keep him in touch with the most important people of all, the pupils.
- Although not all members of staff have come to a view that engagement in research or drawing upon others' research is worthwhile in terms of informing practice and/or affecting pupils' progress, some teachers have become convinced of this, whereas others are somewhat less cynical than they were. In short, there is now a generally more positive response to the notion of evidence-based practice. For those most directly involved in the project, and certainly for the project coordinator, the experience has also been useful in 'de-mystifying' research, in developing research skills and in increasing understanding of many research issues (see Tabberer, 1997) .

This last point leads us to express the fact that, although we realise there would be even greater difficulty in pursuing research-based projects outside of the Manchester and Salford Schools Consortium, the school is keen that the momentum engendered by the project should not be lost and has already discussed possible areas for further research. These include investigations into which teaching techniques are most effective for extending written agility into the children's maths work and into which pupils benefit most from a reduction in formal written calculations in lessons.

Finally, whereas elsewhere in this book attention is paid to lessons learnt by the Manchester and Salford Schools Consortium project as a whole, for its part our school has identified a number of factors that we believe to be of vital importance to the successful mounting of a school-based research project:

- The project coordinator and the project both need a high profile within the school.
- There must be an identified need from the outset that ties in with the school development plan and which the staff as a whole can endorse.
- The support/conviction of the senior management team, especially the Headteacher, is vital.
- Internal as well as external resourcing is necessary.
- Time to meet, plan, reflect and evaluate must be prioritised.
- Training in research design, issues and methodology is essential.

- The support of Governors can be useful.
- Support from outside agencies, whether HEI and/or the LEA and/or other schools is essential; here, the consortium approach has been highly beneficial to the school's project.
- The right choice of project coordinator is fundamental; it must be someone who commands the respect of the staff as a whole and the trust of the Headteacher, and who can forge good professional and personal relationships with all involved parties.
- A longer, rather than shorter, timeframe is helpful. In the context of consortium working, it allows the necessary working relationships to develop; more generally, it allows time for the coordinator to develop confidence and expertise, and it allows for necessary readjustments to thinking, focus and methodology.

References

Askew, M., Brown, M., Rhodes, V., Johnson, D. and William, D. (1997) *Effective Teachers of Numeracy, Final Report*. London: King's College.

Barnes, D. (1992) The role of talking in learning, in K. Norman (ed.) *Thinking Voices: The Work of the National Oracy Project*. London: Hodder and Stoughton.

Department for Education and Employment (1998) *Numeracy Matters: The Implementation of the National Numeracy Strategy*. An Interim Report. London, DfEE.

Corden, R. (1999) Shameful neglect: speaking, listening and literacy. *Forum*, 41(3): 104–106.

HMI (1990) *The Teaching and Learning of Language and Literacy*. London: HMSO.

Kerry, T. (1982) *Effective Questioning: a Teaching Skills Workbook*. Basingstoke: Macmillan Education.

Lee, C. (1997) *Effective Communication in Mathematics*. Research paper commissioned by the TTA as part of the Teacher Research Grant Scheme.

Mercer, N. (1991) *In Talk and Learning 5–16*. Milton Keynes: Open University Press.

Office for Standards in Education (1997) *The Teaching of Number in Three Inner-Urban LEAs*. London: OfSTED.

Muijs, R. and Reynolds, D. (2000) School effectiveness and teacher effectiveness in mathematics: some preliminary findings from the evaluation of the Mathematics Enhancement Program (Primary). *School Effectiveness and School Improvement*, 11: 3.

Straker, A. (1993) *Talking Points in Mathematics*. Cambridge: Cambridge University Press.

Swan, M. (1997) Reflective learning in the mathematics classroom. *Topic*, 18: 1.

Tabberer, R. (1997) Teachers make a difference: a research perspective on teaching and learning in primary schools. *Topic*, 18: 2.

Watson, A., and Mason J. (1994) *Questions and Prompts for Mathematical Thinking*. Derby: Association of Teachers of Mathematics.

Wheeler, D. (1970) The role of the teacher. *Mathematics Teaching*, 50: 23–29.

Chapter 9

'Homing in' on mathematics

Brian Corbin and Sandy Holt

Introduction

This chapter describes some ways in which a school in an inner-city area attempted to introduce changes, particularly in the use of homework as a curriculum tool to provide a basis for improved mathematics attainment. More broadly, these changes also addressed what I, Sandy Holt, the school maths coordinator, regarded as ways of improving home–school links. In terms of the full consortium time span, our involvement was over a comparatively short period of time, and the school was in a particularly difficult phase of development. Given this context, the methodology we adopted involved four complementary data-gathering activities which helped to inform our strategies for improving pupil performance: target-setting on our 'Maths Challenge' sheets to support home–school links; a set of initiatives to raise the profile of maths; the creation of a maths club; and using video to support pupil and teacher talk about maths.

Finding a focus

Several significant factors led to the focus of this initiative. The first factor had been the arrival from Cravenwood Primary School of a new Headteacher, Gudrun Heatley, who had been involved with the consortium previously. Her account of this earlier work is in Chapter 4. So, although our school had not been party to the first stages of the consortium's work, she and I discussed linking possible involvement with the consortium with my priorities, and we agreed that this could benefit our school, especially as there would be some extra funding for the research. The second factor was that even though our recent (1998) OfSTED inspection and report had declared that, in terms of teaching, the majority of children were 'in line with' national standards, our mathematics National Test results were below what might have been expected at Key Stage 2. I therefore felt that improving the teaching and learning of mathematics was a priority not just because the staff generally felt more comfortable with English, but also because the National Literacy Strategy, introduced the previous September (1998), had already given this area a high profile. Also, I knew from general comments that most of my colleagues felt some insecurity about their subject knowledge in mathematics. I wanted to support their work in the context of new demands which would be made by the launch of the National Numeracy Strategy in September 1999. I had become aware in particular of its proposed emphases on pupils' mental strategies, knowledge of number 'facts', such as tables and number bonds, and encouraging pupil talk to make their understanding of these explicit. A third factor was the impact of expectations about school homework announced by the Government: schools were to have an explicit homework policy. Guidelines recommended a sliding scale of homework throughout the primary age range, with a gradual build-up from 1 hour per week in Years 1 and 2 to 30 minutes per day for Years 5 and 6 (DfEE 1998). There was also the DfEE expectation concerning home–school agreements. These impending initiatives were linked with OfSTED (1998) findings about what were considered 'best practices' in schools with successful homework strategies.

These, then, were the main events in my mind at the time of our new consortium involvement: the National Literacy and Numeracy Strategies, and DfEE guidelines about home–school links and homework policies. But, these apart, we had been concerned for some time about home–school links, especially to support pupil and family learning, for the school is located in a deprived inner-city area with a mainly white, working-class population, high rates of unemployment and approximately 90 per cent of the pupils entitled to free school meals.

School–HEI links: helping initial enquiries

There would be no quick fix for addressing the educational implications of these local facts, but what was happening at this particular time gave some opportunity for renewed approaches. I decided, along with my HEI colleague, Ian Stronach, to start with some fact-finding with particular reference to questions such as:

- What had staff been doing about homework (frequency, subject, amount)?
- What did they generally feel about the usefulness of homework?
- How might we improve this aspect of our work?

With these questions in mind, we devised a survey questionnaire about the staff's experiences of, and views on, homework. Our analysis indicated that most staff felt that homework was 'to some extent useful', but there were qualifications, such as: 'For the first few weeks of the year it is done very well then the children lose interest'; and 'Children get little if any help from adults so it is difficult to get any investigations done'. Where homework was seen as most effective was when parents were actively involved. Reading and sharing books helped not only with literacy but with 'number skills' as well. One teacher, in fact, did report a recent improvement in homework, in that she felt her pupils were becoming more 'responsive' and their 'parents more supportive'. More generally applicable however were the words of another (Key Stage 2) teacher: 'some parents who support their children when doing homework have come in to speak to me as they were unable to support their child with the work as it was too difficult.'

So, the problem was not simply parental 'indifference' as much as 'inability to help, especially with number', and 'lack of parental time', especially if they had several children at school and/or were working long hours. These issues also emerged from another research project into Home–School Links based in Manchester (McNamara et al., 2000). But whatever the cause, most teachers believed that the effect was that very few parents in our school were able to support their children's homework. Maths in particular was perceived as 'threatening' by parents, and some teachers had tried to take this into account: 'I try to present practical tasks which parents can help with'. Several pointed out that previous attempts to engage parental support had been unsuccessful. Teachers identified a deeper need for a 'culture change', perhaps beginning with a 'stronger partnership' between parents and school.

In terms of the purpose of homework, colleagues identified three main functions: consolidation, revision (especially for National Tests) and catching up with classwork. Most of the homework they set was 'whole class', but some was differentiated by group. Teachers marked the work and got pupils to mark their own in class in about equal proportions. Overall, it seemed that:

- homework had been regularly given, supported by timetables and letters to parents;
- parents needed guidance and support about how to help with their children's homework;
- initial responses from the children were good at the start of the year, but completion and return rates dwindled very quickly;
- most of the homework given, particularly from Nursery to Year 2, focused on literacy activities;
- the time allocation did generally increase as the pupils got older, but there were surprises in that reception pupils were estimated to spend 100 minutes per week, while Years 4 and 5 spent 30 and 75 minutes respectively.

Assessing the evidence collected to date the Headteacher and I decided to have a staff meeting to explore 'ways forward'. There was unanimity at the meeting about a home–school agreement policy, which we thought should be based on teacher discussion and negotiation with parents and governors. It would have to be 'realistic' in its expectations of parental support, and should offer 'clear expectations' for all concerned.

These were the teachers' views at the time. What about the parents, whose involvement had been seen as so crucial to the success of homework? With this in mind, we decided that Ian Stronach would interview parents during a family evening. One concern of the staff was that this would not give us a representative sample. The parents who came to the meeting would be those who supported the children's homework. This was perhaps also the group most likely to respond to further home–school overtures. In the event fourteen parents were interviewed, mainly from Years 3, 5 and 6. A number of aspects of the school were praised, the most frequent of which was that the Headteacher and teachers were seen as 'approachable': 'They listen. If you're worried they'll ask you what your worries are'; 'If they've got a problem, they'll send a note'; 'Each kid gets listened to, even on a bad day'.

Teachers were also seen as 'committed'. Two parents who had moved from the estate had kept their children at the school because they thought it a 'good school'. Others felt some pupils were 'above what they should be' because of the school. They said the children liked the different subjects and that teachers 'knew what they were doing'. It was felt to be a 'community school', and, since its refurbishment, a 'pleasant place to be'. Overall then, this small sample regarded the school as 'pretty good', although two spoke of children not getting enough attention.

Parents were divided in their more general views about the value of education in terms of 'getting on'. The more negative view was put forcefully by one grandparent:

She passed all the exams, A levels, and now she's just a chambermaid in a hotel. Waste of time qualifications. I mean, look at you [to the researcher] I mean I suppose you have qualifications haven't you? But look at what you're doing.

Despite such a view, and except for Year 1, other parents were critical of what they saw as the small amount of homework set. Others felt the main purpose should include 'fun' ways of doing things to help motivation, and sometimes to give otherwise bored children 'something to do'. So as well as the concern with 'fun' and the caution about the link between qualifications and 'getting on', others with older pupils at school felt that results mattered and that homework counted. Most of these claimed that their children were getting less than the 'half-hour a night', which they thought appropriate.

It is not possible to say whether these views were typical or, as we suspected, skewed. Certainly the parental emphases on 'attitude' was not quite the same as my colleagues' identification of the primary purposes of homework, as 'consolidation, revision and catching up'. I noted that the National Numeracy Framework stated: 'Out of school activities need to be frequent, short and focused. They should be varied, interesting and fun so that they motivate children, stimulate their learning and foster different study skills.' (DfEE, 1999, 16).

In some ways, this seems to reflect both concerns – those of the parents with motivation and interest, and those of the teachers with learning issues. We wanted to keep both these aspects in mind. Few parents had heard of the home–school agreement promoted by the government: those who had heard had done so via their children at secondary school. Most thought it a good idea in principle, as long as it was both 'preached and practised'. Perhaps closest agreement between teachers and parents was that maths was the area in which most of the parents might find difficulty in supporting homework. In such instances, the parents (almost all female) would try to involve 'dad' or older siblings. Although it involved a 'self-selected' sample, what we took from this small enquiry was that:

- the parents saw homework as important;
- parents felt that not enough homework was given, particularly at the end of Key Stage 2;
- maths was the most problematic area for parental support in terms of the skills necessary to help their children;
- there was a positive attitude to the idea of a homework policy with home–school agreements.

In turn these findings led us to think that there were needs for:

- more emphasis on mathematics homework throughout the school;
- a higher profile for mathematics within the school and with the parents;
- greater confidence about maths for both staff and parents.

Home and school: four strategies

The Headteacher and myself felt that the feedback from these enquiries into teachers' and parents' views confirmed our decision that our research focus should be mathematics, and should also look to involve parents. We discussed our ideas at another staff meeting and embarked on a four-pronged strategy, three of which directly related to our focus: the setting of maths targets in homework, raising the profile of maths in the school and the mathematics homework club. All these would contribute to improving the use of the appropriate mathematical language, which we wanted to be reinforced at home. Improving pupil ability to talk about their maths and explain their thinking seemed an obvious way of linking home and school. The fourth strategy also focused upon language in mathematics and involved the use of video to look at my own classroom practice in encouraging 'pupil talk'. I also wanted to use the video footage as a tool to facilitate discussion of mathematics classroom practice with colleagues. Generally speaking, we focused on these issues in the order in which we now describe them, but inevitably there was an overlap.

Target setting

I had read something of the IMPACT scheme and its use in relation to home–school links, and agreed with its emphasis that 'explicit connections need to be made' between home and school maths (Merttens and Vass, 1990). We decided to devise a recording sheet which would relate target-setting to homework activities, and which would be signed by parents. Targets would be set for basic numeracy knowledge and skills, such as tables or number bonds, so the content was what Merttens and Vass call 'bread and butter' maths. Each child would be given a target sheet for mathematics based on the class teacher's particular knowledge of the pupil's classwork.

We decided to call our sheet 'Maths Challenge' and to keep its layout 'homely' rather than too official. If a child achieved the target then either the parent or the child's class teacher would sign the target sheet, which would then be stamped with a special numeracy stamp. This was supported by our draft whole school policy document: 'Partnership agreement between parent, pupil and the school'. All parties would sign and date the agreement, which included the following:

- for the parent – 'to make sure my child does their homework';
- for the pupil – 'to do my homework and hand it in on time';
- for the teacher – 'to set appropriate work which will be marked regularly'.

In a staff meeting I sought the views of colleagues about the early stages of the impact of our 'Maths Challenge' sheets. The homework target sheets were more successful in some classes than others. In part this was related to differences in types of parent–school involvement related to the pupil age. Teachers who had constant access to parents – especially nursery and reception – were regularly able to talk to parents about target-setting in numeracy. These parents were the readiest to support their children with the targets. In Years 1 and 2 mathematics games were already out as soon as the children and parents came into school. Given this, it was quite natural for them to play the games with the children and help them with the targets. So this kind of interaction seemed to have supported the parental involvement with the sheets.

With older pupils at Key Stage 2 the results were more disappointing. The majority of children who completed their target sheets were the children who worked on their targets in class time. Their target sheets were kept by the class teacher who would test them at intervals during the week. Some children who took their target sheets home lost them. Although there was more mathematics homework being set, and completion and return rates had improved, these were still lower than we wanted at Key Stage 2. Another factor, besides the readier teacher–parent contact with the younger pupils, may well have been that as the pupils get older and the mathematics more challenging, parents feel less and less confident about their ability to support their children. In addition, there was some evidence that parents felt their children should be 'weaned away' from their support as they grew older, this was again a finding of the Home–School Links research project based in Manchester (McNamara *et al.*, 2000).

Profile raising

With this feedback in mind, we felt it might be useful to raise the profile of maths throughout the school. In particular we needed more mathematics displayed around the building, especially to show how pupils' work might link to the targets for individual children. For example, displays were mounted: Nursery and Reception children produced one showing counting in ones and two; Year 1 in tens; Year 2 in fives; Year 3 in threes; Year 4 in fours; Year 5 in sixes and sevens; and Year 6 in eights and nines. Also, the entrance hall showed ongoing mathematics work, and the children made eye-catching posters. We wrote a 'Newsletter', which was displayed in large format in the school and was also sent home.

What is also worth mentioning is that the LEA held a 'Numeracy Week', which was well timed for us in terms of our concern with raising the profile of maths in school and with the parents. We met together to try to think of something special we could do during that week and decided to organise a Bingo night to encourage more parents to come into school. Bingo is very popular within the community: there are two national bingo clubs within walking distance and it is played regularly at the local youth club. It was a game in which families with young children could all play together, reinforcing the social aspect of mathematics. The school also had a mathematics-themed assembly, when every class in the school sang a number or counting song. After this parents could go into classrooms to watch a National Numeracy Strategy-style oral and mental introduction to a lesson.

The maths club

In order to address the more general concern with pupils' interest and motivation, we also thought it would help to boost the profile of maths if we had an after-school maths club. We wanted it to involve activities to help parents to support their children's learning. So in another staff meeting we decided that the maths club would be open to all the children in Years 1–6 classes and that target sheets would be used in order to provide continuity with other strategies. A newsletter was sent home inviting parents to the club and all staff available on that day would be involved including a nursery nurse and classroom assistants.

In terms of curriculum content and pedagogy we wanted to support basic skills, especially given the concerns expressed by parents in the interviews regarding the older pupils' performance in the National Tests. It would give the children the opportunity to see the adults in school modelling how to work together. As the club would be voluntary, we would need to make it enjoyable too. We thought that the views of pupils might usefully be sought and so decided that my HEI link should talk to them as he was not a teacher/authority figure. Small groups of pupils were asked what they thought of the homework they were already getting, and their feelings about why they might, or might not, come to a maths club. The interviews were taped and transcribed for analysis. About 20 per cent of Years 5 and 6 pupils were involved in this activity. They tended to be the more motivated pupils, but we felt it would give some ideas about what to do in the club. What these group interviews seemed to suggest was:

- the prospect of mathematics as 'games' and 'fun' seemed appealing especially to the boys;
- many, especially the girls, wanted to come to get better at maths;
- pupils estimated that they currently spent about 10–20 minutes daily doing homework for each subject (mainly English, sometimes maths and occasionally science);
- pupils reported no particular pattern about which parent, mother or father, helped in which area, though some pupils worked alone;
- mathematics homework seemed to be mainly basic work, 'sums' and tables, and some felt they would like something 'new' rather than finishing off classwork.

These comments confirmed that some of the club's activities should involve games, which might be capable of engaging others to make positive use of possible 'disruption' by siblings, as well as provide a natural setting for parents to take part in a way which might help some overcome a lack of confidence about maths. In the event, we discussed the possibility of having four areas:

- a mental maths games area, informed by what we knew of the National Numeracy Strategy and with the concerns of the parents of older pupils in mind;
- a traditional games area (such as cards, chess and draughts), as we wanted to ensure a 'fun' element while we were building up our knowledge and resources of National Numeracy Strategy-style maths;
- a two-dimensional and three-dimensional shape area, as this had practical and visual appeal;
- a computer area.

We decided that the children would work through each area on a rota basis, so that all could access the opportunities and also work with an adult (teacher or parent) other than their usual class teacher. At the end of the half-term, each pupil received a certificate, and those who had successfully completed their targets were given a prize.

As it was not possible to find a regular day which did not clash with some other activity, such as staff meetings, sports matches, dance clubs, etc., we chose the one which offered the best opportunity for pupils. In the event, the take up for the club was very positive, involving just over half of Years 1–6. Surprisingly perhaps the take up for boys was slightly more than for the girls, except for Years 5 and 6. This might be because the club was attended by approximately half of the children on the school's Special Educational Needs register for either learning or behaviour difficulties, and boys make up over two-thirds of this register.

A few weeks at the maths club began I decided to evaluate its impact and devised the simplest of questionnaires. The questions were as follows:

- Did you go to the mathematics club?
- Why did you go/not go?
- If you went, which activity was your favourite?

Two-thirds of the school's pupils, half of whom had attended the club, were reached. I also decided to use Year 6 pupils as researchers: they read the questionnaire to Key Stage 1 pupils and recorded their responses. I think this was a good experience for the general language and social development of Year 6 pupils as well.

In the main, those children who did attend said that they came because they wanted to improve their mathematics to help them in their classwork, others came because they liked mathematics as a subject anyway and thought it would be fun. A few children wanted to work with other teachers in the school. Those children who did not attend mainly felt they were good enough at mathematics and did not want what they saw as just extra practice. Some did not come because they do not like mathematics and thought it would be boring. For a few others there were alternative activities on the same afternoon or early evening. What was encouraging was that some comments indicated that the use of computers was very attractive, especially for the older boys. This last finding was good news, especially given that the school was to upgrade the availability of computers the following year. This future possibility reminded me that a link between target-setting and new computer software was being used successfully in an inner-city authority in London (Neumark 1999).

We had expected two levels of parental involvement. The first was the more specific: parents who supported their child with mathematics targets. The second level was more general: to increase parental involvement by working informally with the children and the staff. The first week, only two parents came to the club; however, numbers increased as parents who came early to pick up their children were naturally drawn in to sit down and work with the children. The following week, five came to help in the club, and eventually twelve parents became involved. This was a gradual and modest progress, but it was in the right direction.

As I felt our perceptions as a staff might benefit from some kind of shared reflection, we evaluated the activities of target-setting, profile raising and the maths club. In general terms, it was felt that we had become more willing to reassess the kind of mathematics we were doing in school and opportunities for its use outside. Homework club and classwork activities began to be linked more in early Key Stage 1 and at the end of Key Stage 2. Although the club's activities had led to a better use of existing, even sometimes neglected resources, we identified a need to purchase more interactive games for use in both the school and the home. The forthcoming upgrading of the school's computer facilities would also present an opportunity. We have just introduced a reception pack, which includes resources suitable for use both in class and at home to support the children with their interactive homework. Creating a lending library of games was a possibility.

Some of the number-related games used in the club began to be used in the classroom, during regular class time. Several of these could be photocopied for use at home. Especially high rates of homework return and completion were noted with those games which had been enjoyed in class – sometimes after having been 'piloted' in the club.

My Year 6 children also planned and designed their own activities (which we called 'games') such as 'Magic Squares' and variations on 'Number Lines' for use with specific younger classes in school. They then went to the classes to play the games with the children. I regarded this as another way of helping the development of maths vocabulary, as well as perhaps a way of interacting with others on maths activities which might be transferable to their home context. Five of the pupils did subsequently talk about using these with younger siblings at home and explaining them to parents.

It was also agreed that the maths club was very relaxed. Children with emotional and behavioural difficulties seemed to benefit from the lower adult–pupil ratios, and displayed more independence in choosing what to do, working purposefully and clearing up later. The children were also able to see the staff working in pairs and demonstrating with parents how to play games. Experiencing these activities might also have helped some parents. On the whole, we felt that this would contribute to a change in the relationship between teacher and pupil, pupil and pupil and parent-educator and child, although, again, these are longer-term issues.

This is not a 'success against all the odds' story of a hard-pressed school in a deprived inner-city area, but encouragement can be found in several ways. In terms of my original concerns it seemed that:

- the initial surveys of parental opinion showed our efforts were appreciated;
- we had made progress with the target sheets as a way of linking home and school, and there was the possibility of investigating more individualised support via software (such as 'Successmaker' used in the Haringey account in Neumark 1999);
- a heartening increase in involvement of parents with the early years pupils had been identified and could be built on;
- we had raised the profile for mathematics throughout the school;
- older pupils had been involved in data gathering.

Maths talk

The fourth of our strategies involved working with a video to develop the pupils' language in maths. Although I knew that there was much work to be done here, I agreed with the idea that 'numeracy teaching is based on a dialogue between teacher and pupils to explore understandings' (Askew *et al.*, 1997, p. 2). I thought that this would indirectly feed into the kinds of activities discussed above, in that improving pupil talk in class would have some carry-over to home and again, might be helpful to parents who lacked confidence about mathematics. As Merttens (1999, p. 79) has written 'the biggest single factor in children's educational success is their parents'. I was also aware that in my role as maths coordinator I would be responsible for supporting colleagues, and the National Numeracy Strategy seemed to have a special emphasis on language. Developing maths 'talk' with colleagues would, we hoped, improve our 'talk' with pupils and thereby improve pupils' 'talk' and subsequently their 'talk' with parents.

By now (academic year 1999–2000) the National Numeracy Strategy had arrived, and it was clear that it would reinforce our emphases on home–school relations and language interests, especially in its use of 'whole class interactive teaching' and pupils' explicit use of various mental strategies. I knew all this would be a long-term process, and decided to start by looking at my own classroom practice first, and then begin to work with other members of staff in a more explicit way. At this stage I began to work with another HEI link, Brian Corbin, as he had the experience of working on a related project mentioned in the Introduction. It was funded by the Economic and Social Research Council and involved mathematics coordinators looking at their practice using video evidence. The use of video with an emphasis on 'speaking and listening' was a general feature of the consortium's work and an account of this broader context was given in Chapter 3. We decided to video some of my lessons and to support my particular intention I initially decided to concentrate on the 'mental–oral' start to the lesson with my Year 6 pupils. I was interested in seeing how my use of various types of questions, initially broadly categorised as 'closed' and 'open', worked in this whole class context, especially to engage everyone in a class with a wide range of abilities. I also wanted to be able to show colleagues how various visual supports and activities might be used in relation to developing language.

Looking at the position of the video, enabled me to notice what was difficult to pick up in the to-and-fro of teaching this 'mental–oral starter' from the front. I was pleased with the variety of questions and the way I spread them around the room. The pause for a particular pupil to stumble through his explanation did not seem as long as in the lesson, when I felt under pressure about the 'pace'. Also, there were some responses which I might have explored with the pupil a bit longer, as on reflection I began to see how a particular misconception had been hurried over. I was satisfied to confirm that I had given opportunities for pupils to explain their thinking when challenged, but thought that next time it would help if they wrote on the blackboard at the same time, so they could see their own thought sequence as they were trying to articulate it. I also noted that the chanting of tables using my pendulum and the number line was a support for those unsure of some of the number bonds at certain places – they got 'carried along'. However, I could see that I needed to increase the support offered to my special needs pupils when it came to quick calculations to help them keep up with the pace at these times.

In another video session I looked at my work with a small group, whose activity was to find a systematic way of recording data when working and discussing a number problem. During the session I felt that it was not going as well as planned. On reviewing the session on video I realised that that part of the problem arose from my explanation of the task. Hearing it from the pupils' point of view, it was not as clear as I had thought, so I arranged to video this same activity but with a different group and a revised introduction. I was also beginning to think that some sections of these videos might be useful in INSET (in-service training) sessions, not just as a demonstration but as a focus upon which to discuss practice. I therefore watched this third video with Sarah, a colleague who in the following year would be teaching a similar year group for the first time. We audio-taped our subsequent discussion and had it transcribed.

I was surprised at Sarah's interest in the earlier parts of the lesson, particularly I think because of her concerns with questioning and differentiation in her class. She remarked on the use of calculators with my special needs pupils, to help them keep up with the lesson pace at some points. She found my use of digit cards helpful, not just because the pupils could work with concrete materials but because I could link this with asking them to explain their thinking rather then just 'show' the response. This led to questions about where I got my ideas from, and I was able to remind her about school resources which, though supportive of the National Numeracy Strategies, might have become neglected.

Watching the video again with her also enabled me to notice things I had not caught in my first viewing of it, perhaps because our own talk helped me see it anew. For example, when we did get around to looking at the small group activity, she spoke about what she really found difficult in encouraging pupil talk in problem-solving activities: 'I always find that you end up doing it altogether because they just can't do it independently'. As I was assuring her that this would take lots of modelling, I noticed a point on the video I had missed in my first viewing. A pupil was giving an explanation, we paused the video at that moment, and I noted that the 'pupil has got the idea, and it shows the process of thinking'. We then discussed the teaching opportunities of such moments. Recording and analysing video is obviously heavy on time and resources, but we felt that there was value in our use of video evidence. Helpful features included:

- use of 'clips' for demonstrating and focused talk during INSET with colleagues;
- noticing things about one's own practice not caught when teaching – and having that practice available for further reference;
- helping to think about what to do next time when things went wrong;
- recognising one's own good practice (sometimes a fresh angle is needed for this, which might involve a 'critical friend').

Reflections

These various activities of target-setting, raising the maths profile, homework club and using video evidence amounted to a set of complementary strategies related to our concerns to improve pupil performance and home–school links. In terms of their possible impact, they have different time scales. For example, we hope that the 'Maths Challenge' sheets and supportive teacher–pupil contact in the early years can be sustained as cohorts move up and that the 'Maths Club' might become more associated with National Test 'booster' classes.

The activities have involved data-gathering, some of which would not have not been undertaken without our involvement in the consortium. They provided different kinds of evidence to inform our decisions. For example, at the level of the school, the variations in amounts of time allocated to homework and the degree of emphasis on literacy came as something of a surprise. The discussions of this feedback had raised our awareness about some relevant factors, which seemed obvious once stated, but giving them a school-wide airing was helpful. At the level of home–school links, surveying teachers and interviewing parents had shown commonalities and differences, which we tried to take into account. A pupil age-related difference in opportunities for teacher–parent talk about the 'Maths Challenge' sheets also became more evident. This contributed to our 'Reception pack' of resources. The common concern with maths as a more 'difficult area' for parents had led to some of our 'raising the profile' activities.

At the level of the teacher, the opportunity to watch one's own teaching on videos and to start to use them in developmental work with a colleague, was daunting, but did make available some relevant material for reflecting on one's own practice and for subject coordinator work. And, of course, at the level of our primary concern with pupils, we did have evidence about improving their opportunities for learning both in and out of class. These included the differential impact of the homework club on the involvement of those at various ability levels, ways of involving older pupils in data gathering and simple maths 'games' development for use at home and in school.

There are other kinds of data from feedback about pupil performance in National Tests which were increasingly beginning to inform our decisions. Our experience of incorporating the National Numeracy Strategy has been encouraging, especially for me in its emphasis on the development of mental strategies and pupil explanation. These are major emphases, and working to them certainly does feel like a 'sea-change' in teaching mathematics (Merttens and Wood, 2000, p. 17). These changes might be a context in which more focused data-gathering can take place, drawing also on our experiences in the consortium.

References

Askew, M., Brown M., Rhodes, V., Johnson, D. and Wiliam, D. (1997) *Effective Teachers of Numeracy: Final Report*. London: Kings College.

Department for Education and Employment (1998) *Home–School Agreements: What Every Parent Should Know*. London: DfEE.

Department for Education and Employment (1999) *The National Numeracy Strategy*. London: DfEE.

McNamara, O., Hustler, D., Stronach, I., Rodrigo, M., Bereford, E. and Botcherby, S. (2000) Room to manoeuvre : mobilising the 'active partner' in home–school relations. *British Educational Research Issues*, 26(4): 473–490.

Merttens, R. and Vass, J. (1990) *Sharing Maths Cultures: IMPACT, Inventing Maths for Parents, Children and Teachers*. Basingstoke: Falmer,

Merttens, R. (1999) Family numeracy. In: I. Thompson (ed.) *Issues in Teaching Numeracy in Primary Schools*. Buckingham: Open University Press.

Merttens, R. and Wood, D. (2000) Sea changes in mathematical education – an elaboration of the National Curriculum Strategy. *Mathematics Teaching* 172: 13–17.

Neumark, V. (1999) Everyone can share in success. *Times Educational Supplement*, 21 May 1999, Mathematics supplement, pp. 24–25.

Chapter 10

Balancing the forces

Researching primary science in the classroom

Dave Heywood and Ann-Marie Roberts

Introduction

I initially became aware of the Manchester and Salford Schools Consortium in September 1997 when I, Anne-Marie Roberts, arrived in Manchester to take up my new position as the Deputy Headteacher in St Chad's RC Primary School. The Headteacher 'invited' my participation, with the words: 'It won't mean any more work, and it's a good way of getting to know people ...'

The school had been involved in the bidding process from April 1997, although the focus for the project was not confirmed until June when we received the results of the National Tests. The science results gave considerable cause for concern: only 29 per cent of pupils achieved Level 4 or above at Key Stage 2. Our results for science in Key Stage 1 still remained good and we wanted to find reasons for, and address, the slump in performance from Key Stage 1 to Key Stage 2. As well as my role on the Senior Management Team at the school I was Science Coordinator and in addition had responsibility for Key Stage 2. It did seem that the role of research coordinator had my name written large upon it!

The school is a one-form entry primary and the area is one of severe social and economic deprivation. A second major challenge is the transient nature of the local population and the presence of a relatively large proportion of traveller children. The school had also experienced major staff changes in the 2 years prior to the commencement of the project in autumn 1997: there was a new Headteacher, a new Deputy head (myself) and four other new class teachers, all of whom were newly qualified. In addition, two of the staff who had left over the previous 2 years had only been in post for a year. In April 1998 as we were trying to get the project going the school was inspected by OfSTED, which, despite the added pressure for the teaching staff, fostered a spirit of working together and helped to build a sense of collective responsibility. This was beneficial for individual staff and the school as a whole. The following year, when staff were well involved with the project and felt they were making progress, there were further staff changes: two more teachers left to be replaced again by newly qualified teachers. It takes time for new staff to be assimilated within the structure of a school and such frequent changes in personnel in a relatively small primary school affects the stability and sense of continuity of the whole school community. This was also, of course, a time of curriculum upheaval: the arrival of the Literacy and Numeracy Strategies meant that even more experienced staff were experiencing considerable change in their professional lives. In order to accommodate these changes, most of the staff went on a team-building weekend during the second year of the project, which enabled us to strengthen relationships, discover individual strengths and weaknesses, and develop our ability to work together as a team.

Focusing on forces

The context for the research was to raise the level of achievement in Key Stage 2 science. Our project benefited at different times from the support and expertise of two HEI link colleagues: Alan Cross from the Victoria University of Manchester, a specialist in primary science who had extensive experience supporting practitioner research projects, and Dave Heywood from Manchester Metropolitan University, who was also involved in primary science education and had specific research interests in forces and teacher subject knowledge. Both contributed a great deal to this project.

It was decided that all the teachers in Key Stage 2 should become involved and data collected from all classes, but for ongoing measurements of improvement, changes in attitude, etc., we decided to focus more on the children in the then Year 3 class, who were to be tracked through to Year 6. I would have liked to have taught this focus group in the first year, but of course other factors had to be taken into account when allocating teachers to classes and I had to take over Year 5, a class that were proving very challenging in their behaviour.

In order to evaluate the difficulties which Key Stage 2 pupils were experiencing in science, we felt it was necessary to initially blanket-test all the children in Years 3–6 using a standardised test. The time-consuming process of searching for suitable age-standardised tests proved an enormous hurdle as there seemed to be a scarcity of such published materials. Finally, the decision was taken to use the tests published by Letts, rather than allow more valuable time to be wasted.

The assessment and analysis of the test results confirmed much that we already knew, and a number of patterns were confirmed across the key stage:

- attainment based on the tests was generally low compared with national expectations;
- the format of written tests, in particular the written language, was a significant barrier;
- children were better at describing effects than describing causes;
- children had difficulty with questions involving more than one concept;
- children had difficulty with questions which went beyond a simple causal relationship.

Our initial focus was to be the children's understanding of the concept of forces. In Year 3 the children had not yet covered this topic, but in later years all children should have had some knowledge of forces from previous science lessons. The Letts test gave us some information on the understandings/misconceptions that children throughout the school had regarding forces, for example:

- Many children, presented with a football being kicked, were able to draw an arrow saying which direction it would travel, but when asked to say why this happened, most had no ideas.
- When asked about a ball thrown into the air, children were confident about it

going up but less so that it would slow down, and very few could offer an explanation of the reason.

- A typical response from a child explaining why a car's wheels spun when the car entered a patch of mud, was simply 'its wheels would spin'.

In order to obtain some more specific and detailed information on their understanding of forces all the children within Key Stage 2 were asked to undertake a concept-mapping exercise. Many of the children had no experience of using a concept map to explain their ideas, and therefore needed help to understand what it was and how it could be used to demonstrate their knowledge and learning. The concept map required the children to show what they knew about various forces, e.g. push, pull, gravity, friction, air resistance, etc. These words were written on a large empty piece of paper, and in a box at the bottom of the paper were further key words: car, slow down, balance, change direction, stop, speed up, ramp, ball, door, moves, attract, repel, etc. The children were asked to show what they knew about forces by linking words, drawing pictures or diagrams, adding arrows, writing sentences, etc., or by explaining orally.

The concept maps were very revealing of the children's conceptual understanding and misunderstanding and provoked a great deal of teacher discussion. The open format allowed children to be expansive and follow through their ideas, whether in pictures or words, and where their responses were not clear, teachers could subsequently ask children to talk through what they had drawn/written and expand it further, which revealed more of their thinking. This exercise on its own illumined for teachers the misunderstandings that could go unnoticed, the areas that children found particularly difficult and the misconceptions that needed to be addressed. Teachers began to discuss and explore ways that they could alter their pedagogy to address the particular problems of their year group. After the concept maps had been completed in Year 3 and the class teacher and I had had time to explore them in depth, the class teacher and I swapped classes for 3 weeks so that I could teach Year 3 the topic of forces. This enabled me to get acquainted with the children, as people and as budding scientists.

The focus shifts to language

The initial test results and the concept maps had shown that throughout Key Stage 2 the children's knowledge of science was patchy. We were interested to explore further the possible misconceptions in the children's understanding of the various physical processes represented in the questions that had occurred in the Letts tests. We decided to interview a sample of children from each year group. During these interviews it became apparent that the children's understanding of the concepts involved was not the only problem. Not only did they lack scientific vocabulary, but also they had great difficulty expressing their ideas, even in everyday language. Thus, as we approached the second year of the project we began to focus our inquiry on the use of language, both that of the teacher and that of the children, in the classroom. We sought to answer the questions:

- How do children come to understand scientific terms?

- In what ways can their understanding become confused?
- What strategies do teachers currently use to introduce and explain scientific terms?
- What strategies could teachers adopt to develop children's understanding of scientific concepts and their use of scientific vocabulary?

We acknowledged across the key stage that it was necessary to examine the ways in which we, as teachers, introduced and explained key scientific words to the children. Our strategies clearly needed to be rethought, and we felt it was appropriate to call on outside expertise to assist us and give us fresh ideas.

An in-service workshop was planned for the school, run by our HEI link, Alan Cross, and attended by all teachers. This session offered us a number of approaches to the teaching of primary science, but particularly focused on acquiring scientific understanding and language through investigational work, and strategies that would emphasise scientific language in the classroom. The outcome was a more confident commitment from all staff to a more practical, investigational, hands-on approach in science that would support a great deal of scientific talking by the children. It also led teachers to focus more on the language we, and the children, used in science lessons. After the workshop Key Stage 2 teachers had a brainstorming session to come up with some instant action we could take that would support the work in lessons. We all agreed to try:

- bombarding the walls of the classroom with key words;
- sending words home with the children;
- sending letters to the parents/carers informing them of the topic;
- sending homework sheets to focus parents/carers support in helping their children;
- reinforcing science vocabulary with games and quizzes.

This was useful as an awareness-raising exercise and also effective as reinforcement. Previously, children below Year 6 had rarely had science homework, and we felt we had been missing out on the possibility of parental support.

Our skills in planning and managing practical science activities had increased, along with our understanding of the logistics of resourcing, storage of apparatus and the practicalities of investigational science group work in small and sometimes overcrowded classrooms. Our emphasis on linking vocabulary to practical experience of scientific concepts was, we believed, central to promoting effective learning. The language barrier that the teachers had earlier experienced was beginning to be addressed.

At the end of the first year of the project the success of the work done so far was evident in the improved National Test results, which in Key Stage 2 Science were 56 per cent at Level 4 and above in June 1998, a rise of 27 per cent. And in Years 3–5 all teachers felt that their children now understood how to use concept mapping skills to explain, explore and discuss their understanding of scientific concepts.

Using video evidence

In the long term, however, the teachers within Key Stage 2 felt that they wanted to look in more detail at the language difficulties of the children, and at the effectiveness of their responses to children who were struggling. It was thus decided to make video-recordings of some lessons in order to collect hard evidence of both teacher and pupil talk that could subsequently be analysed and shared. In the first instance we decided to record two lessons, one by the teacher of Year 6 and the other by myself in Year 5. With the help of Alan Cross, we taped both lessons on the same afternoon. The Year 6 teacher had used video as part of her initial teacher training, but many of the children had never experienced being videoed, and neither had I as a teacher. I was surprised at the degree of anxiety the idea provoked in me. The aim of the video-recording was to capture episodes of classroom interaction that would give us insights into the ways in which the children's understanding of concepts, and their ability to explain them, developed, and identify ways in which we, as teachers, might facilitate the process.

The Year 5 lesson was on the topic of solids, liquids and gases, the particular focus being on how some solids dissolve in liquids. The Year 5 class concerned was streamed and consisted of eighteen children of average and lower ability, including some children with special needs. There was to be a practical session in groups, and the resources for each group had already been prepared and awaited the class on the tables. Then the whole class engaged in sharing and discussing their activities, defining, explaining and using the scientific vocabulary connected with the lesson.

Analysis of the video evidence confirmed that the significance of language, both ours and that of the children, was a core issue. For example: children used scientific terms incorrectly; they were reluctant to speak and hesitant when they did; they stumbled over vocabulary, scientific and non-scientific; they appeared not to have full command of the way they were expressing their ideas; they could attempt description, but requests for explanation merely produced more description. In addition, we recognised that the language we, as teachers, used in explanation was central to developing children's thinking and understanding of the scientific vocabulary and concepts. This too needed sharpening up at times. The need to focus on the specific language used and its scientific meaning became apparent when I asked the children the meaning of the word 'solution'. Daniel, who was, within this group, a bright and articulate child, proposed that: 'a solution is when you find the answer to a problem – you have the solution'. Such a response made me, as a teacher, think about the interdependence of language, thinking and context. The response would be seen as entirely appropriate in a maths lesson, or elsewhere, yet in this science lesson it became the 'wrong' answer. The child was confident that he knew the meaning of the word, unaware that it could have a different definition in the world of chemistry.

As the discussion progressed it was noticeable how many children bided their time before answering. Often when they did answer they provided an accurate prediction of what would happen in the chemical processes – but they were not able to describe what was meant by the term 'dissolve', mainly because they lacked a specific and accurate vocabulary for defining scientific concepts. The lesson concluded by recapping what had been introduced earlier: a focus on the key scientific terms used, and the specific meanings of those terms in a scientific context. During this plenary session the children were given a worksheet containing key vocabulary and they were asked to colour in each word that they had come across during the lesson. This not only highlighted the importance of the key words – and their spelling – but it also focused the children's attention at the end of the lesson, when their concentration was in some cases beginning to wane.

Video provides an ideal opportunity for teachers to become aware of their practice, consider possible ways to improve it and identify how children's thinking is developing during lessons. It provides important evidence upon which to base judgements on aspects of practice. It is easy to misinterpret the input of individual children in a busy classroom. For example, the video revealed that some individual children remained in command of the task and the discussion at a conceptual level although they appeared to be off task. This was exemplified in the case Steven, who although bright had a very poor attendance record and consequently was almost always in a state of having to catch up. As some of the children in the class were on the school's Special Educational Needs register for behavioural as well as learning difficulties, the lesson had been very structured, offering little opportunity for distraction and diversion. Nevertheless, during the lesson Steven was restless, appeared distracted and displayed attention-seeking behaviour. In spite of what appeared to be off-task behaviour for much of the lesson, however, his answers were often accurate, showing clear understanding of the concepts; for example, he described 'condensation' as 'what you get on the windows when it's cold outside and warm in the house'.

Children, as well as teachers, can learn from watching themselves on video: they can observe themselves and others engaged in on-task and off-task behaviour, see how groups interact, helpfully or not, watch themselves developing understanding, noting what helped them and what did not. Steven watched part of the video soon afterwards, and we discussed how many of the questions he had answered correctly, which helped, I hoped, to raise his self-esteem.

The availability of video, and the time to examine it carefully, enabled the teachers to focus on many different aspects of pedagogy within the lesson. However, although videos allow classroom experiences to be relived, they are still at life speed, i.e. too fast for the viewer to take in all the details. In order to facilitate further analysis of these lessons I transcribed sections of video that seemed of particular interest. This allowed us to focus in detail on who was doing the talking, and the language used, and we subsequently worked with episodes from the videos, and/or the transcription, both with staff in the school and with colleagues in the consortium. More of this story was related in Chapter 3.

Implications: clarifying the problem

The key issue here is that of meeting children's needs and developing interest and enthusiasm in science learning, while at the same time increasing their ability to describe and explain their thinking. Initially these two tasks seemed both overwhelming and incompatible to us as teachers and the challenge of achieving the aim within the constraints of the school timetable seemed immense. During the project the focus on science was sometimes difficult to maintain alongside the increased emphasis on literacy and numeracy. We were sustained by the knowledge that the attention we had given to science teaching and our efforts to change our pedagogy had produced worthwhile results: performance in National Tests at Key Stage 2 had risen to 73 per cent at Level 4 and above by June 1999, a rise of 44 per cent in 2 years. We clearly perceived the value of spending significant time on supporting children's language development, because we knew, from our own work, that where this is possible pupil outcomes are likely to be significantly improved.

We found that when teachers probed more deeply into children's responses, the children based their ideas on their experience of the world, as is shown, for example, in the Year 5 children's comments on change of state when investigating dissolving and their use of the word 'solution'. The children were able to offer sensible suggestions why certain events occurred. Not surprisingly, children were more confident in offering ideas about effects rather than causes in expressing their thinking about forces. This was because most children intuitively knew the effect of forces from their experience of the world (most of them at some stage have fallen off a bike or kicked a ball), and they therefore drew on this experience when asked to describe events. When it came to explaining why things happened, however, the causal mechanisms involved in terms of forces are notoriously difficult to articulate and cause most of us problems (Parker and Heywood, 2000). As adults and teachers we needed – as much as the children – to have opportunities to think through, discuss and check our ideas with others, and this indeed was an invaluable element of the in-service sessions. The children also needed to be given this opportunity, because not only were the ideas difficult to explain in a purely theoretical way, but with abstract notions, such as forces, the problem was made worse because the scientifically accepted ideas are often counterintuitive (Wolpert, 1992).

For example, it is natural to think about forces as belonging to a body rather than acting on a body, and this affects the way that children perceive the causes of movement. In explaining the forces acting on the football once it has been kicked, the most likely interpretation is that the person who has kicked the ball has applied a force to the ball that remains with the ball until it runs out and the ball comes to rest. This is a persuasive explanation in terms of commonsense reasoning, but is unfortunately one that contradicts the scientific version of events, which is that the instant the ball is kicked the forces acting on it are gravity and air resistance. When faced with questions that require a scientific interpretation, it is difficult to give a response which seems in conflict with common experience. Certainly, 'coaching' involving drawing force arrows in the correct position on force diagrams can be helpful but is limited in supporting children in reasoning in different contexts. This implies that there needs to be both practical exploration of ideas and the time in which to articulate, discuss, compare and question views (Heywood, 1998). Both of these activities need to be built into planning for science.

Where we go from here: practical experience as a support for language

The focus on language that we see as critical in supporting learning in science, so that children can express their ideas in ways that address the requirements of National Tests, is not simply a case of reinforcing definitions of words (Sutton, 1992). The 'bombardment' of words referred to earlier in the display work and the 'blitz' in learning these with parental support played a very important part in raising awareness of the vocabulary that children encounter in formal science assessment. This strategy seemed to affect performance, but the problem of reasoning about more abstract scenarios and applying learning across contexts is not addressed solely through an approach that focuses on the acquisition of vocabulary. Accepting that there is no simple solution to the difficulties concerned with language and learning in science, we believe that the insight gained from exploring the issue more closely in this project provides some possible practical strategies.

The first of these relates to the structure of teaching sessions. There are currently materials available that offer some guidance in respect of this. The QCA scheme of work (DfEE, 1998) is a reasonable starting point, because it explicitly outlines learning objectives and the expectation of what children should be able to do as a result of the unit of work. However, there are implicit assumptions that need consideration in translating the content and concepts into productive science lessons. To illustrate this we will examine the unit of work on forces in Key Stage 2.

It is useful to identify the key ideas that underpin learning about forces and structure units of work which explicitly relate to and reinforce these concepts. There are implications in doing this in regard to teacher subject knowledge, but knowledge of science alone is not the only factor in the complexity of learning in science. It is necessary to combine subject knowledge with an understanding of what is involved in the teaching and learning process. Here is the significant professional dimension of pedagogic knowledge and its relationship to subject knowledge (Parker and Heywood, 2000). It is not just knowing the science, but concerns knowing what is involved in the teaching and learning of it. Primary teachers working with children from deprived backgrounds recognise the need to provide experiences that the children can relate to and build upon, because this enables them to clarify their ideas. This is where practical investigational work in science becomes so critical.

However, it is not just practical opportunity that is the solution to the problem. Doing practical work does not necessarily equate to learning in science. Practical activity needs to provide a reference point for both learner and teacher to which they can relate their ideas and explore them in discussion. Such an approach makes clear the link between practical investigation and language in science learning (Heywood, 1998; Parker, 1995). As an example, consider the ideas that underpin some of the requirements in understanding the questions in the Letts' assessment materials and those that pupils should be taught as part of the programme of study in the Key Stage 2 National Curriculum. The current National Curriculum (DfEE, 2000, p. 88) requires that children be taught:

- about forces of attraction and repulsion between magnets, and about the forces of attraction between magnets and magnetic materials;
- that objects are pulled downwards because of the gravitational attraction between them and the Earth;
- about friction, including air resistance, as a force that slows moving objects and may prevent objects from starting to move;
- that when objects (for example, a spring, a table) are pushed or pulled, an opposing pull or push can be felt;
- how to measure forces and identify the direction in which they act.

There are changes in the 2000 curriculum on forces, the most significant being the omission of balanced and unbalanced forces and the idea that weight is a force. The concept of balanced and unbalanced forces causes considerable difficulty, particularly when applied to objects in motion, and it is therefore understandable that the teaching of this has been deferred to Key Stage 3. The idea that weight is a force is counterintuitive, since weight is often conceptualised as 'heaviness'. Although these omissions appear to simplify the curriculum, we suggest that it can still be productive for investigating the ideas through activities that can be explored in floating and sinking.

Although floating and sinking is no longer explicitly mentioned in the National Curriculum programme of study, it remains a useful context in which to explore the forces curriculum at Key Stage 2. These include the concept that forces occur in pairs (usually, but not always, referred to as pushes and pulls), and that when objects are pushed and pulled an opposing push or pull can be felt. More subtly, the reference to gravitational attraction implies the idea that weight is a force, and the conceptualisation that forces act on (rather than belong to) a body is explicit in the requirement that children should be able to identify where forces are acting.

When working on activities in floating and sinking such as pushing an inflated balloon in a tank of water, we offer children direct tactile experience of forces acting in pairs. The push down on the balloon is resisted by a push back of the water, and the children recognise that the more push (force) they exert, the more the water pushes back. This is significantly more important than introducing just the vocabulary used to describe the phenomenon (e.g. upthrust), and illustrates that the real issue is not simply that of learning vocabulary but is concerned with understanding through experiencing and being given the vocabulary to describe your experience. Children need the opportunity to test their ideas and talk about them (Harlen, 2000). In the case of the submerged balloon, the idea of opposing forces can be discussed and related to other examples in different contexts where opposing pushes and pulls are acting on objects. The foundation for recognising these forces and the effect that they have on objects is developed through such practical reference. This is much more likely to promote understanding and support children in recognising forces acting where it is not possible to have direct tactile experience of them (i.e. in diagrams that require the inclusion of force arrows acting on the object).

In addressing the idea that objects are pulled downwards because of the gravitational attraction between them and the Earth, children are introduced to the abstract concept of forces acting at a distance. Although the work on magnets provides a context for experiencing such a phenomenon, the application of the idea across contexts seems to be particularly problematic. This was evident in our own findings in which the children experienced difficulty in expressing their understanding of a moving ball. In reasoning about gravitational attraction there is again opportunity to introduce the conceptual framework in exploring the behaviour of objects in water.

One way of doing this is to encourage children to investigate a floating object whose weight can be changed relatively easily (a screw-top glass jar is ideal for this). If the jar is empty it floats high in the water and when relating this to the floating balloon the children's attention can be focused towards recognising the forces acting on the jar. That is, the jar is pressing down on the water in the same way as they were pressing down on the balloon and the water is exerting a force back on the jar (of course this is an example of balanced forces). If the jar is filled with a small amount of water then a prediction can be made about its floating position and this can then be tested. In such a focused activity the teacher can control the learning agenda more easily and refer to the 'downward' force of the jar being increased. That is, the jar is being pulled down through the gravitational attraction of the Earth on the object. The downward force can be gradually increased until the jar is just about floating. In increasing the 'downward' force we are increasing the weight of the jar and it is important to draw attention to this, since the notion that weight is a force is a concept that children have difficulty with later in Key Stage 3.

There is a wide range of activities that are possible in floating and sinking that support thinking about forces in a more general way and support the learner in reasoning about forces acting on objects in different contexts. Making these links is a critical skill in pedagogy that we as teachers need to work at developing (Heywood and Parker, 2002). If the vocabulary used in science is to have meaning then it is necessary to offer learners the opportunity for practical experience of the concepts involved. This is likely to promote success both in enhancing children's performance in national tests, and, more importantly, in their understanding of science.

Reflections

The research has highlighted significant factors that impact upon effective learning in science. The language focus has enabled us to look closely at how we might improve our science teaching. An important element of this concerns developing structure in our planning and implementation of the science curriculum. The opportunity to examine our practice more closely has proved extremely valuable, and consultation with colleagues with particular expertise in science education has developed our awareness of a range of issues. These include developing our subject knowledge through reflection on practice to determine appropriate action steps in which we can address the particular language needs of our children. This would support them in being able to illustrate more fully the level of their understanding in more formal settings such as that required in summative assessment procedures. These are demanding and exciting challenges that confront us, and we have welcomed the insights gained from examining our own practice in detail to determine a way forward.

References

Qualifications and Curriculum Authority (1998) *A Scheme of Work for Key Stages 1 and 2.* London: DfEE.

Qualifications and Curriculum Authority (2000) *The National Curriculum. Handbook for Primary Teachers in England.* London: DfEE.

Heywood, D. S. (1998) Spreading the message: exploring language and learning in science, in Cross, A. and Peet, G. (eds) *Teaching Science in the Primary School.* Plymouth: Northcote House.

Heywood, D.S. and Parker, J. (2002) Describing the cognitive landscape in learning and teaching about forces. *International Journal of Science Education* (in press).

Harlen, W. (2000) *The Teaching of Science in Primary Schools.* London: Fulton.

Parker, J. (1995) Words on paper. *Primary Science Review,* 36 (February): 18–22.

Parker, J. and Heywood, D. (2000) Exploring the relationship between subject knowledge and pedagogic content knowledge in primary teachers' learning about forces. *International Journal of Science Education,* 22(1): 89–111.

Sutton, C. (1992) *Words, Science and Learning.* Buckingham: Open University Press.

Wolpert, L. (1992) *The Unnatural Nature of Science.* London: Faber and Faber.

Chapter 11

Streaming reviewed

Some reflections from an inner-city, multi-ethnic primary school

Mike Berry, Helen White and Peter Foster

Introduction

The multiplicity of reforms in education in recent years – the National Curriculum, National Tests and their publication in the form of league tables, increasing competition between schools for pupils, greater accountability of schools to parents, scrutiny of school performance via inspection and more recently the impending introduction of target setting and the National Literacy and Numeracy Strategies – have focused the minds of primary school heads and teachers on increasing standards of educational achievement, particularly in the core subjects of English, maths and science. Moreover, the guidance coming from government and other influential figures is that improved standards can best be achieved by moving away from individualised, child-centred forms of teaching towards a greater emphasis on whole class teaching. One result of these developments is that the issue of grouping pupils in classes by ability has reappeared on the policy agenda of many primary schools.

Our story

This was the case at Cheetham CE Community Primary School in Manchester in 1995. We debated the issue and decided to introduce ability grouping in the junior section of the school in September 1995. Our intake of approximately forty-five children each year already dictated vertical grouping so that Years 3 and 4 pupils and Years 5 and 6 pupils were taught together, giving us three mixed-age classes in Year 3/4 and three in Year 5/6. We decided to stream these classes so that each age band had a top, middle and lower stream.

Our decision was influenced partly by a concern about the achievement levels of our pupils at the time (see p. 144), which we thought were disappointing, given that our district inspector had praised the quality of teaching and learning in the school. However, it was also swayed by the distinctive nature of our intake, which has implications for the distribution of resources in the school. Cheetham's intake is primarily (95 per cent) from ethnic minority backgrounds, particularly children from Pakistani/Muslim backgrounds and children of more recent (and sometimes temporary) migrants from Libya, Iraq, Iran and Malaysia. The children's competence in spoken and written standard English therefore varies enormously. Some children, particularly those who have recently arrived in the UK, have very little English. Others have achieved relatively high standards when they reach the junior years. We also have the usual range of general ability found in most schools. Because we cater for so many children from ethnic minority backgrounds we receive extra resources provided under Section 11 of the 1966 Local Government Act. These consist of 1.5 additional teachers and five part-time support teachers, some of whom are bilingual. In order to target these teaching resources more effectively at children whose English is particularly weak, we decided to place these pupils together in the lower stream. Our Section 11 teachers could then spend the bulk of their time in two classes, rather than continually switching between six classes, liaising with six teachers, as had been the case in the past. We also felt that our teaching could be more effective if we had children with broadly similar achievement levels in the same class. We thought the methods of teaching and the work which children were expected to do could be more effectively tailored to the needs of the children. With our previous mixed-ability classes many children with low levels of competence in English struggled to understand, and keep up with, class activities and work, whereas those with greater competence often appeared to be bored, under-stretched and frustrated.

For the last 3 years, then, we have placed our pupils in one of three streams when they enter the junior section. Placement decisions are made by the Deputy Head in consultation with class teachers and Section 11 staff. Judgements are made largely on the basis of a child's level of achievement in English assessed using the SELA (Stages in English Language Acquisition) scale, but we also take into account National Tests results, teacher assessments and information supplied by other schools. Continual assessment also forms part of the material at Key Stage 1 that is used to place children in their classes. Where children have been in England prior to their attendance at Cheetham Community School, all efforts are made to interact with the previous school, using any assessments they may have made. There is considerable flexibility in the system. The pupils' progress is reviewed every half-term and pupils are moved to alternative streams if this is appropriate.

After running this system for 3 years we felt it appropriate to undertake a review and reflect on its merits and limitations. Our aim in this chapter is to report these reflections in the hope that others will find them informative when making their own policy decisions. Our review has been facilitated by involvement with the Manchester and Salford Schools Consortium. This has given us some time and resources and access to research expertise.

The review took place in the later part of the 1997/98 academic year and utilised a number of sources of evidence. First, we looked at the findings of existing research on ability grouping in schools. We were helped considerably here by two already published reviews of research on this issue (Harlen and Malcolm, 1997; Hallam and Toutounji, 1996). Second, we examined data on educational outcomes in the school over the 3 years our streaming system has been running and, in the case of academic outcomes, compared these with data from earlier years. Third, we elicited the views of the teachers in the school, exploring what they thought were the advantages and disadvantages of the system. Finally, we looked at the views and perceptions of some of the pupils in the school. In what follows we report what we found out from these different sources and the general conclusions of our review.

Existing research on ability grouping in the primary school

The two reviews we looked at, which are in part based on previous reviews (especially Gregory, 1984, and Slavin, 1987), cover a large and complex field of research. Clearly a substantial number of studies, especially in the US, have focused on the impact of different forms of ability grouping. However, as the reviews point out, there are complex methodological problems in researching these issues, and consequently the results of individual studies are often inconclusive. Moreover, different studies tend to point in different directions so that it is difficult to synthesise findings and extract clear or conclusive lessons from the body of research.

This said, our impression on reading the reviews was that most studies have found that streaming, when compared with mixed-ability grouping, has no significant overall effects on pupil achievements. Where there are effects streaming seems to benefit more able pupils, who make better progress than their counterparts in mixed-ability classes, and disadvantage less able pupils, who make worse progress than their counterparts. Another common finding seems to be that streaming tends to result in more favourable treatment for pupils in higher-ability groups. These groups tend to develop more academic and work-orientated cultures, and their teachers tend to be more enthusiastic, more motivated and have higher expectations. Some studies also seem to suggest that streaming tends to have a negative effect on the attitudes, self-esteem and consequent motivation of pupils placed in lower-ability groups, and that some polarisation of attitudes between pupils in high and low groups occurs. Overall the research suggests that there are no significant advantages in terms of achievement to be gained from streaming, but several possible negative consequences in terms of equity and pupil attitudes.

The two reviews also discussed a smaller study carried out, mainly in the USA, on setting for particular subjects in primary schools. A number of studies (though not all) here report that on average pupils make more progress in setted groups than in mixed-ability groups for maths and reading, as long as the teaching and teaching materials are adjusted for the pupils' needs.

Thus, as far as we could tell from these reviews, previous research provided no support for our streaming policy. Indeed, it raised significant doubts in our minds about the appropriateness of our policy. It did, however, suggest that setting for key subjects could be a positive alternative.

Educational outcomes for pupils pre- and post-streaming

Academic attainment

Table 11.1 shows the Key Stage 2 National Test results for three different cohorts of our children – the 1995 group who had been taught in mixed-ability classes, the 1997 group who had been taught for two of their junior years in streamed classes and the 1998 group who had been streamed for most of their junior years.

Table 11.1 Key Stage 2 national test results showing percentages with Level 4 and above

	1995*	1997†	1998‡
English	41%	70%	72%
Maths	50%	91%	88%
Science	52%	86%	84%

*Mixed-ability classes in Years 3–6.
†Classes in Years 5 and 6.
‡Streamed classes in Years 3–6.

These data show a considerable difference in the Key Stage 2 achievement levels of the mixed-ability and streamed cohorts. Much higher proportions of the 1997 and 1998 streamed cohorts achieved Level 4 and above in the core subjects than in the 1995 mixed-ability cohort.

Our first impressions were that these data indicated that our streaming policy had had a quite dramatic effect on the levels of children's attainment, and that this contradicted the findings of previous research. Perhaps in our particular case streaming had led to better pupil performance. This view was supported by the views of several colleagues (see pp. 146–148), who argued that streaming allowed more effective planning and teaching, and a more efficient distribution of resources, and that these resulted in better Key Stage 2 results.

However, further reflection led us to temper this judgement. We recognised that there were several other factors that might explain the different performance of the cohorts. One is that there could have been substantive differences in the ability levels in the different cohorts; however, on investigating teacher assessments and the external tests used in school such as NFER, no such significant evidence could be found. One important factor that may have affected results was a change in national regulations that allowed for the 'disapplication' of some Year 6 children who had been in the country less than 12 months in the 1995 mixed-ability cohort. A decision at senior management level was made not to exclude children for future tests. There is some evidence to suggest that those children from 1997 onwards who were in danger of not achieving Level 4 actually received extra, more focused teaching in English, which resulted in approximately half achieving Level 4. In 1995 a similar group of children had no such extra support. Another possible factor is that the teachers in the school became more adept at preparing children for Key Stage 2 National Tests. Certainly, over the years we are discussing, this was probably the case at Cheetham. Anecdotal evidence from discussions suggests that teachers became more aware of what the tests measured and how they were conducted, and this probably affected their teaching and the ways they prepared children. There is also the possibility that changes in the Key Stage 2 tests, their administration and marking mean that the results do not provide the basis for valid comparisons between the cohorts.

We recognised that these possibilities could not be discounted, and so we became much more sceptical about our initial conclusion that streaming had had a positive impact on attainment levels at Key Stage 2.

Attitudes to school

The other outcome we considered was the children's attitudes to school. Some of the previous research on ability grouping had suggested that streaming tends to result in a polarisation of children's attitudes to school, such that those placed in top streams develop positive attitudes and those assigned to low streams develop negative attitudes (this is also related to subsequent differences in academic achievement). We did not have the time or resources to test this causal hypothesis in a detailed way. This would have required monitoring changes in children's attitudes from the beginning of Year 3, when they were placed in streams, to the end of Year 6. All we were able to do was to compare the attitudes of Years 5 and 6 children in different streams. We felt this would at least give us some clues about whether streaming had had an impact on attitudes. We speculated that if we found no significant differences in the attitudes of children in the different streams then we might reasonably conclude that streaming had not had an impact. On the other hand, we felt that if we did find a difference then streaming might be implicated.

In order to examine children's attitudes we utilised a slightly adapted version of 'The Smiley Scale' questionnaire developed by Mortimore *et al.* (1988) during their research on school effectiveness to measure primary school children's attitudes to school (see also West and Sammons, 1991; Davies and Brember, 1994). The questionnaire was administered in each class with the assistance of the class teacher. Children were asked to rank their feelings towards twenty different aspects of school life, including various subject activities, homework, school rules and teachers, on a five-point scale: 5 indicated that they felt very positive and 1 indicated that they felt very negative. They were also asked to rank their feelings about two further items in the same way: how they felt about school in general and how happy they felt in school. We used these rankings to produce two scores for each pupil. One scored the pupils' attitudes to aspects of school life on a scale ranging from 20 (negative) to 100 (positive). The other scored the pupils' general attitudes on a scale ranging from 2 (negative) to 10 (positive).

Table 11.2 Year group data showing attitudes of children in each year group

	Year 5	Year 6
Negative attitude (< 60)	3	2
Moderately positive attitude (60–80)	8	6
Very positive attitude (> 80)	33	37

Table 11.3 Class data showing attitudes of children in the three streams across Years 5 and 6

	Class 1 (top)	Class 2 (middle)	Class 3 (bottom)
Negative attitude (< 60)	1	2	2
Moderately positive attitude (60–80)	4	5	5
Very positive attitude (> 80)	28	23	19

Table 11.2 shows the average of the two scores for the children in each year group, and Table 11.3 the average of the two scores for the children in each stream across the two year groups. Numbers of children with negative attitude (below sixty), moderately positive attitude (sixty-eighty) and very positive attitude (eighty plus) are shown.

These figures suggest that the vast majority of the children had positive attitudes to school. In fact most had very positive attitudes. More significantly for our purposes, there was little significant difference in the attitudes of children in the three streams. The mean scores on the two scales were very similar for each class, as were the proportions of children falling into the three attitude categories. The data showed few signs, then, of any polarisation effect.

This was confirmed by the accounts of the three class teachers who reported that most of the children in their respective classes were positively orientated to school, and by general observations of children's behaviour in school which did not suggest any great difference between the three classes in terms of pro- or anti-school behaviour.

Teachers' views of the streaming system

To discover the teachers' views about the streaming system we distributed a questionnaire to all staff. This consisted of nineteen open questions, which encouraged teachers to give their views in detail. Nine teachers completed the questionnaire. We supplemented this with data from informal conversations and a discussion at a staff meeting. We divided the data into three broad categories: teachers' perceptions of the effect of streaming on their teaching; teachers' views about the benefits of the system; and their views about its limitations. One problem we experienced in analysing these data was of differentiating teachers' perceptions of the system in operation at the school from their views about ability grouping in general. As far as possible we concentrated on the former.

Seven of the teachers who completed the questionnaire felt that streaming had affected their teaching methods. One said his methods had changed very little and the other (a newly qualified teacher) said she was unable to comment because she had no experience of mixed-ability teaching. Most of the seven mentioned utilising more whole class teaching and being able to interact for longer with larger groups of children. Some also said that they were more able to keep children together on common tasks so that the class worked more as one, and that classroom management was therefore easier. Several also commented that where tasks were differentiated, a narrower range and fewer in-class groups were needed. One teacher suggested less time was wasted continually repeating explanations and instructions, and another that children spent more time on task as a result. Two teachers of the top groups commented on being able to work at a faster pace, covering more material, with children working more independently of them. A teacher of a lower group said she was able to break down learning tasks into smaller, more manageable units, and could provide resources which were more understandable for the pupils.

Six of the teachers also said that streaming made their planning easier and more effective. They felt that, because they were catering for a narrower range of ability and needed to give less attention to differentiation, their planning, and the materials they used in class, were of better quality. Two teachers of the lower groups, however, mentioned increased demands preparing appropriate materials and liaising with Section

11 support staff. The latter was a key issue for one teacher who felt the job of teaching the lower groups was much harder.

With the exception of these last two comments, the changes mentioned were seen as beneficial. In fact most teachers emphasised the positive impact they felt streaming had had on their teaching and consequently on the learning experiences of the children. A number of other advantages were also mentioned. Three teachers pointed to the advantages of being able to target Section 11 resources more effectively at children in the lower stream, thus providing children who were at a disadvantage in terms of English with more support. Two teachers argued that the system introduced greater competition, which encouraged children to aspire to a higher group (or fear allocation to a lower group) and pushed all children to work harder. They emphasised the benefits of a meritocratic hierarchy, especially in a situation where children's achievement levels were relatively fluid. Another teacher said she felt that the system stretched the most able children while enabling targeted support to be provided for the least able. Another pointed to the challenges which she felt teachers could provide for those in the top groups while ensuring a secure environment for those in the lower groups. Similarly, one teacher claimed that lower-achieving children were less overawed in streamed groups, and another that streaming avoided the dominance of mixed-ability classes by the able, articulate few. In lower groups, this teacher suggested, less able children could experience success without attention continually being drawn to their relatively low level of achievement.

However, most of the teachers also recognised problems with the streaming system. The concerns raised were mainly about equity. Three teachers suggested that the children in the lower groups were disadvantaged because they had few high-achieving role models and a less stimulating linguistic environment. Two teachers argued that allocation to a low group sometimes had a negative impact on pupils' self-esteem and motivation, and pointed to the dangers of 'type-casting' pupils at an early age and of consequent self-fulfilling prophecies. Two others commented on the way streaming reinforced status hierarchies among the pupils and influenced pupils' perceptions of each other, sometimes causing 'nastiness' and 'unkindness' in their relationships. Another teacher felt that, despite the targeting of Section 11 resources at the lower groups, the top classes enjoyed more favourable opportunities (for example, in Music and out-of-school activities). This teacher also drew attention to what she thought was the inequity of the system for teachers. She claimed that certain teachers had been given the lower-ability classes for a number of years while others stayed with the top classes. She felt that this was unfair because the preparation workload required in the former classes was much higher, and because teaching these classes was more difficult. She also argued that teaching the lower groups was less rewarding in the long term, and that there was a danger of teachers' losing enthusiasm and consequently providing less effective teaching for the pupils in these groups.

Another problem recounted by three teachers concerned the practice of placing pupils in a stream for all their subject work on the basis of their competence in English. They felt this was sometimes inappropriate because a pupil's capability in other subjects could be very different. In fact, they pointed out that in reality the streamed classes contained a wide ability range, particularly in maths and science. This range was made wider by the mixed-age nature of classes. They suggested that sometimes streaming gave the impression that classes were more uniform than was actually the case, leading teachers to neglect differentiation.

So on balance how did the teachers feel about the streaming system? The final question on our questionnaire asked them to say whether they felt the advantages of the system outweighed the limitations or the reverse. Five teachers thought that, on balance, the system had been beneficial, although one said that there was relatively little to choose between streaming and mixed-ability systems. She felt that the quality of teachers was a much more important issue. Only one teacher felt that the system's limitations outweighed its advantages. Two teachers said they were undecided and one (the newly qualified teacher) said she did not feel able to make a judgement.

Pupils' perceptions and views of the streaming system

In order to explore the pupils' perceptions and views of the streaming system we conducted group interviews with all Year 5 and 6 children. Each class teacher selected groups of three or four children at a time and we asked them to ensure that the children they chose represented as far as possible the range of children in their class in terms of ability. Peter, Mike or Helen, who utilised a short list of common questions, conducted the interviews in a quiet area adjacent to the children's classroom. The interviews were tape-recorded and partially transcribed.

Several themes emerged from the analysis. The first was that all the children (as far as we could tell; note the problems of judging the perceptions of individual children on the basis of group interviews) recognised that there were three hierarchically ordered classes in Years 5 and 6 and three similar classes in Years 3 and 4, and that there were clear differences between them. All recognised too that the classes were differentiated in terms of some notion of academic ability or achievement. The children utilised dimensions such as 'clever ... not so clever', 'better able .... less able', 'speak English well ... cannot speak English well', 'successful with their work .... struggling with their work', 'doing harder work ... doing easier work', and so on to describe the differences between the three classes, and provided generalised descriptions of the three classes in these terms.

Thus, the children saw the streaming system as a status hierarchy in which those in the top class were seen as better than others in terms of the qualities valued in school. They had clearly learned some lessons from aspects of the school's 'hidden curriculum'. It seems logical to deduce from this that class placement framed the children's perceptions of each other, and of themselves. There were some indications of this in the data. For example, some of the children in Class 1 spoke in rather condescending terms about 'Class 3 kids', and about themselves in rather superior ways. And one Class 3 group spoke of being regarded as 'the baby group' by others and of being upset by this. However, we did not explore this issue in great depth.

A second theme that emerged was that most children seemed to see the streaming system as fairly fluid. There was quite a lot of talk in the discussions about the movement of children between streams, especially from Class 3 to Class 2. Several groups explained that children were placed in Class 3 because their English was poor, sometimes because they had recently arrived in the country, and that once their English had improved they were able to move up to a higher class. So despite their use of terms such as 'clever' or 'bright', the children did not seem to see the attributes which gave individuals status in the system as necessarily fixed. Several also noted that children in Class 3 were often very good at subjects such as maths and science (a point which several in that class were keen to emphasise), which suggested that they recognised various lines of differentiation and that stream placement was not an overriding academic label.

Most children also seemed to regard the allocation of places in the streaming system as meritocratic and fair. There were no complaints by children that they or others had been wrongly placed, and most thought the way places were decided was legitimate. However, some children did complain that the top class sometimes had more opportunities to 'do interesting work', 'to do things like Music and Art' or 'go on trips and visits'. And there was very definitely a feeling among many children (particularly in the top and middle class) that the top class had a better teacher and in this sense perhaps received more favourable treatment. On the other hand, some children pointed out that Class 3 was much smaller and had more teachers so the children got more individual attention. As one Class 3 child said, 'There's sometimes four teachers in here. You can't get away from them!' What the children seemed to be saying was that, although there was inequality in some senses in the treatment of the three classes, it was balanced by inequality in other senses.

Another theme which emerged in these group interviews was that streaming had an effect on children's social relationships. Most children said that they spent their free time and were most friendly with others from the same class. Unsurprisingly, this was particularly the case with children who had remained in the same group during their junior years. Several children also commented on animosities between the different classes, which seemed to have been influenced by the status differences between them. They explained that there were sometimes outbreaks of name-calling, with Class 3 children calling Class 1 children 'snobs' and 'big-heads', and Class 1 children calling Class 3 children 'thickies' or 'dummies'.

What then did the children think about the merits of the streaming system? In all the discussions the children emphasised what they felt were the system's benefits. The most common view expressed was that grouping children in this way allowed teachers to set work and activities at the right level for all the children in the class. Most of the children felt that the work they were given in their class at the moment was about the right level for them, although a few children in Class 3 complained that their work was sometimes too easy and some in Class 1 said that their work was sometimes too difficult. A related benefit, which was frequently mentioned, was that the teacher could teach all the children together. Here most of the children seemed to feel that whole class teaching was more effective than teaching individuals or groups at different levels. One Class 2 group said that they thought teachers would waste a lot of time explaining things in different ways to different groups and to children who did not understand. Another common view was that in a mixed-ability class 'clever children would get bored or held back' and 'not so clever children would get left behind or struggle to keep up'. One of the Class 1 groups also argued that there would be more 'jealousy and arguments in a mixed class because people would be at different stages'. Thus, the children's views were very much in favour of the streaming system. This said, we should recognise that very few of the children had had recent experience of anything else, and their comparisons were therefore hypothetical.

Reflections

We have tried to review our system of streaming by utilising a number of different sources of evidence. What, then, have we learned from this review? Perhaps the first thing we have learned is how difficult it is to establish with confidence whether or not such a system brings benefits. Our reading of academic research suggests its findings are equivocal, and the data we were able to collect in school were inevitably limited. Nevertheless, we believe that these sources of evidence did encourage a higher level of discussion about the issue than would have occurred had they been unavailable, and they did allow us to make a more informed judgement.

We concluded from our review (somewhat tentatively) that our system had avoided some of the problems that previous research has associated with streaming. For example, we felt on balance that there was little evidence of serious inequity in the treatment of different classes, or of a significant negative effect on pupil attitudes. We also felt that streaming had brought some positive gains. Most staff felt that they were able to teach more effectively with a more limited achievement range in the class, and the children seemed to favour the whole class teaching that resulted. Some staff also felt that the system enabled a more effective targeting of additional Section 11 resources. To what extent these benefits resulted in the increased levels of performance indicated by our National Test results is difficult to tell, but we think there is a possibility that they played a part.

However, we also concluded that our system had drawbacks. Some teachers expressed concerns about equity of treatment in certain respects, and about differences in the workload between teachers. Doubts were also raised about the merit of grouping children for all their lessons on the basis of their competence in English. Our reflection on the data from pupils also raised concerns about what the system of streaming communicated to them about status in general and their own worth in particular, and about its impact on social relationships.

For these reasons, and also because of the impending introduction of the National Literacy Strategy in 1998 and the National Numeracy Strategy in 1999, the outcome of our review was a decision to change our system somewhat. We decided from September 1998 to introduce a system of subject setting in the junior school for core subjects, which would be taught largely in the mornings. Our hope is that this will preserve what we think are the advantages of grouping children at similar achievement levels together, but at the same time eliminate some of the disadvantages of the streaming system.

Note

We are sad to say that both Peter Foster and Helen White died before this book was published.

References

Davies, L. and Brember, I. (1994) The reliability and validity of the 'Smiley' Scale. *British Educational Research Journal*, 20(4): 447–454.

Gregory, R.P. (1984) Streaming, setting and mixed-ability grouping in primary and secondary schools: some research findings. *Educational Studies,* 10(3): 209–226.

Hallam, S. and Toutounji, I. (1996) *What Do We Know About the Grouping of Pupils by Ability: a Research Review.* London: Institute of Education.

Harlen, W. and Malcolm, H. (1997) *Setting and Streaming: a Research Review.* Edinburgh: Scottish Council for Educational Research.

Mortimore, P. , Sammons, P. , Stoll, L, Lewis, D. and Ecob, R. (1988) *School Matters: the Junior Years.* Wells: Open Books.

Slavin (1987) Ability grouping and student achievement in elementary schools: a best evidence synthesis. *Review of Educational Research,* 57(3): 293–336.

West, A. and Sammons, P. (1991) *The Measurement of Children's Attitudes Towards School. The Use of the 'Smiley' Scale.* London: Centre for Educational Research, LSE.

Part 3

Reflections upon collaborative research

Chapter 12

Working together

The long spoons and short straws of collaboration

Ian Stronach and Olwen McNamara

Introduction

We have two purposes in this chapter. Our primary intent is to think about 'partnerships' such as our own by exploring what the word means for externally funded research projects involving schools, HEIs and LEAs. What is a 'partnership'? When do you know you've got a good one? Were we good partners, the TTA, the LEAs, the schools and the HEIs? It's such a delicate balance. 'Not good enough', and of course we fail; 'too good' and we fail again, promoting the partnership as an end in itself instead of as a means to an end. 'Just right' and we still fail, inventing some impossible spot beyond uncomfortable compromises: a place where all may pirouette without prejudice.

We may, for example, begin to see a glimmer of 'partnership' – casting an educational light – that makes it possible to say things in school meetings that were not otherwise said:

> ... those interviews that Dave did with different staff members on professionalism ... he took them out and just presented them as quotes at a staff meeting. Everyone looked and said, no, I never put children under pressure and Tony the Head said, 'hang about, but surely that is what we do do'. We all turned round and said, yes, we actually do ... It went on for days. It was brought up at coffee-time and the infants [teachers] got involved then and wanted to know what we were all talking about. It was quite interesting to see that, sort of, flourish really – apart from what are you doing at Asda today, what is your shopping list? We were professionally discussing the quotes.

The above quotation is about successful collaboration, at least on the surface. We would argue that 'real' partnership (never a stable or final achievement, always a work in progress) began in moments like these, but it is important to get behind the rhetoric. Our secondary intention in this chapter then is to delve beyond the notion of partnership, in order to understand what it really means, in the turbulent context within which innovations such as ours have to develop.

We want to start, however, with the idea of partnership – as a problem to be solved – and not assume that it is a fantasy solution of some kind (like a 'perfect marriage'). As with most things in education, the notion is both complicated and contradictory. To start with we will take a look at partnership from a number of different angles in order to get contrasting perspectives on the problem – ideological, social, philosophical and educational. Having skirted the problem from a number of these viewpoints, we will then take Bratman's (1992) account of 'partnership' as a useful philosophical starting point, although eventually we will try to go beyond his ideas. But we can give you most of our answer now: 'partnership' is not really about consensus. Rather, it is a paradox – more like managed difference or productive dissonance. And that becomes a problem only when partnership is portrayed as unproblematic, because hidden in that pretence is a power-play. (If I can make you do what I say and persuade you to call it partnership, I double my hold over you. A 'perfect marriage' indeed!)

Ideological

The most obvious angle of 'partnership', perhaps, is that it belongs in the 'first eleven' of political weasel words (the rest might include such notables as empowerment, effectiveness, quality, transparency – see Strathern (2000) for a sceptical team selection). In such company, partnership might be seen as a good word more in appearance than in reality; for as Edelman (1972) observed in his book subtitled 'words that succeed and policies that fail', it can offer 'disguised coercion'. It is a word that may mean a lot more than it says. But it is certainly a word that succeeds.

What is the track record of education 'partnerships'? Crozier's study of Initial Teacher Education partnerships (Crozier *et al.* 1990) identifies it as a 'slippery and imprecise word'. She concludes that teacher trainers found that their 'good' word was hijacked and used to hide the change to a model of school-based 'apprenticeship'. In this interpretation partnership was used to disguise a shift from 'professionalism' to 'vocationalism'. This version of 'partnership' views it as the handshake that turns out to be an arm lock. Similarly, education/business partnerships have been seen as attempts to vocationalise the curriculum, and to shift the balance of power from the education profession to the business world, via happy talk of joint ventures between educators and employers to raise the performance of learners. In the USA, Klein has recently offered powerful criticism of business intrusion into schools and universities: she accuses corporate business of seeking to colonise the 'unbranded space' of public institutions (Klein 2000, p. 105). She sees an unequal 'partnership' whereby global 'brands' like Nike and Coca Cola buy their way into the school or college with information technology inducements. Moving into the arena of home–school liaison, Crozier (1998) identifies 'partnership' as a surveillance mechanism. It extends the reach of the school into the home: 'partnership' as the inspectorial eye. Vincent and Tomlinson (1997), on the other hand, compare the 'soft' talk of partnership with its increasing use in 'home–school' contracts as a way of making parents act as, and on behalf of, teachers. This time, it's the invisible hand (made invisible by the glove of partnership), but in each case there is a power struggle going on. The ways in which such 'partners' seek to manipulate each other are complex and contradictory (McNamara *et al.*, 2000).

Partnership, then, is a good word that often keeps bad company. It is alleged to get up to some nasty tricks on behalf of the state (Todd and Higgins, 1998), with the language of 'stake-holders' and 'business partners' sometimes acting as code for the attempted transfer of power from one institution or group to another. Such power struggles were integral to our project both across, and within, institutions:

HEI/LEA staff: What do you want out of it [the project]?

| Teacher 1: | We wouldn't have been allowed to be involved in any way ... if it wasn't an idea to get better SATs results in the year 2000 ... |
| Teacher 2: | If they wine you and dine you like this I don't mind.' [Friday evening writing weekend, close to the end of the project]. |

It is also worth looking at research on 'partnership' with an eye to how various authors 'rescue' this fallen word – e.g. 'real' partnership, 'genuine' dialogue, 'flexible mutuality' (Todd and Higgins, 1998). The formula always promises a sort of utopian cure, where words will come to have their true meanings once more/at last. Yet the idea that partnership is necessarily about disagreement, always in need of re-negotiation, never fixed in meaning, is seldom considered.

Such a perspective has implications for how we go about accounting for ourselves as a 'partnership'. If we see the word as highly ideological, and part of a contest (for power, the intellectual high ground, resources, etc.) between government and profession, between school and HEI, between HEI and LEA, or even between teachers and pupils, then it follows that we must take an interest in how the idea is put into practice, and to what end. We may need to focus on the implicit meanings of the word, over time and across sites. For example, the two extracts below illustrate both something of the suspicions early in the project, and of the changing relations between the various parties:

Teacher 1:	I look at you and think 'what are you getting out of this?'
HEI/LEA staff:	Yeh, we're all in the ring looking fairly suspiciously at each other.
Teacher 1:	I know that the conversations that we have in the car park are very different to the ones that go on in the room. With the LEA involved, some things cannot be said ...

Teacher 2:	The data [pupil interviews] were really good. It brought me up short. There was a point when I looked at it and I thought 'here I am doing this for them [the pupils]' and, you know...
HEI/LEA staff:	... ungrateful sods ...
Teacher 2:	Yeh, exactly ... then I looked at it again and I thought well they've got a point. And the whole thing is that if you're going to have children who feel part of their learning, you acknowledge that. So I discussed it with them.

Social

Almond (1991) identifies three human bonds, in which we may include partnership:

- biological and natural (e.g. sister);
- legal and artificial (e.g. apprentice);
- social and voluntary (e.g. friend).

She points to the tendency of bonding attempts of one kind (say, religion) to talk the language of another kind (family – father, son, brethren, etc.). Definitions of 'partnership' in education belong, of course, to the 'legal and artificial' category but are similarly attracted to 'family' relationships or 'friendship' metaphors (e.g. 'critical friend'). Similarly, industrial mentors form 'Big Brother and Big Sister partnerships' (O'Connell, 1985). Thus the metaphors of partnership are worth looking at for the ways in which they conjure up notions of relationship. In this way, 'partnership' may have a different meaning at the level of apparent purpose (what is supposed to happen, and to what effect) than at the level of actual relationship (how people really feel about their involvement, and on what grounds). We believe that our project had considerable success in translating its own 'legal and artificial' bonds into 'critical friend', 'peer' relationships or indeed ordinary friendships (without inverted commas). The evidence for such change lies in the crucial trivia of tea and biscuits, get-well cards, and so on. For the school teachers in the project, more than anyone else, this stood in direct contrast with relationships elsewhere:

HEI/LEA staff: One of the things I am hearing from you is, the loneliness of the long distance teacher.

Teacher 1:   Decisions are made for me and I become the implementer of those decisions. The things that I used to enjoy very much about teaching, thinking about ideas and ways of moving things forward, those decisions are already made for me and I am just the work-horse along with the staff really

Teacher 2:   The only time I feel anything about autonomy is when I deliberately disobey what someone else has told me to do.

It was a paradox of the project's 'confessional space' that it offered teachers the chance to express their feelings about a more general lack of autonomy.

Anthropologists also have a great deal to say about how human bonds and partnerships are created. They claim it is important to attend to the 'social' nature of such links and the need to convert 'artificial' into 'natural' bonds (Almond, 1991). For example, among the Desseneth (Ethiopia) successful partnerships tended to offer reciprocal assistance; warmth of relationship; exchange of goods (Almagor, 1978). Business management literature on partnership ('alliance' building) would also emphasise the first two of these (see Forrest, 1992), but we would not wish to ignore the value of an 'exchange of gifts' in a work context which was increasingly defined in terms of sticks rather than carrots:

Teacher 1:   ... provision of laptops, videos, subsequent discussion of practice ... being able to work with people as an activity.

Teacher 2:   [re recruiting colleagues to the project] ... they have not blackmailed them enough, I don't think. It obviously needs a cake on the staff-room table and a bottle of wine....

Such exchanges could even result in teachers trading their most precious 'gift', that of time:

Teacher 1:   Do you remember you said that it [the project] *gave* you time? I feel now that we *made* the time.

Teacher 2:   Yes, we prioritised where we wouldn't have done.

Teacher 1:   But I do think that we had the freedom to do that with the extra support that was there.

The argument so far suggests that we need to attend carefully to what 'partnership' both implied and came to be in reality. We have suggested that it is a complicated word that has to be read ideologically and socially and we will now explore in some detail a philosophical slant on partnership.

Philosophical

Bratman (1992) argues that partnership is a kind of shared cooperative activity. We will portray Bratman's argument and illustrate it with examples relating to partnership issues in the consortium. Bratman's account is useful because it directs our attention to some of the things that may be crucial in the establishing and maintaining of 'partnership'. He identifies three aspects of 'cooperative activity' that we find easy to illustrate from our experiences in the project. These are the notions of *mutual responsiveness; commitment to joint activity; commitment to mutual support.* Our intention is to use this philosophical clarification in order to explore the much muddier realities of 'partnership' in practice. This is necessary because, as we mentioned earlier, words like 'partnership' (or 'research-based', or 'school-owned') do not have 'meanings' so much as 'leanings', in one ideological direction or another. However, taken along with a careful examination of the different roles and levels in any partnership it may help us to provide richer possibilities for thinking about notions of partnership in future.

Mutual responsiveness

Bratman's first criterion is mutual responsiveness, in which each party responds to the intentions and actions of the other, knowing the other will behave similarly. But mutual responsiveness, Bratman suggests, is not enough: *enemy soldiers may behave in such a way towards each other.*

The research-based consortia initiative sprang from a heated national debate about educational research begun by the TTA – self-styled 'catalyst for change' in this highly political arena. In promoting 'teaching as a research-based profession' the TTA (1996) sought to 'improve the accessibility of the existing stock of knowledge; improve the quality and relevance of research; [and] help teachers play a more active role in conceiving, implementing, evaluating and disseminating research'. This led to claims by some educational researchers that the TTA wanted to 'get its hands on' university research funding (Millet, 1996). Allegations about the relevance, quality, accessibility, credibility, applicability, etc., of educational research for teachers were made by other educational researchers (e.g. TTA Annual Lecture, Hargreaves, 1996). Battle ensued, with heated responses (Hammersley, 1997) and rejoinders (Hargreaves, 1997).

Such was the educational research landscape in autumn 1997 when the 'school-based consortia' initiative began. Battle lines were quickly drawn. Did 'research-based' mean 'evidence-based' and did it mean better outcomes, or another quick fix? Did evidence-based approaches add to professional autonomy and status, or were they a technology that denied 'craft' knowledge and made a technician out of the teacher? Surely teachers' broad 'repertoire' of skills could not be reduced to a 'recipe'? Summer 1998 saw the launch of two further criticisms of educational research: Tooley and Darby (1998) , funded by OfSTED, were closely followed by Hillage et al. (1988) , funded by the DfEE. Both criticised the relevance and utility of educational research to policy and practice, but in different ways, adding to the negative perceptions of educational research. Reynolds (1998), launching the TTA Corporate Plan 1998–2001, then waded in, denouncing D-I-Y and prescribing a 'technology of teaching'. Our project both gained and lost from these conflicts. Clearly, we were trying to be relevant and classroom-focused, but teacher-researchers could be criticised for offering an amateur, 'cottage-industry' solution.

In the early days of our partnership, direct encounters with the protagonists in the debate included regular, but relatively minor, confrontations in the boardroom of the TTA where 'key contacts' of our consortium (Bill Rogers, Olwen McNamara and the elected chair), and the other consortia, met with the National Steering Group. The latter included representatives of all the major educational stakeholders (HEIs, LEAs, schools, OfSTED, DfEE, QCA, TTA, etc.). They were not immune to the controversy, and nor indeed were we as a team. A further, and to us, rather more distressing assault came when we (two HEI researchers) and two teacher colleagues offered a presentation of work in progress at the CARN (Collaborative Action Research Network) conference in October 1998. It was a hostile reception. How could this be called proper research? Was it supposed to be generalisable? Were we not traitors to the cause of educational research accepting funding from the TTA? It was not exactly CARNage, but some did have to lick their wounds, while others were 'bloody but unbowed'!

So there was no shortage of 'mutual responsiveness', and we could quite see the force of Bratman's observation that such a criterion might include hostile relationships with our various 'partners', broadly defined. Indeed, we could also see that neither were 'we' united in our beliefs. There was no shortage of potential conflict between partners.

Commitment to joint activity

Bratman's second criterion is that the participants should share an appropriate commitment to the joint activity, but not necessarily for the same reasons, and their mutual responsiveness should support this commitment. There are two aspects to this:

(a) An 'appropriate' commitment may mean that each intends to carry out the joint action, but perhaps for different reasons. In which case, there must be *meshing sub-plans*. That is, sub-plans may be different so long as they are not mutually exclusive, and each party must be committed to the fulfilment of the other's sub-plans as well as to the joint activity. It is also a condition that there is common knowledge of these joint intentions.

An appropriate commitment to joint action will include the public and contracted goals, and, inevitably, the individual sub-plans of the participants, made up of multiple agendas, some of which will be kept private. For example, a common suspicion in education partnerships is that the partners harbour unexpressed grievances about the other, concerning their location, e.g. 'ivory tower academics'; motives, e.g. promotion, deficit budgets, falling roles, resources, the Research Assessment Exercise, inspections; different work patterns, e.g. holidays (or lack of them); and different assessments of potential costs and benefits. In particular, the parties varied in terms of their commitment to the project, in relation to other demands (clashing sub-plans) in school, LEA or HEI.

Even if the joint intentions of the four partners initially 'mesh', over time events will occur that cause tensions. For example, sub-plans may change, e.g. initial school commitments with regard to research focus shift in response to external forces and internal redefinition of priorities. OfSTED inspection is an example of this. Clauses in the contractual agreement may cause tensions between partners, e.g. it became apparent that aggregate 'consortium interests' at times conflicted with individual 'school-ownership' of research. The meanings which individual partners bring to the contractual agreements may become clear only in its enactment, e.g. discrepant notions of pedagogy held by the partners became apparent. Subtle shifts may occur in the nature of partners' engagement with each other (as 'legal and artificial' bonds acquired a 'social and voluntary' dimension) enabling them to revise the initial plot.

In general, this meant that 'implementation' of the project was always a matter of negotiation and compromise, not with the outcome of actually 'meshing sub-plans' so much as minimising 'clashing sub-plans' and creating a spirit of creative compromise in which 'social and voluntary' ties could prosper. For example, a variety of relationships emerged among the TTA, LEA, HEI and teachers. These included HEI/LEA working with schools to establish research design and process, assist the school in data collection and analysis, provide literature, write and present joint papers or almost wholly conducted the research themselves.

The changes in school priorities, the demands of OfSTED inspections and other innovations, such as the Literacy and Numeracy Strategies, all resulted in clashing sub-plans that had to be fairly frequently renegotiated. Sometimes these were individual renegotiations, sometimes between the HEI researcher and the teacher-researcher, or the project coordinator and the school. Sometimes they were collective decisions. And, of course, it was not just the schools that were subject to multiple and shifting demands; both the LEA and the HEI faced new demands on their commitments over time.

(b) Partnership must mean the *free agency of each party* and the *absence of coercion and* manipulation.

The notion of 'free agency', as we have already noted, is particularly utopian, and the circumstances in which the LEA and the HEI initially recruited the group of schools in order to bid for TTA funding were far from ideal. Notions of autonomy ran thin. There were inevitably top-down coercive influences implicit in the power structures of the negotiating parties (Bill Rogers was Head of the Manchester Inspection and Advisory Service). There were probably also sideways pressures ('I'll do it if you will', 'if St Cuthbert's are involved we don't want to be left out') from other schools in the group, all of which were in a tightly knit geographic and economic area. LEAs wanted to invest in a deprived area. Heads sought resources. Teachers were more or less committed, according to the initial nature of their recruitment. A further layer of potential coercion was apparent between the initial and the final bid: it was felt that classroom teachers not Headteachers should be centrally involved and so Headteachers had to recruit staff to lead the research. Thus elements of coercion and manipulation were endemic to the 'partnership'.

Power was also unequal within individual school projects. Each operated independently, linked with an advisor from the HEI/LEA. This proved to be a strength and also a weakness. HEI/LEA staff find it difficult to avoid a paternalist 'partnership' with individual teachers, in which their perceived superiority is defined in terms of things like hierarchy, research experience, professional status, etc. Attempts at empowerment of teachers, therefore, could easily fail. Again, a power dynamic inevitably operates between employers (the LEA) and employees (the teachers). Put another way, the scriptwriters (HEI) were privileged over the producer/directors (LEA) and the actors (teachers). Gender inequities added a further dimension to the developing picture. In its original formulation all but two of the teachers were women; all but one of the HEI/LEA were men. In addition, the seven men from the HEI/LEA were in positions of considerable power (inspectors, professors, principal lecturers, etc.); the eighth (a woman) breached convention in that she was at one and the same time the most powerful (as project coordinator) and the least (as Senior Research Fellow). Apart from the teachers that is.

A tempting conclusion would be that teachers end up bottom of the pile, whatever the talk about partnership, empowerment, critical friends, action research, co-researchers, and so on. But not necessarily. A judicious reading of the TTA might see it making all partners equal but some (teachers) more equal than others. Teachers, it will be recalled, in the TTA grand plan were to play a larger role in all phases of research – 'conceiving, evaluating, implementing and disseminating'. Again, a different power relation between teachers and the HEI can be seen in the TTA 'teacher research grant' partnership agreements in which the grant holders (teachers) use funds to buy support from HEI colleagues. In so doing the TTA disrupts the unequal relation between teacher and HEI and rebuilds instead a 'different-but-equal' model. The teacher, in this account, becomes more of a 'free agent', the HEI colleague less so. We might speculate whether the equality spawned by such a voluntary agreement, regulated by contract, brought an increased subordination to the TTA.

We concluded that the notion of 'free agency' was the least useful of Bratman's categories. Obligations were many, various in kind, and conflicting. More important was the way in which participants 'grew spaces', dealt with 'clashing sub-plans' and traded commitments against restraints. In our account, freedom was not the absence of coercion, so much as its subversion.

Commitment to mutual support

Bratman's third criterion is that each partner supports the efforts of the other in the joint activity, and so makes possible a successful performance. There are three aspects to this:

(a) Each agent must look out for and support the goals of the other, as well as their own.

(b) Such support must not be restricted to 'pre-packaged' cooperation at the beginning of the joint activity. That is, not only must there be 'mutual responsiveness of intention' but support offered must include 'mutual responsiveness in action'. It must be an ongoing concern.
(c) Support cannot mean cooperation at one level and competition at another – as in a game of chess where rules are a cooperative agreement and the 'game' is a competition.

> The eight initial research pairs had a shared research goal in the need to produce an account of their research, and a measure of some kind of outcome. Positively and negatively, it locked them together, even when each had obvious 'clashing sub-plans', as for example when partners had priorities elsewhere, in teaching, OfSTED concerns, other research projects or support obligations. The identification of a common research theme across the schools also developed a more collective loyalty across the projects, and gave the teachers more reasons to cooperate. It gave the projects more of a shared agenda, within which 'mutual responsiveness' developed. So too did it assist with the change from 'artificial' to 'friendship' bonds. The emergence of the 'book project' – to which all would contribute – as well as a CD Rom increased both individual and group motivation by promising (and threatening) a public arena in which the pairs' and the group's work would be visible. The prospect of an eventual public scrutiny was a powerful prompt for an ongoing 'reflexive' concern for each other's progress in individual and group research work.
>
> 'Mutual responsiveness' was also evident in some of the consortium's failed initiatives. For example, supply cover quickly became an important issue for schools. It was hard for class teachers, especially those with Year 2 and Year 6 classes, to rely on supply cover that was scarce and not always sufficiently competent. The pressures of the Literacy and Numeracy Strategies added to this reluctance. In addition to moving most meetings to the twilight slot, the consortium developed a bid to fund classroom assistants through the Government 'New Deal' initiative. The bid was foiled by factors outside its control, but it illustrated for everyone the willingness of the partners in the consortium to acknowledge and try to address each other's needs, to be a little speculative. Even its failure contributed to the fund of goodwill.

To conclude this section on partnership, Bratman's break-down of cooperation into components is a useful start to an in-depth understanding of an educational partnership. Criteria such as 'mutual responsiveness', 'joint action', 'meshing sub-plans' and ongoing commitment to the other's goals as well as your own are useful in analysing the conditions for successful partnership, and going beyond the empty calls for 'real' partnership and 'genuine dialogue'. But, as we suggested at the beginning of this chapter, it has its weaknesses. The most important of these is that Bratman builds his theory on assumptions of stability (relations stay the same), transparency (each can have perfect knowledge of the other) and ideal conditions (which can be separately defined and fostered). Our experience of partnership would put much more emphasis on the importance of how instability, uncertainty, difference and less than satisfactory conditions were handled.

Centrifugal versus centripetal pressures

Our own theory of how our 'partnership' developed has already illustrated centrifugal aspects (clashing sub-plans, pressures from other initiatives, promotions elsewhere) and centripetal features (moves from 'artificial' to 'friendship' links; successful joint completion of research tasks; the role of the coordinator in pulling people into the action and motivating them). So we need an account of partnership that has more movement in it than Bratman allows, or indeed most aspects of the 'ideological' and 'social' perspectives permit: these categories pin things down and pigeon-hole them too much. Like all multi-layered relationships we could think of the consortium as a social galaxy whose objects move in individual trajectories according to simultaneous forces of attraction and repulsion. The trajectories are not controlled by 'free agency', although they are always open to that possibility: there are almost always choices within limits as well as limits to choices. The coordinator, armed with the 'gravity' of will-power, strives to sustain as it were two orbits of participants: teachers who are pulled away by the overriding demands of everyday teaching, OfSTED pressures, promotion, etc; and HEI/LEA colleagues who accumulate new responsibilities and projects and therefore have to juggle with their commitments to the initiative. But as time goes on, the changing of the nature of the bonds from artificial to social (never complete or irreversible) strengthens the centripetal nature of the project. In this upending of the model, our partnership is better defined as collective activity in a permanently threatening state of unrealised dissolution, held together both freely and against its will. Such partnership is always a compromise within conflicting demands: it can only, therefore, be a risky business. More generally, it is a view of successful partnership that cannot be reduced to the sorts of formulae for 'good practice' so glibly represented in both the literature and the rhetoric of cooperation.

It also follows that consortium members can never have the perfect knowledge of each other's intentions etc. that Bratman as a tidy-minded philosopher would like. Those in the HEI/LEA colleague orbit know more about their partners in school than they do about other 'research linked pairs', including those involving their colleagues. They also attend to the nature of the school context since that is part of the research remit. The teachers on the other hand, have no project-based interest in the contexts within which the HEI operates. Thus the pairs do not look at each other in quite the same ways, leaving aside the other differences of hierarchy, status and gender. Those in the schools, through growing collective involvement, get to know each other much better. Thus the dynamics of partnership allocate different perspectives to the different partners. All have a partial view (in both senses of 'partial'). From Olwen's point of view, as coordinator, she has more information and personal knowledge than anyone else about both orbits, 'warts and all'. Such knowledge both informs and deforms a 'dispassionate perspective'. So if research implies a 'detachment', she is awkwardly placed for objective evaluation. In addition, of all the participants, she has the most at stake in this innovative enterprise, including a direct line of accountability to the TTA. Innovators fly in the face of considerable odds, and need to believe in their ability to do so successfully (just ask Icarus). Olwen must be Janus-like in her response to these pressures. First, as coordinator, she is drawn to think and then tell a corporate story as expressed within the language of the game that the project officially represents. Second, as researcher, she is drawn to join with others in talking *about*, rather than *within*, that game-playing, examining presentational surfaces, rhetorics of success, relating the case to others in the innovation literature and so on. That too is a legitimate and overt aim of the project. But the problems do not stop there, because those least caught up in the action are by definition poorest informed. It follows, certainly, that the 'true story' of the consortium is the one thing that cannot be told because it never happened (not as a single 'true story' at least). Any account that seeks to be comprehensive, then, has to treat partnership and project development as essentially a thing of differing perspectives. Preserving and re-telling these differences, and the dynamics behind them, is the task of this chapter. Ian felt 'ventriloquised in the first chapter ... uncomfortable with the "we" voice'. Olwen responded by writing a section at the end of the Introduction which drew the readers' attention to the inherently problematic nature of the authorial voice in both that chapter and subsequent ones. Another voice, however, is missing from this account: that of the most 'ventriloquised' and yet least spoken partner. That absence is about to be remedied too; now, as they say, 'a word from our sponsors' – the TTA – in the guise of Philippa Cordingley.

Scepticism and aspiration (a reflection from Philippa)

From a TTA perspective, this chapter reflects, in both content and style, the nature of its partnership with the consortium. The discussion about the nature of partnership encapsulates the 'pessimism of the intellect and optimism of the will' that Anton Gramsci (1971) refers to as a precondition of change in his *Selections from the Prison Notebooks*. It contains challenges to intentions and interpretations of core concepts and positive support for high expectations in the descriptions of goal setting and effort expended. This mix of scepticism and aspiration has characterised many aspects of working relationships between the consortium and the TTA. For example, when the TTA encouraged the consortium to identify a unifying core theme their first reaction seemed to be anxiety about central dictatorship but debate soon centred around how such a theme might work efficiently and effectively within the grain of teachers' classroom experiences. 'Speaking and listening' emerged as a root concern of teachers about raising standards and the TTA highlighted it as a possibility for building a critical mass of interest across the schools. The key issue is that through dialogue all partners' views about problems (the pessimistic views) were heard and were subsequently built into goals and the programme of work.

This mix of scepticism and optimistic planning was also evident in the consortium's responses to TTA efforts to spread good and interesting practice across the four consortia. At the first residential conference where the four consortia worked together, all participants were necessarily and genuinely focused upon taking their own work forward. The potential for learning from each other was difficult to assimilate because there was still so much start up work to do. If it was to happen it had to happen through TTA officers' cross-consortia knowledge. By the second conference there was greater trust. This seemed to derive from experience and from the TTA officers' decisions to ask each consortium to present to the others a concrete example of an effective approach to working collaboratively. This meant that sharing good practice could be seen as a teacher-to-teacher and consortium-to-consortium endeavour rather than an orchestrated one. There were, of course, other propitious factors, including the fact that effective practice was by then better developed and all parties were more confident and therefore more able to take risks. In this context the Manchester and

Salford Consortium chose to start to experiment with the use of video recordings of classroom teachers as a means of capturing classroom data that were useful to teachers at the point of collection. This was already a strong (and strongly commended by TTA) feature of the work of the Northeast Consortium.

A third example of Manchester and Salford Consortium's challenge/support or optimistic/pessimistic approach lies in the way in which support tutors were recruited and the way they worked. As can be seen from other chapters, individual HEI/LEA staff from a wide range of backgrounds and with a wide range of interests and preferred ways of working were attached to each school. Their roles seem to have led to the pursuit of a similarly wide range of strategies and projects. One of the benefits of this was the development of a capacity to respond sensitively to the specific needs and pressures experienced within each school. Given the intensity of social and economic pressures in the local environment and the external demands on and direction given to these particular schools in the period concerned, this has almost certainly enabled some individual schools or teachers to stay with the work 'against the odds'. Some of the debate and counterdebate about the most effective models for supporting this collaborative research work between HEI/LEA link tutors has also greatly developed our understanding of the research/practice interface. But from an outside perspective the whole seems to have been greater than the sum of the parts when all the partners across the consortium came together to pursue a unified aim in an integrated way, as in, for example, establishing a baseline of teachers' attitudes to research; preparing papers for BERA; involving teachers in bidding for externally funded research; and preparing this book or the CD Rom. Tension can be creative, but so can pooling efforts and suspending scepticism.

Context is so often central in education, and this was no less true for this consortium. The political context of educational research is portrayed vividly at the start of this chapter. The pressure on time and human resources in the schools is depicted, alongside huge local efforts to overcome it, in earlier chapters. One story that seems, from a TTA perspective, to be missing and yet to be a strong feature of the partnership is that of the energy, determination and high self-expectations that lay at its administrative and support core. Challenging and fierce in demanding clarity about what was expected in terms of public and collective accountability, the consortium was also punctilious about delivering practical and well-crafted outputs to agreed deadlines. It also seems to have been able to maintain an objective understanding of demands made on others including the TTA. One very practical example can be found in its efforts to secure in-classroom support for teachers engaging in and with research. The LEA and the consortium central team thought hard and laterally about how to respond to a crisis in access to supply teachers. An imaginative and rigorous set of proposals for training and recruiting classroom assistants who could and would support consortium work was the result. Although this model was ultimately foiled by inflexible local politics, it remains as a hopeful potential model for the future. So perhaps the conclusion about the TTA's experience of working with and in many ways within the Manchester and Salford partnership is that there has been challenging critique and scepticism in both the content and process. These have often produced the creative fusion which led to successful cooperative joint working and which gave rise to a fresh set of such challenges.

Reflections

Offering many thanks to Philippa for sharing her insights about our school/LEA/HEI/TTA partnership, our final actions, as authors, might be to reflect upon the nature of these words as we write them at the end of this project. The act of writing a book could be seen – in the terms we have been using above – as a very centripetal activity. We came together, we wrote our case studies and reported our conclusions. There is commonly an expectation at such times that a 'we' will be produced – a 'partnership' that has arrived at a consensus about its processes and outcomes: idiosyncrasy and mess 'tidied up'; generalisations big enough and smooth enough to be called conclusions reached; and quality assurance successfully negotiated. (The TTA have a 'contractual right to be consulted about separate publications, a commitment to contributing to the accessibility of all consortia writing and a quality assurance responsibility for the final written report'.) We have, however, resisted the temptation to write too tidy a concluding account – one that would be a retreat to just the sorts of oversimplified 'blame and cure' discourses that bedevil educational development in the UK.

Evidence-based approaches to educational development may or may not be possible, although we are fairly sure in the light of our experiences that research can make a difference to practice. But it will not offer easy formulae. Change in schools is complex, and just as there is no 'recipe' knowledge for good teaching and learning in a classroom, so too there is no simple formula for making change succeed in complex social and organisational settings. 'Good partnerships' are not made in the heaven of the ideal. But that is good news rather than no news, at least for all those who believe that educational practices cannot be reduced to simple slogans and facile soundbites.

Notes

Stronach initially employed Bratman's philosophical analysis of 'partnership' in order to portray aspects of the Initial Teacher Education strategy at Stirling University (in Brown *et al.*, 1993). More recently, William Taylor has drawn on that analysis in order to look at current dilemmas in understanding educational partnerships in the UK, and in Northern Ireland in particular. In this third deployment of that analysis, we would very much agree with Taylor's conclusion that '[a]s in most things educational, there are no quick fixes, no complete or assured solutions. Partnership is a process not an outcome' (Reid, 2000, p. 55).

References

Almagor, U. (1978) *Pastoral Partners. Affinity and Bond Partnership among the Dessenetch of S.W. Ethiopia*. Manchester: Manchester University Press.

Almond, B. (1991) Human bonds. In: Almond, B. and Hill, D. (eds) *Morals and Metaphysics in Contemporary Debate*. London: Routledge.

Bratman, M. (1992) Shared cooperative activity. *Philosophical Review* 2, 101: 327–341.

Brown, S., McNally, J. and Stronach, I. (1993) *Getting it Together: Questions and Answers about Partnership and Mentoring*. Stirling: University of Stirling Department of Education.

Crozier, G. (1998) Parents and schools: partnership or surveillance? *Journal of Educational Policy*, 13(1): 125–136.

Crozier, G., Mentor, I. and Pollard, A. (1990) Changing partnership. In: Booth, M., Furlong, J. and Wilkin, M. (eds) *Partnership in Initial Teacher Education*. London: Cassells.

Edelman, M. (1972) *Political Language: Words that Succeed and Policies that Fail*. New York: Academic Press.

Forrest, J. (1992) Management aspects of strategic partnership. *Journal of General Management*, 4(17): 25–40.

Gramsci, A. (1971) *Selections from the Prison Notebooks*. London: Lawrence and Wishart.

Hammersley, M. (1997) Education research and teaching a response to Hargreaves TTA lecture. *British Educational Research Journal*, 23(2): 141–161.

Hargreaves, D. (1996) Teaching as a research-based profession: possibilities and prospects. Teacher Training Agency Annual Lecture 1996. London: TTA.

Hargreaves, D. (1997) In defence of research for evidence-based teaching: a rejoinder to Martyn Hammersley. *British Educational Research Journal*, 23(4): 405–418.

Hillage, J., Pearson, R., Anderson, A. and Tamkin, P. (1988) *Excellence in Research on Schools Research*. Report RR74. London: DfEE.

Klein, N. (2000) *No Logo. Taking Aim at the Brand Bullies*. London: HarperCollins.

McNamara, O., Hustler D., Stronach I., Beresford E., Botcherby S. and Rodrigo, M. (2000) Room to manoeuvre: mobilising the active partner, in home–school relations, *British Educational Research Journal*, 26(5): 473–489.

Millett, A. (1996) A plus for the sum of knowledge. *Times Educational Supplement* Nov 8, 1996.

O'Connell, C. (1985) *How to Start a School/Business Partnership*. Blacksburg, VA: Phi Delta Kappa Educational Foundation.

Reid, I (ed.) (2000) *Improving Schools: the contribution of teacher education and training*. An account of the Joint UCET/HMI Symposium held in Edinburgh, December 1999. Loughborough University.

Reynolds, D. (1998) Teacher Effectiveness Teacher Training Agency Corporate Plan Launch 1998–2001. London: TTA.

Strathern, M. (ed.) (2000) *Audit Cultures: Anthropological Studies in Accountability, Ethics and the Academy*. London: Routledge.

Tooley, J. and Darby, D. (1998) *Educational Research: A Critique*. London: OfSTED.

Todd, E. and Higgins S. (1998) Powerlessness in professional and parent partnerships. *British Journal of Sociology of Education*, 19(2): 227–236.

TTA (1996) *Teaching as a Research-based Profession: Promoting Excellence in Teaching*. London: TTA.

Vincent, C. and Tomlinson, S. (1997) Home–school relationships: 'the swarming of disciplinary mechanisms'? *British Educational Research Journal*, 23(3): 361–377.

Toolkits

Toolkit 1

Questionnaire for Staff in MSSC Schools

The Manchester and Salford Schools' Consortium (MSSC) wishes to elicit the views on educational research of all teachers in the project schools. Thank you, in anticipation, for the time and effort you have taken in completing the questionnaire.

Please circle or tick the answers as appropriate and, where a scale is given, circle the number in the grid which best represents your views.

Age group	20-29	
	30-39	
	40-49	
	50-59	
	60-65	
Sex	Male	
	Female	

Length of teaching experience		years
Length of time in present school		years

Post of responsibility in present school	
(with subject if applicable)	

1. Have you any experience of doing educational research?   **Yes / No**

    Please specify context ... .
    (e.g. Initial Teacher Training, Continuing Professional Development, Universities)

    What was the research about?..

2. Have you any experience of being involved in research with other organisations?   **Yes/ No**

    If so, with whom? (e.g. LEA/IAS, OFSTED/HMI, Universities) ....

    What was the research about? ....

3. What image does educational research conjure up for you? ....

4. In your opinion who
    (a) is **currently** doing most educational research?(b) would you like to see doing it in the **future**?

None	A little	Some	A lot		None	A little	Some	A lot
1	2	3	4	Universities	1	2	3	4
1	2	3	4	LEA/IAS	1	2	3	4
1	2	3	4	Schools and Teachers	1	2	3	4
1	2	3	4	NFER	1	2	3	4
1	2	3	4	OFSTED/HMI	1	2	3	4
1	2	3	4	(other)......................	1	2	3	4
(a) Currently					**(b) In the future**			

5. How do you find the thought of being involved in educational research?

No practical help	1	2	3	4	Practically helpful
Too much work	1	2	3	4	Easily manageable
Waste of time	1	2	3	4	Valuable
Very boring	1	2	3	4	Very interesting

6. Do you think teaching would be improved if teachers knew more about using research findings?

Not at all	A little	Some	A lot
1	2	3	4

Why? ....··

7. Where do you gain information about teaching from?

	None	A little	Some	A lot
Professional journals	1	2	3	4
OFSTED/HMI	1	2	3	4
DFEE	1	2	3	4
LEA/IAS	1	2	3	4
TTA	1	2	3	4
Books	1	2	3	4
Press and media items	1	2	3	4
Professional unions	1	2	3	4
Universities	1	2	3	4
Other colleagues	1	2	3	4
Professional conferences	1	2	3	4
(Other)..	1	2	3	4

8. In your opinion what impact does research currently have on teaching?

	None	A little	Some	A lot
Improves the effectiveness of teaching	1	2	3	4
Makes teachers think more about teaching	1	2	3	4
Increases teacher knowledge	1	2	3	4
Raises public esteem of teachers	1	2	3	4
Underpins development work in schools	1	2	3	4
Increases teachers' promotion prospects	1	2	3	4
(Other)..	1	2	3	4

9. Has any research you have read, or done, impacted directly upon your teaching?   **Yes / No**

What was the research about? ....

10. How much do you know about the MSSC project?

Nothing	A little	Some	A lot
1	2	3	4

11. What benefits do you hope your school will derive from being involved in the MSSC project?

	None	A little	Some	A lot
Professional development of staff	1	2	3	4
Pupil gains	1	2	3	4
Underpinning development work	1	2	3	4
Good publicity	1	2	3	4
Raised esteem from the local community	1	2	3	4
Increased self confidence	1	2	3	4
More money for the school budget	1	2	3	4
Better collaboration within the school	1	2	3	4
Better collaboration with HE	1	2	3	4
Improved management of school/subject area	1	2	3	4
Better collaboration with LEA	1	2	3	4
(Other)	1	2	3	4

12. Do you support your school's involvement in the MSSC project?   **Yes / No**

Any further comments ....

Toolkit 2

Please Help!!

You were kind enough to give us your views about educational research and your school's involvement with the <u>*Manchester and Salford Schools' Consortium*</u> *(MSSC) at the beginning of the school-based research project. We now want to know how those views have shifted, if at all, towards the end of the project. Thank you, in anticipation, for the time and effort you have committed to complete the questionnaire.*

Please circle or tick the answers as appropriate and, where a scale is given, circle the number in the grid that best represents your views.

1. What image does educational research conjure up for you now? ....

    ....

2. In your opinion who
    (a) is <u>currently</u> doing most educational research?   (b) would you like to see doing it in the <u>future</u>?

None	A little	Some	A lot		None	A little	Some	A lot
1	2	3	4	Universities	1	2	3	4
1	2	3	4	LEA/IAS	1	2	3	4
1	2	3	4	Schools and Teachers	1	2	3	4
1	2	3	4	NFER	1	2	3	4
1	2	3	4	OFSTED/HMI	1	2	3	4

             (a) <u>Currently</u>   (b) <u>In the future</u>

3. How do you feel about the thought of being involved in <u>doing</u> educational research?

No practical help	1	2	3	4	Practically helpful
Too much work	1	2	3	4	Easily manageable
Waste of time	1	2	3	4	Valuable
Very boring	1	2	3	4	Very interesting

4. What, if any, recent changes in education have made you feel differently about <u>doing</u> research?

    More inclined to be involved..

    Less inclined to be involved...

5. Do you think teaching would be improved if teachers knew more about <u>using</u> research findings?

Not at all	A little	Some	A lot
1	2	3	4

    Why? ....

6. In your opinion what impact does research currently have on teaching?

	None	A little	Some	A lot
Improves the effectiveness of teaching	1	2	3	4
Makes teachers think more about teaching	1	2	3	4
Increases teacher knowledge	1	2	3	4
Raises public esteem of teachers	1	2	3	4
Underpins development work in schools	1	2	3	4
Increases teachers' career prospects	1	2	3	4

7. Has any research you have read, or done, impacted directly upon your teaching?   **Yes / No**

What was it about? ………………...…..

8. Where do you gain information about research and teaching from?

	None	A little	Some	A lot
Professional journals	1	2	3	4
OFSTED/HMI	1	2	3	4
DFEE	1	2	3	4
LEA/IAS	1	2	3	4
TTA	1	2	3	4
Books	1	2	·3	4
Press and media items	1	2	3	4
Professional unions	1	2	3	4
Universities	1	2	3	4
Other colleagues	1	2	3	4
Professional conferences	1	2	3	4
The internet	1	2	3	4

9. How much do you know about the MSSC project in which your school is involved?

Nothing	A little	Some	A lot
1	2	3	4

10. Have you been directly involved in   (a) collecting and interpreting the data?   Yes/No
    (b) using the findings?   Yes/No

11. What benefits, if any, do you think your school has derived from being involved in the MSSC project?

	None	A little	Some	A lot
Professional development of staff	1	2	3	4
Pupil gains	1	2	3	4
Support for development work	1	2	3	4
Good publicity	1	2	3	4
Raised esteem from the local community	1	2	3	4
Increased self confidence of staff	1	2	3	4
More money for the school budget	1	2	3	4
Better collaboration within the school	1	2	3	4
Better collaboration with HE	1	2	3	4
Improved management of school/subject area	1	2	3	4
Better collaboration with LEA	1	2	3	4
Raised esteem from OFSTED	1	2	3	4

12. What costs, if any, have there been for the school as a result of their involvement in the project?

……..

……..

13. Overall has your school's involvement in the MSSC project been worthwhile?   **Yes / No**

14. Any further comments ....……………..

Many thanks for your help in completing this questionnaire

Toolkit 3

corner	racer	another
monster	saucer	whatever
never	grocer	discover
letters	ginger	computer
whiskers	manager	carpenter
spider	register	October
waiter	passenger	surrender
lobster	anger	remember
chapter	foreigner	manufacturer
suffer	wonder	housekeeper
weather	wander	kingfisher
temper	answer	disaster

favour	colour	behaviour
humour	flavour	endeavour
rumour	odour	demeanour
labour	armour	neighbour
harbour	honour	
vapour	splendour	

collar	sugar	popular
nectar	cellar	calendar
pillar	nuclear	regular
burglar	circular	vinegar
vicar	muscular	particular
dollar	similar	familiar
beggar	caterpillar	peculiar

sailor	doctor	radiator
mirror	actor	indicator
terror	tractor	illustrator
horror	collector	duplicator
major	inspector	creator
traitor	projector	governor
editor	instructor	survivor
visitor	author	

cactus	famous	generous
bonus	jealous	dangerous
fungus	joyous	tremendous
focus	nervous	treacherous
circus	fabulous	ridiculous
radius	poisonous	courageous
octopus	vigorous	outrageous
	numerous	contagious
	humorous	religious
		marvellous

serious	obvious	victorious
furious	previous	luxurious
glorious	tedious	injurious
odious	hideous	ingenious

precious	delicious	luscious	cautious	obnoxious
gracious	suspicious	conscious	infectious	anxious
spacious	officious	unconscious	nutritious	
atrocious				ambitious
ferocious				superstitious
vicious				conscientious

decent	resident	basement
recent	president	movement
innocent	confident	enjoyment
adolescent	superintendent	excitement
agent	ancient	amusement
urgent	patient	department
intelligent	impatient	argument
different	efficient	instrument
convenient	sufficient	entertainment

station	imitation	mention
relation	situation	invention
invitation	education	attention
information	congratulations	option
investigation	conversation	caption
starvation	congregation	addition
explanation	coronation	condition
examination	compensation	position
preparation	celebration	exhibition
declaration	application	lotion
organisation	illumination	emotion
operation	levitation	solution
imagination	hesitation	pollution
cancellation	generation	contribution
population	donation	caution
action	direction	destruction
fraction	election	instruction
subtraction	inspection	introduction
reaction	correction	production
attraction	injection	addiction
distraction	protection	fiction
question	reflection	junction
exhaustion	affection	reception
passion	mission	tension
profession	omission	extension
procession	admission	comprehension

impression	permission	mansion
expression	transmission	expansion
depression	discussion	expulsion
	concussion	compulsion
	percussion	submersion

vision	confusion	invasion
division	transfusion	occasion
provision	conclusion	explosion
television	illusion	erosion
decision		
collision		

criminal	musical	special
personal	magical	official
festival	logical	beneficial
normal	comical	financial
national	physical	artificial
several	electrical	essential
local	political	circumstantial
final	medical	confidential
natural	technical	initial

ability	normality	popularity
capability	brutality	charity
availability	fatality	clarity
visibility	mortality	electricity
mobility	reality	felicity
nobility	morality	ferocity
audibility	hilarity	capacity
probability	gravity	curiosity
responsibility	depravity	veracity
credibility	agility	facility
feasibility	practicality	hostility
importance	evidence	difference
assistance	confidence	conference
attendance	impudence	circumference
appearance	obedience	preference
distance	experience	reference
balance	science	patience
ambulance	prudence	innocence
disturbance	absence	

Toolkit 4

Framework for assessing pupils' speaking and listening

Levels 1 to 4 indicate rough equivalence to corresponding NC level descriptors at KS2. Level 0 indicates the lower KS2 baseline of our cohorts and levels 4+ and 4++ (listed at the end of the framework) indicate enhanced competence.

Coherence of response – listening

Level 4

The child's contribution, as a consequence of listening carefully to the discussion, is focused and relevant. Ideas are clearly and logically expressed, in a range of different contexts, and through discussion lead to a logical and consistent conclusion. Where appropriate the child is able to respond in a personal way that reflects his/her unique experience.

Level 3

The child's contribution to the discussion is relevant with perhaps occasional lapses due to inattentiveness or lack of understanding. Ideas are clearly and logically expressed demonstrating an understanding of the main points.

Level 2

As a result of listening more carefully the child selects appropriately from, and exploits, the ideas in the stimulus materials and others' contributions.

Level 1

The child makes occasional and appropriate reference to what has been said but, perhaps as a result of ineffective listening, demonstrates no clear sequence.

Level 0

The child has failed to make use of the ideas in the stimulus materials in any relevant way.

Fluency in speaking

Level 4

The child accurately and confidently uses a range of vocabulary and speech style appropriate to purpose: developing ideas thoughtfully, describing events and conveying opinions clearly. In particular the child shows an awareness of, and demonstrates competence in, standard English vocabulary and grammar.

Level 3

The child uses confidently a wide range of accurate, consistent and fluent vocabulary in different contexts. Use of stress, intonation and tone is appropriate.

Level 2

The child rarely has difficulty in making him/herself understood and attempts to use a developing range of vocabulary and syntax but these are not always accurate.

Level 1

The child generally speaks audibly and is comprehensible, though vocabulary and syntax are limited.

Level 0

The child fails to make him/herself understood, even in a very limited way.

Interaction in the classroom

Level 4

The child takes account of the needs of others and builds on their contributions. (S)he defends a point of view when challenged, and shows willingness to make a reasoned compromise in order to reach an agreed conclusion. Eye contact and body language are used effectively.

Level 3

The child takes an active part in discussion, contributing where appropriate, provided that the audience is supportive and cooperative. Eye contact and body language indicates readiness to communicate.

Level 2

The child contributes to discussion when prompted to do so but shows limited awareness of the audience. Eye contact and body language indicate willingness to communicate.

Level 1

The child responds when spoken to but is very reluctant to initiate or sustain speech without frequent prompting. Eye contact and gesture are minimal.

Level 0

The child is extremely reluctant to take part in any sort of exchange.

Descriptors for Levels 4+ and 4 ++ - additionality to be demonstrated in the following respects in a variety of contexts, including formal situations.

Speaking	Listening	Interactive skills
Confidence	Attention to others	Engagement with others – shows interest
Range of vocabulary, syntax and grammar	Appropriateness of response	Takes account of others' ideas/views
Fluency in use of standard English	Engagement with and development of ideas	Effective use of body language
Context relatedness	Engagement with and development of arguments and discussion	Effective use of expression

Adapted from the Assessment of Achievement Programme (1988) and the National Curriculum AT1: Speaking and Listening

Toolkit 5

A guide to reflection

Teacher's style of questioning

- Open (e.g. requiring extended answer – the teacher might use prompts and probes to encourage the child).
- Closed (e.g. requiring factual response).
- Thinking time allowed?
- Differentiation built in? (e.g. are questions phrased/posed differently in order to accommodate ability levels of the children?).
- Purpose (e.g. management strategy)?

Children's responses

- 'Quality' of response indicating listening skills (e.g. gives brief but factually correct response/ extends answers to include additional knowledge and understanding) i.e. Level 1 to 4 of 'coherence of response' framework.
- 'Quality' of response indicating speaking skills (e.g fails to make himself understood/ accurately and confidently uses a range of language) i.e. Level 1 to 4 of 'fluency in speaking' framework.

Inclusion strategies

- Who answers? Who does not answer?
- Who is reading aloud? Who isn't? Why?
- What kind of verbal teacher strategies are used to include/exclude the children? (e.g. affirmation of children's correct responses/ praise or reaction to incorrect responses/muddled thinking/ misconceptions).
- What kind of non-verbal teacher strategies are used to include/exclude the children? (e.g. body language).
- What strategies are used by children to include/exclude themselves? (e.g. sitting at the back, hands up, eye contact, etc.), i.e. Level 1 to 4 of 'interaction in the classroom' framework.

Strategies for stimulating/encouraging listening

- What teacher strategies have been developed in order to develop an ethos so that children feel able to listen? (e.g. tone/volume/non-verbal/humour etc.).

Strategies for stimulating/encouraging speaking

- What teacher strategies have been developed in order to develop an ethos so that children feel able to speak? (e.g. Is the group dominated by particular children? Is silence used effectively by the teacher?)

Toolkit 6

Pupil log

Thinking about speaking

1 How many questions did you *answer* in the lesson today?   none/a few/a lot
2 Do you like *answering* questions in lessons?   yes/sometimes/no
3 What feels good about *answering* questions? ....
   ....
4 What feels bad about *answering* questions? ....
   ....
5 Did you get a chance to *ask* any questions in the lesson today?   yes/some/no
6 Were there things you wanted to say and didn't get the chance?   yes/no

Thinking about listening

7 Are you a good listener?   very good/quite good/not that good/poor
8 What makes listening hard? ....
   ....
9 What makes listening easy? ....
   ....
10 What are you good at remembering? ....
   ....
11 What are you poor at remembering? ....
   ....

Thinking about lessons

12 How do you most like working in lessons?
   in groups/on your own/in pairs/as a class

13 Why? ....
   ....
14 How do you least likeworking in lessons?
   in groups/on your own/in pairs/as a class

15 Why? ....
   ....

Toolkit 7

'Temple goes mental' project observation sheet

Research into reflective teaching methods in mathematics (with particular reference to speaking and listening)

Year group   Lesson focus   Teacher

Set: No. in set: Date: Time:

Type of interaction/ questioning	By teacher	By the children
Asking questions		
Answering questions		
Reflecting/imagining		
Calculating mentally		
Describing methods or thinking		

Index